# THE *Journey*

# THE *Journey*

### a novel by

## ANNE CAMERON

author of *Daughters of Copper Woman*

spinsters | *aunt lute*
SAN FRANCISCO

Spinsters/Aunt Lute Book Company
P.O. Box 410687
San Francisco, CA 94141

Printed in the U.S.A.
First Spinsters/Aunt Lute printing, September 1986
10-9-8-7-6-5-4-3-2-1

Cover design by Pamela Wilson Design
Cover art by Kristen Throop

Publication of this book was made possible through
the continuing generosity and crucial support of Angels Ink.

*For*

Alex, Erin, Pierre, Marianne, Kim, Jeff, Charlotte,
Audrey, Barbara, Nancy, Stanley, Jimmy, Anna, Vivienne,
JaneOgle, Liz, Louise, Judith, Shirley, Mom, Judy,
Heather, Nancy H., BJ, Shirl, Michelle, Maggy, Brenda, Osa,
Eve, Daffodil, Maria, Sunshine, Ferron, K-O, Breezy,
Charby, Vina, Janaree, Shane, Sandy, Trish, Joyce, Roberta,
Frances, Tara, Luna, Eileen, Kathy, Valerie, Eleanor

and for all the little girls
who always wanted to be
and never could grow up to be
cowboys.

*I see by your outfit that you are a cowboy*
*I see by his outfit that he's a cowboy true,*
*I see by their outfits that they are all cowboys,*
*If I get an outfit can I be cowboy, too.*

> (as sung by those of us tied for
> too long to trees and stereotypes)

●

> Sincere thanks to Jean Feiwel,
> speaker of those immortal words
> "What's a jamtart?"

●

"Considering how dangerous everything is, nothing is really
very frightening."                                    —*Gertrude Stein*

"If you don't know how ... fake it; who'll know the difference,
anyway?"                                              —*Liz Brady*

"Consider the source and ignore it; them as can, does,
them as can't, criticize."                            —*My grandmother*

D edicated critics and committed historians will quickly
find that this novel does not pay particular attention
nor give much respect to the recorded version of history.

*—Pickypicky!*

When one is re-inventing the world one cannot be
concerned with minor details, and when one has become
convinced, over a number of years, that the privileged
patriarchal perspective is sick, one looks for alternatives.

When I was a girl, Saturday meant movies. Roy
Rogers, Gene Autry, Hopalong Cassidy, Cisco Kid, and the
Lone Ranger were all as much a part of our lives as school
and the after-dinner dishes. Guns, horses, trail drives, danger,
adventure, challenge, and the heroic overcoming of all odds.

The boys could identify with the heroes. We had
Dale Evans. She was the one with no guns, the one on the
slower horse, who rode behind Roy just in time to catch the
mud flying from his gallant steed's hooves. Not much of a
role model.

And so, because I had long hair, worn in pigtails,
and the stereotype did not allow me a six-gun, a rifle, or a
knife, I spent many hours tied to trees, the captive Indian.
Perhaps that was the beginning of this story.

# THE *Journey*

# Chapter 1

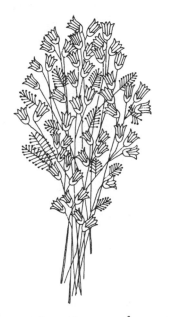

Dry and ugly, whipped by a constant wind, the stark barren flatlands lay baked by a hot copper sun, the dust rising in whorls, the sparse yellow grass bending stiffly. Thinly scattered scrawny little trees tried to pretend they were something they weren't, and in the distance the pall from the quarry lay like an unanswered insult in the gritty air.

A rickety split-rail fence surrounded the forlorn cemetery. One or two stone markers stood guard over the graves of the well-to-do, but, for the most part, the plots were marked by weathered wooden slats on which were inexpertly carved a name and some dates.

A young girl and a weary woman stood beside one of the graves, hands folded stiffly across the skirt fronts of their worn dresses, the wind pulling and teasing at the much-washed fabric. The dust whirled around their bare feet and their hair loosened and trailed after the ceaseless tugging fingers of the wind. The girl, a tall, skinny fourteen-year-old with corn yellow hair, looked down at the wooden marker.

"John Gray," she said softly, "1823 to 1847 . . ."

"He was a good man," her mother said wistfully, a faded smile pulling at the corners of her bloodless lips. "He was loving . . . gentle . . ." She raised her eyes from the shabby mound and looked into her daughter's eyes, remembering those other deep blue laughing ones. "He could always find something to laugh at, Anne. He sang, he teased, he made each day something new, something to get out of bed for." They moved away from the grave, talking quietly. "He worked the farm, and when we needed cash money, he worked the quarry." Her eyes found the dust cloud in the distance. She looked away quickly, too tired to even bother accusing the rockworks.

"I don't remember him at all," Anne prompted, wishing she could remember, or even pretend to remember, the man who had been her father.

"No, you wouldn't." Again her mother sighed. "You were too young. Everything was better then. The grass was green and the wind didn't blow as much. Or if it did, we didn't notice it."

They walked slowly down the twin ruts that were the wagon road, their bare feet swishing in the dust and sand. Once in a while Martha would stop for a moment, her hand pressing her side, her breathing suddenly ragged.

"You ought to see a doctor," Anne said suddenly.

"He can't help me."

"You don't know that. He's awful smart. He helped Jenny Logan when her baby wouldn't come." She wanted to say more, wanted to argue the point, but her habit was to do what she was told. At first she had done what she was told because she was little, and small children want to be obedient. After her father died she did what she was told because if she didn't Uncle Andrew would yell, or slap, or grab for his belt. If her mother tried to interfere, he would slap at her, too, likely as not, and, angered at her defiance, the beating would be twice as bad as if she had never contradicted him. Now Anne did what she was told because her mother was so very obviously sick, and Anne didn't want to add to her worries.

"He costs money." Martha put the real reason into words, and they hung in the air like sharp stones. "Uncle Andrew says we don't have the money . . ."

"I don't see how, if Poppa was so nice, Uncle Andrew can be his brother!"

"You have to be grateful," Martha said, her voice suddenly as dry and lifeless as the land around them. "He came to help us."

"He came to take over the farm, that's all," Anne said flatly. "He never got a place of his own. He had nothin'." She grinned suddenly. "He made a poor bargain. He always makes poor bargains. That's why there's never any money. Except when he wants a jug . . ."

"Now, now." Martha's voice was weak, her face beaded with sweat, and Anne put her arm around her waist, pretending the gesture was a cuddling, not a supportive, one. Martha didn't like to feel she was a burden to anybody.

"Tell me about when you went to school," Anne urged. "Tell me about the books with the names of places."

"The library." Martha's face relaxed, her eyes softened. "The library was full of books. Maybe two hundred of them. And my favorite had a soft brown leather cover, with pictures to start every chapter. Pictures of places beyond the sea, places with green grass and soft blue skies, and beaches stretching as far as forever . . ."

They made their way down the wagon road toward the small farm that was home. A little cabin, never properly finished, a barn in dire need of repair, a small parched garden for family food, and a couple of weed-choked fields of hay, another of wheat.

"He didn't get to finish anything," Martha said suddenly. "He was going to add another piece onto the house, finish the barn, run irrigation to the garden and put in good fences. We needed cash money to buy material . . . that's why . . ." Her eyes flooded suddenly, and, shamed, she turned her face away.

"We're nearly home, Momma. It won't be long now."

"He said . . . he said 'Back before dark' . . . but he wasn't. They brought him back before noon . . . what was left of him."

"Where in hell you been?" Andrew's voice roared at them, startling them as he shot his words from somewhere behind his bushy black beard. "Do I have to do everything myself?"

"It's Sunday!" Anne protested, feeling her mother shrinking beside her, drawing away from the noise Andrew always made, hiding inside herself from the constant dissatisfied uproar of the man.

---

3

"Sunday, Tuesday, what's the difference? There's work to be done."

"We'll do it," Martha said calmly. Anne wished that once, just once, Martha would tell Andrew to shut up. All he did was yell, shout, aim slaps and kicks and complain. For all the help he was, he wouldn't be missed and with what it cost to keep him in tobacco, moonshine and food, they could hire a good handyman to get some of the work done. But Andrew was her dead father's brother and that made him family. That made him the man in the family as surely as if he, not her father, had filed and homesteaded this tatterpatch farm.

It was cool in the barn and old Bess whickered softly, her damp brown eyes shining as she nuzzled hopefully at Anne's pockets.

"Nothing there for you," Anne said softly. "You just behave yourself until feedtime." She patted the old mare, then took a minute to rub the thick tar salve onto the sores on the bony old back, sores where the ill-fitting, poorly tended harness rubbed. She wished she could turn the skinny old thing loose to graze but Andrew's fences were such a mess there was sure to be trouble if she did. The last time, he'd threatened to shoot Bess, and Anne wasn't convinced he wouldn't enjoy the chance to do just that.

"Hey, Dan, y'ole fool." She turned to the other horse, a total contrast to poor worked-to-a-standstill Bess. "Feelin' pretty proud of yourself today, aren't you? Enjoy your week over at Sampson's place? Bet they gave you a nice stall full of fresh straw and let you run around all you wanted with those pretty young mares, huh?" The big stud tossed his head, pressed against the bars of his stall, inviting her touch as much as he rejected Andrew's.

Anne was watering the garden, hauling buckets from the well, struggling to carry the heavy load to the parched rows of withering vegetables, carefully trickling water to the scrawny plants. She was careful not to waste any of the water on the dirt between the rows; only the plants themselves got watered. The well was low and the creek provided just enough for the stock, so she had to be careful. They all had to be careful with water. Every drop not used for drinking was used more than once: The dishwater and laundry water was hoarded for the garden, and lately, the water from their infrequent baths had been saved for the laundry.

"Where's your mother?" Andrew asked suddenly.

"Doing the wash."

"You sure?"

"I said so, didn't I?" she answered tartly, reaching out to prop up a wilted bean plant. Andrew backhanded her casually, hitting her on the side of the head, knocking her sideways. The force of her fall tipped the bucket, spilling the precious water.

"See what you did?" he roared, kicking her backside and sending her back into the dust she was rising from. "How many times you been told not to waste water?"

He stalked off, aiming a stream of tobacco-stained spit at a fence post and for a moment Anne had to fight the impulse to send the bucket after him, aimed at his head. Sometimes, at night, when the soft darkness hid her face and nobody could read her unspoken thoughts, she dreamed while awake, dreamed of being big enough, strong enough, hard enough to just kick Andrew where it would hurt the most. Even as she dreamed she knew it was a hopeless dream. Now she got up, dusted herself off, picked up the bucket and headed back toward the well for more water.

Halfway there, on impulse, she put down the bucket and raced around the side of the house to where her mother was doing the wash. Two large tubs rested on an old makeshift table of planks laid across two sawhorses. Martha, face white and beaded with sweat, scrubbing determinedly, rubbed a pair of Andrew's work pants against the ribbed side of the washboard. Andrew was glaring at Martha, his eyes lidded and red-rimmed from the blowing dust and the jug he kept close to hand all the time.

"Momma, sit down," Anne said.

"Leave her alone!" Andrew commanded.

"She's sick! Look at her!"

"I'll be all right!" Martha insisted faintly. "I'm just a bit short of breath." She tried to smile, her lips drawn tight against her teeth.

"Uncle Andrew, she's sick. She needs a doctor!"

"Rake the hay," Andrew said shortly.

"You go lie down, Momma. I'll do this."

"No, you won't!" Andrew roared. "She'll do this, you'll rake the hay!"

There was no use arguing. Anne knew it would only make more trouble. She turned unwillingly, tearing her eyes away from the sight of her mother's gray, sweat-beaded face.

She was following the horse and the rusted hay rake across the field, her nose prickling with hayseed, her skin itching, her feet scratched by thistle and weed. She looked over at the cabin, a sagging shed beneath the brassy sky. She wanted a drink of water, but Andrew would only yell about that, too, so she licked her dust-caked lips and urged old Bess on, the hay rake bumping inadequately across the field. It wasn't much of a crop for first haying: The rains hadn't come on time or adequately, and, like the garden, the crop was puny and weak. Some of the tines on the hay rake were missing and the dry hay was being drawn into irregular rows. She knew she would have to make another pass of the entire field and maybe even wind up going over it yet again with a hand rake. She had spent most of yesterday out here with a scythe, swinging and cutting until her arms ached and she was sure her fingers hung down to her ankles. Her mother had brought her lunch to her in the field and they had barely enough time to eat before Andrew was screaming at her to get to work again. By suppertime she could hardly move. Her back felt as if a hot iron band was clamped around her spine, and her shoulders ached so much she doubted if she'd ever stand straight again. But supper was no more than in her belly when Andrew was cursing at her to finish the field. He was so anxious for the hay to be cut he had even come out for a while in the cool of evening and helped. Andrew was so obsessed with this first crop of hay she wondered if he meant it when he said there was no money.

By midafternoon her head was aching and she was too numb to even notice when Andrew joined her in the field. Together they wielded pitchforks, rolling the hay into piles, forming haycocks. In a few days they would be back out here, swinging the haycocks up onto the wagon, and the first crop of hay would be ready. Andrew said he could get a good price for it. Maybe then they could afford a doctor for Martha.

She looked toward the house. No smoke coming from the chimney. No wash flapping on the line behind the cabin.

"Get busy!" Andrew snarled.

"Fire's out," she stuttered and then she was running toward the house, ignoring the shouts of rage as Andrew ordered her back to work.

She ran into the kitchen. The cabin was empty, the silence hanging like dust in the air. No fire in the stove, no meal being prepared. She ran out the door and along the side of the house toward the washtubs. Martha was lying in the dust, her chest moving shallowly. When Andrew came around the side of the house to order her back to work, he found the young girl holding her mother, staring at him dry-eyed and filled with raw, naked hate. Andrew lifted Martha easily, shocked at how thin she was, and carried her to her room, placing her on her bed. When Anne led the big stud from the barn and jumped on his back Andrew could only stare.

Andrew sat at the table nursing his jug of cheap moonshine, staring down at his chipped glass, trying to convince himself there was no way he could have known the woman was really sick. Sometimes, no matter what a man did or tried to do, he was going to be wrong, one way or the other. Because when it was time for the devil to shit on your head, he'd shit, no matter what. Once in a while he would look toward the small back bedroom where Martha lay, eyes closed, breathing in quick raspy breaths, her lips pale, the veins in her forehead showing blue against the gray-white of her skin.

7

The sound of wagon wheels outside drew his gaze to the front door. Soft muted conversation, and then the door opened and Anne came in, followed by the young doctor with his already battered black bag. "She's through in the back." Anne ignored Andrew, and led the doctor to the small bedroom. "I didn't know what to do for her so I just covered her up warm."

The doctor looked down at Martha. "I want you to help me," he said carefully. "I want you to build up the fire and boil lots of water . . . it's getting chilly in here and . . ."

"You just want me out of here," she said coldly.

"No," he sighed. "But I didn't have any lunch, and supper is three hours away, and I could sure use a cup of coffee."

"I'm sorry." Anne looked suddenly like a very little girl. "She'll be all right, won't she?"

"I hope so," he answered, and she smiled slightly, appreciating his frankness. He went into the small bedroom and closed the door carefully, then moved to the bed, already knowing what he would find. He remembered his own mother and sisters, glad they lived in the East, where a woman didn't have to be a beast of burden, glad he had no wife. He cursed this hard frontier land and its extremes of temperature and unforgiving harshness.

In the kitchen, Anne struggled with the stove until the fire was blazing. Then she made several trips out to the well, filling the pots and tubs, heating the water the doctor said he needed.

Andrew watched her resentfully. There she was, working like two people, working more willingly for a doctor she didn't know than she ever had for him, her own father's brother. Peeling and slicing potatoes, cooking them in the frying pan with thick slices of ham, the last ham in the house, ham from their own pigs, slaughtered last fall. "Never a word of thanks from you," he growled. "I didn't have to come here, you know. I could'a gone south, to California . . . they say there's gold in California . . . but you were my brother's family."

"That's not true," she said coldly. "If you'd been goin' to California, you'd have gone, brother or no brother, family or no family. Family never meant anything to you, anyway. You came here because it didn't cost anything to get here. You never had anything but the clothes on your back until you came to take over my dad's farm."

"That's a lie." But his voice was surly and he wouldn't look at her.

She took the platter of food into the back room, and Andrew had to satisfy himself with the few scraps left in the frying pan. He cut a slice of bread and folded it around a hunk of ham, then sat at the table eating, sipping his moonshine, and feeling sorry for himself, feeling trapped.

When the doctor had finished his lunch, Anne came back out of the room with his empty plate and coffee cup. Then she cleaned up the kitchen, using some of the hot water the doctor hadn't really needed at all. She washed the table, carefully avoiding Andrew or his glass, then she swept the floor, and, nerves jangling, butterflies dancing in her stomach with each sound, real or imagined, from the bedroom, she got down on her hands and knees and scrubbed the floor, again staying away from Andrew or his big new heavy boots.

The floor was dry, and she was sitting on a chair beside the stove, concentrating on her bare toes, watching them wiggle, waiting, just waiting, when the bedroom door finally opened.

"I'm sorry," he said softly, and he stepped aside when she ran toward him. Anne stopped at the door, stared at the frail husk on the bed. "She started to hemorrhage," the doctor said gently, reaching out to touch the small, stiff shoulders. "I couldn't stop it . . . I'm sorry."

"That's okay." Anne's voice was dry and brittle, her eyes bright with tears he knew she was not ready to shed. "It's not your fault. Maybe it's better this way."

After the doctor left, Anne used the rest of the hot water to bathe her mother. Andrew sat in the kitchen, drinking the faintly yellow liquor and ignoring the sound of the wind. When Anne came out of the bedroom he tried to take her hand, but she pulled away from him, blaming him silently.

"I can't afford much of a funeral," he blurted.

"Sell the hay as it is," she replied coldly.

"Not to pay for a funeral," he protested. "Not my hay!"

---

"*Your* hay!" She glared at him, face frozen. "And your farm, too, I suppose?"

"You can't work it alone," he growled. "It'll be yours one day, but until then, don't worry. I'll look after you."

"Like you looked after her? Too cheap to get her a doctor, too cheap to get her medicine, too cheap for much of a funeral, and now she'll wind up in a pauper's grave!"

There was no use talking to her, he knew, so he took what was left of his jug and went to his room in the loft. He fell asleep quickly, sucking his teeth, tasting the faint oily residue of the corn liquor and the bitterness of trying to live with an ungrateful child. Hours later he was awakened by the sound of laughter, and Anne jabbing his ribs with her bare toes.

"Can't you hear it?" she laughed.

"What?" he mumbled, sitting up and cursing as the liquor in his head exploded and the bile rose in his belly.

"*Your* hay, Uncle Andrew," she crooned. "It's *your* hay!" And then he heard the sound of rain on the roof above him, a steady drumming rain, and he knew she had sat in the kitchen grinning to herself, sat through the first few drops, the first half hour of sporadic showers, sat waiting for the rain to settle in before waking him to gloat as his dreams were washed into the ground.

"Don't just stand there," he roared, reaching for his boots. "We can still save some of it!" But she just laughed. Even when he slapped her face, she just stood laughing maliciously. He ran out into the downpour and stood cursing, staring out at the hayfield, staring and knowing the hay would go to mold and be good for nothing but bedding. She had waited so long the ground was already turned to mud. The haycocks would be soaked to the middle.

It was still raining when they buried Martha. The friends and neighbors stood around the muddy hole and tried to hold their umbrellas over the dry-eyed young girl. They looked at her dress. Undoubtedly the best she had, it was too short for her, but it was carefully mended and patched. They knew the shoes on her feet had belonged to someone else first, and probably pinched her toes painfully. Andrew stood beside her in his one suit, the backside worn shiny, the elbows and knees baggy. He had trimmed his beard and taken the scissors to his hair, but the odor of moonshine hung around him like a cloud. He wore his new sturdy boots and tried to look pious and sad, but his eyes slithered sideways to where Anne stood, and when he wasn't careful, a small smile played at the corners of his mouth. The preacher finished speaking, something about a good woman being worth more than pearls and diamonds, and a family being the greatest treasure in the world. Then someone handed a shovel to Anne. She dug the shiny blade into the pile of mud beside the grave, her eyes narrowing slightly when the mud splattered the lid of the coffin. Andrew reached out, took the shovel from her and shoveled more mud into the grave. One by one the neighbors, men and women alike, helped to fill Martha's grave, and those who would have wept didn't, because Anne's eyes were dry and glittered like crystals from the quarry.

Back at the cabin there was food enough for two weeks. Meat and potato pies, cooked ham, chicken, pork roast, a big pot of stew and a small mountain of pies and cakes. The neighbors stayed a while, trying to find something reassuring and comforting to say to Anne, telling her not to worry, there was no rush for the pots, platters and bowls in which they'd brought the food. They'd be dropping around often, to be sure things were fine with her, and could pick things up then. The women stared thin-lipped as Andrew got out several jugs and sat on the porch with the men, drinking and talking of who had lost their entire hay crop, who had saved some, who had escaped the storm. Elizabeth Conroy, who had been a good friend to Martha from the first, moved to stand by Anne where she was pouring coffee for the women.

"You can come and live with us, dear," she said softly.

"He wouldn't let me," Anne replied calmly.

"I spoke to Angus about it and he says it's your decision, and yours alone." The other women were listening, faces revealing nothing.

"He'd only come and get me and make a big stink. He needs

---

11

someone here to do the work while he talks about how he's going to spend the crop money."

"Angus says if there's trouble he can handle it," and all the women nodded.

"Thank you." Anne tried to smile. "But you don't know how much trouble Uncle Andrew could make." Just then Andrew walked into the house, went to the table, and began to load food onto his plate.

"Andrew," Elizabeth spoke softly, "Anne needs a woman with her for a while, yet . . . it's no place for her here, now. She can stay with us and go to school in town."

"She don't need school." Andrew grinned widely, enjoying his power, knowing nobody was going to dare argue with him, the man of the family, her last living relative. "She can learn everything she needs to know right here." Then he walked over and put his heavy arm across Anne's shoulders, smiling down at her, his eyes enjoying the way her face paled suddenly. "We'll make out just fine, won't we, honey?"

The women all looked away suddenly, the way people do when they happen by accident upon an owl-killed hen or a hoof-crushed toad, the way people do when they turn over a rock and find something flabby and spineless wriggling underneath it.

"We'll make out just fine," he repeated, laughing. "We're family."

Everyone left shortly after, the women rock-faced, waiting until they were out of sight, out of earshot before telling their men what had happened. The men sighed, but only Angus, who had been a friend to Anne's father, wanted to go back and take Anne away then and there.

"A good dose of buckshot will move him," he growled.

"Wait," Elizabeth said firmly. "Anne can handle him for the next little while. Wait until we've got a paper from the judge."

When everyone had left, Anne changed her dress and started doing the chores. The garden had benefited from the rain, at least, all the plants standing up straight, already greener and healthier. The rain had stopped and the sun was already peeping out from behind the clouds. In a day or so the dust would start blowing again, but for now there was an illusion of something softer, something better in store. The hens were picking their way out of the barn, avoiding the puddles, searching for the drowned worms that always lay on the ground after a rain. Anne moved toward the barn, the mud squishing between her toes, glad to be out of the cramped and uncomfortable shoes she had worn for the funeral.

In the barn she moved to the back where the nesting boxes were, and gathered the few eggs the hens had left. Two of the hens were sitting on the boxes, eyeing her suspiciously. "Oh, don't worry," she said softly. "I'm not taking your eggs. I'm taking the fresh ones. You just sit there and cluck until you've got chicks." The sound of her voice soothed them, and the old gray hen ruffled her feathers, her eyes turning glassy again, and the soft low clucking started deep in her throat. Every year for as long as Anne could remember the old gray hen sat on eggs until her underside was bare and featherless, and then she would appear one day with her brood, and strut proudly around the barnyard. As the rooster kept his eyes on the sky, watching for hawks and owls, the old gray hen clucked and guided her chicks to the best scratching spots. By Christmas, most of her young ones would be total strangers to her, the cockerels winding up on the table, the young hens left to lay eggs the following year. Every few years the proud rooster became stew and a young cock from Elizabeth Conroy's flock would take his place, so the chickens never got too inbred the way some did.

She took the eggs into the house and began tidying up the kitchen. Andrew sat at the table, staring at her, and when he finally got up and moved toward her, her hands betrayed her, and she dropped and broke a cup. Andrew slapped her face.

"Leave me alone!"

"You do as *I* say, now! You've had it soft, lady, but no more."

"It was an accident."

"Don't talk to me like that, Missy. You're not the Queen of England. It's time you learned who you really are. Just because your hard little titties are pushin' against the front of your dress don't mean you're a full-grown woman. And if you were, you'd still do what you were told!"

He pulled off his belt and began to strap her across the shoulders and back, and though she tried hard not to, she began to cry. He beat her with the belt until his arm was tired and her dress was torn. Then he grinned down at her until her blood ran cold with fear.

"That's just a sample, Missy. From now on, whatever I tell you to do . . . you do! You do it and keep your mouth shut to the neighbors or you'll get more of this." He reached down and took her chin in his hand, his big fingers squeezing cruelly. "You're a big girl now. Time you learned your place. Time you learned what a woman's place is. And I'm gonna teach you. Damn quick!"

She crouched on the floor, the tears drying on her cheeks, watching as the new sturdy boots moved to the table. There was the sound of Andrew's jug scraping against the tabletop, then the boots moved toward the ladder to the loft. "You finish what work you got to do, and if I think of something else, I'll let you know. And whatever I think of, you'll do. You'll do'er, smart Missy, because you know what you'll get if you don't," and then he was climbing the ladder, laughing softly to himself.

There wasn't any use going into town, he'd only follow her and bring her back. There wasn't any use going to Angus and Elizabeth Conroy. That would be the first place he'd look. She either had to go so far away he'd never find her or stay and put up with it all. She got up off the floor, her back aching, and stared around at the cabin her mother and father had built, the cabin Andrew now ruled.

In the back bedroom she took her mother's prized quilt, the handmade double wedding-ring design, and into it she placed the big Bible, the picture of her parents taken on their wedding day, and one or two pieces of jewelry. She folded it all up as small as she could, and tied a piece of cord around it. There wasn't much else there, some blankets, so thin as to be com-

14

fortless, a couple of worn and faded house dresses and a thread-bare coat.

In the barn, the big saddlebags Uncle Andrew used to bring home his jugs hung from a wooden peg on the wall. The quilt fit easily into one of them, and that seemed to decide everything for her. She took the big saddlebags back into the house with her and began to pack quietly and quickly.

The hens were too dazed by the dark to make any sound at all. She picked up the nesting boxes one by one and moved them to where the few skinny trees tried to protect the house. The cow didn't understand why she was being taken from the barn, why she was being taken to the one place she had never been allowed to graze, the garden, but she was too old and too docile to do anything except stand where she was left. After a few minutes she lowered her head, her soft brown eyes watching in puzzlement.

Anne wasn't sure Dan would accept the bridle. He was uneasy with all the unusual comings and goings in the dark, but she patted him gently, as Andrew never did, and spoke softly. He calmed at the sound of her familiar voice, and the bit slid into his mouth easily. She had to stand on the box to get the saddle blanket in place and the saddle on him, and then she had to put her knee against his side and jab him in the ribs to tighten the cinch. She tied the roll of blankets from her mother's bed behind the saddle, put the bulging saddlebags in place and then, using a piece of rope from the wall of the barn, she tied the pillow slip filled with roast chicken, pork and ham to the horn of the saddle.

Uncle Andrew's nearly new rifle fit neatly into the scabbard on the saddle. Every shell he owned went into one of the saddlebags. There was no money to bother taking, but she had his warm winter jacket and his near-new hat. And his big knife. She used it to split open the grain sacks, then she shoved the knife in the sheath on Andrew's belt. She grinned slightly, remembering how he had slid off the sheath to use the belt on her, then left both of them on the table when he went upstairs to bed.

---

The moon was full in the sky as the horse picked his way carefully past the mud puddles and stood waiting, reins hanging. Anne went back to the barn and put a halter and lead rope on old Bess, and led her from the barn, whispering softly to her, tying the rope to a round shiny fastening on the saddle. Then she went back into the barn for the last time and deliberately spread kerosene all over everything. As she was leaving she saw her father's small hatchet hanging on the wall, and she took that, too; she wasn't leaving anything for Andrew, not even a hatchet head.

She moved to the cabin, went inside stealthily, and spread kerosene all over everything. She wished there had been time to move the dishes and bowls in which the neighbors had brought the food, but it would take too long to wash them, and Andrew might wake from his shine-sodden sleep and catch her before she was finished.

She came back outside again, moving quickly, trailing a thin stream of kerosene behind her, then splashed the sharp-smelling liquid on the weather-dried sides and roof of the small cabin. There wasn't much left in the can, now, and she sprinkled it carefully on the ground, moving back toward Dan. It was a struggle to get up on his back without the box. Andrew had bragged he was probably the biggest and strongest riding horse in the district, and Momma had only shaken her head when she looked at him and realized what he had cost. When Anne was safely settled in the saddle, she took a piece of paper from her pocket, struck a wooden match against a metal stud on the saddle, and when the match flared, she lit the paper and dropped it on the ground. Instantly the kerosene caught fire, racing back toward the cabin and barn like a snake's tongue flickers when you hold him up by the tail. "Get up, Dan," she urged, and the big stud moved away quickly, old Bess following contentedly at the end of the lead rope.

Anne stopped once and looked back. The cow was standing in the ruins of the garden, staring with mild concern at the fire that was devouring the barn and the few sacks of stored grain, spreading and already licking at the wall of the cabin. Anne didn't like the idea of Uncle Andrew maybe roasting in there, but she wasn't going to wake him up and give him a chance to beat her again. Or worse. And she wasn't leaving a stick for him to claim as his own. "Move along, Dan," she urged, and they were off, heading in the direction the sun took when it went down at night.

She didn't look back again. Didn't see the cow chewing the bean plants, confusing the light from the blazing barn for the daytime sun. She didn't see the chickens sitting in their nesting boxes under the trees, ignoring the sparks heading up to the sky. Didn't hear the shout of surprise, the clatter of a body tumbling down the ladder, didn't see Uncle Andrew come flying through the window, glass showering into the yard. Didn't see him land on his belly in the mud and slide almost to where the hens sat staring at him. Didn't see the look on his face when he lifted his eyes and saw the old gray hen staring at him, blinking slowly and crooning to her unhatched chicks.

When the neighbors arrived in the morning, alerted by the pall of smoke, they found Andrew sitting in his long johns, wearing only one of his sturdy new boots, staring at the charred ruin of the barn. The hens were pecking in what was left of the garden, scratching happily in the ground pitted and chewed by the cow's hooves. The cow was lying under the trees, chewing her cud, chewing for a second time the young corn she had eaten.

"Where is the child?" demanded Angus Conroy.

"Gone," Andrew moaned. "All gone. Everything."

The neighbors stared down at him, then over at the ruins of the cabin. The stove, charred and blackened, some heat-shattered dishes, the metal springs of the beds.

"My God!" Elizabeth began to weep. "He saved himself and left that poor child to perish." They all stared at him. Stared grim-faced and disgusted until he rose to his feet, trying to stammer an explanation, already knowing there would be no place in this community for a man who saved his own skin and left a little girl to die in a fire.

"The poor child," Elizabeth sobbed.

# Chapter 2

Miles away the poor child was doing quite well, thank you. Not caring that her skirt was hiked up in a most unladylike way, not caring that her bare feet barely reached the stirrups, she was stuffing her face with meat and potato pie, letting Dan pick his own way across the miles of rolling yellow grassland. Old Bess ambled along behind, occasionally tossing her head. This was better than pulling a rusty hay rake through the dusty meadow.

They stopped at the banks of a stream when the full heat of day was upon them, and Anne tethered the horses in thick rich grass, and took off Dan's saddle and blanket so he could roll in the grass. She swam in the creek and used a strip of her petticoat to wash the horses' faces, paying particular attention to their eyes where the flies gathered.

"There, you old fool, you look a lot better. If I had a comb, I'd make you beautiful," she crooned to Bess. "You look like you're having fun. We should have done this a long time ago." Then she fussed over Dan so he wouldn't get jealous, and then, because it had been a long and busy night and she was still just a little girl, she curled up and went to sleep, leaving the horses to graze and drink, rest and swish flies.

When she woke up, the skin on her face was dry and hot so she had another swim. Then she finished the last of one of the meat and potato pies and gave each of the horses a cookie from the saddlebag. Dan nuzzled her with his big head. Cookie was something new to him and he wanted some more. She gave him what was left of her own cookie, then saddled him, put the lead rope on Bess, and rode off after the sun which was already dipping toward the far-off hills.

They spent the night behind a natural windbreak, an outcropping of rocks pointing like fingers to the sky. There was grass for the horses and she gave them water to drink from the water canteen that had been her father's, pouring the water into Andrew's near-new hat and letting them drink from that. She spread Dan's saddle blanket on the rocks to air and made sure both horses had everything they needed and were securely tethered. Then she gave them each half an apple from the food the neighbors had brought, wrapped herself in the blankets from her mother's bed, lay down and went to sleep immediately.

Several times during the night Dan moved to stand near her, sniffing her hair, nuzzling her body with his big pink muzzle, and Bess made soft whickering noises the sleeping girl did not hear.

In the morning Anne gave them a drink, saddled Dan and rode off with the sun at her back, chewing happily on a piece of roast chicken. She stopped anytime the horses seemed to want to stop, filling the water canteen at a deep pool, where she swam and again bathed the horses. She made camp early and spent some time figuring out how to make the rifle fire. She lay down on her belly and aimed at a large rock, took a deep breath, pulled the trigger and thought her shoulder had been knocked loose from her spine.

"Doing something wrong, Dan. Must be doing something wrong. If a damn fool like Uncle Andrew can hit what he aims at, there's no reason I can't." And she tried again. She remembered he had seemed to cuddle the gun, so she held it close to her shoulder and laid her cheek along the smooth stock. She could see in her mind how his finger had curled, softly, not tugging at the trigger but squeezing it, and she tried to do what he had done. This time her shoulder was only half ripped away, and there was a satisfying ping! and a scratch on the rock.

Dan wasn't very impressed. He was tearing hungrily at the

grass, trying to eat it all before Bess could. Bess didn't seem worried. She was rolling on her back, her legs stuck up in the air, the memory of the hay rake already dimming in her mind.

Anne wakened once that night, sat up and spoke softly to the horses, then stared out across the prairie, her eyes straining. Nothing. Nothing to look at, nothing to see, and if anything or anybody approached, Dan and Bess would let her know. She lay back down, pulling the blankets up under her chin, and went back to sleep.

The saloon at Feather River was brightly lit, the noise from the piano fighting with the noise that passed for conversation from the crowd of cowboys, railroad workers and ranchers. Against the back wall a table of serious-faced poker players squinted at their cards, then at the well-dressed, handsome man who had most of the chips in front of him. He looked up briefly, his eyes scanning the crowd, resting momentarily on the bright professional smile of his woman, Sarah, who was dancing with a very young, very awkward teen-aged cowboy. Then he looked back down at his cards, his face betraying nothing.

Sarah, for the fifteenth time, coached the young cowboy in the mysteries of dancing. "One and two and one and two." She smiled, pretending to gaze deeply into his infatuated eyes. He nodded, his tongue licking his lips, too young and too inexperienced to realize she would be far prettier if she weren't so tarted up and covered with powder and paint.

Suddenly he whirled her off her feet, holding her tight, and she laughed happily, her arms wrapping around his neck. Spurred by his success, he headed across the dance floor with her, carrying her easily, grinning proudly as the older men called comments and advice on what to do once he got her upstairs. Sarah continued to smile over his shoulder, her eyes resting on the gambler, wishing again he didn't accept this so readily, knowing he would never understand what she was saying if she told him that just once, just once, she wished he would object. But she knew he wouldn't. He would ignore it, except when he held out his hand for the money.

"The third door," she said, and the young man, the boy, grinned again, and carried her down the hall toward the door of her room. He opened the door, carried her inside and placed her gently on the bed. "Close the door," she reminded him, and he blushed, stumbling in his eagerness, and not only closed the door but locked it. Then he turned toward the bed, suddenly frightened. She smiled and patted the bed. He moved to sit beside her.

"What's your name?" she whispered, beginning to unbutton his shirt.

"Johnny . . . John." He licked his lips again.

"John. That's a nice name. I had a cousin named John," she lied, her fingers moving to another button.

"What's your name?" he mumbled.

"Sarah," she answered, smiling at him brightly. He reached out and stroked her arm. "You have to promise," she urged, reaching for him, "that you'll be . . . nice . . . about this . . . don't grab at me or . . . be too eager."

"I won't," he blurted.

"Because I'm not very experienced at this," she lied again, "and I know you probably are."

"Not too," he contradicted, beginning to feel less awkward and stupid. "Not too much."

Luke Wilson marched down the main and only street of Feather River with his badge securely pinned to his vest, his gun riding low and comfortably on his hip and a dozen respectable members of the community backing him up, walking down the street with him. He had vowed to clean up the town if elected, and he had been elected and tonight he would clean up the town. All his life Luke Wilson had waged war against sin and trashy behavior, and Feather River was but one of several towns which had felt the power of his dedication. Ahead of them the lights of the saloon spilled into the street, the noise and laughter dared and insulted them. Luke Wilson led them to the gates of Sodom and Gommorah, the swinging doors of the saloon. He stepped inside, drawing his gun.

---

"Hands off the money, cardsharp . . . just stand up slow," he barked. The gambler froze, nodded once, politely, and then stood up. Carefully. The piano player let his hands fall to his lap. Several of the posse men ran up the steps, smashing open the doors, ordering the girls and their thwarted customers to head downstairs.

The young cowboy had his pants half off when the door began to shake and shudder under the repeated kicks of the posse. He raged with frustration and anger, dragging his pants back up, reaching for his shirt.

"Damn them," he muttered. "Damn them," and then the door burst and the righteous citizens were ordering him and Sarah to join the others.

"Oh, for God's sake," Sarah muttered to herself, shaking off the hand of one of the deputies. "If it's not one damn thing it's another."

She followed them downstairs, ignoring Luke Wilson and his cleanup crew. She could see Keno standing by the poker table, calmly watching the uproar. Then Keno caught her gaze, and smiled broadly. She stopped at the foot of the stairs, surprised, her heart thumping suddenly. The smile lingered on his face, his gaze seemed riveted on her. Luke Wilson turned to see what the gambler was looking at and in that moment Keno's hand darted out, covering and taking the pile of money from the table.

"My wife," he blurted, moving toward Sarah.

"Take it easy!" Luke warned, but Keno paid no attention.

He crossed the few feet of floor, grabbed Sarah and held her against his chest. "Cry, for chrissakes!" he commanded.

"Why?" she blurted.

"Dammit, do it," he snarled into her hair, and the sudden change from broad smile to heartless snarl made the tears flow. She wept on the front of his shirt, her makeup smearing against the carefully ironed ruffles.

"Come on," Luke ordered. "The jail's waiting."

Sarah moved obediently toward the door, wiping her eyes, smearing her makeup even more. Luke watched her, wishing a man was allowed to teach these tarts a real lesson. What she needed was a good beating and some strong yellow soap to get the signs of sin and devil worship off her face. In the moment Luke watched her, Keno made his move. He grabbed and swung the closest table, sending it crashing into Luke Wilson. Luke's gun went off with a loud crash and the young cowboy grunted, grabbed his belly, staring with disbelief at the widening stain of blood.

"Oh, my God!" Sarah screamed, trying to hold the boy upright. Keno raced past her, dove through the big window, landed like a cat and started to run off through the night. Luke's gun barked again and Keno grabbed at his leg and fell to the street.

"Get that gambler," Luke snarled. Then he turned and looked down to where the young cowboy, looking like a little boy, was bleeding his life into the sawdust on the floor.

"It hurts," John said faintly, "and I never even got a kiss."

"You're going to be all right, Johnny," Sarah sobbed, her lips brushing his cheek. "You'll see. We'll go on a picnic and I'll hold your hand. We'll laugh and . . ." Her voice trailed away, his eyes glazed over and he was dead.

"Look what you did!" she screamed accusingly. "Look what you did to him!"

"Not me," Luke grunted righteously. "Your man did it."

They sent the railroad workers and ranchers home, sent the cowboys home with the body of young Johnny, locked the piano player, bartender and the girls in the jail, and then dragged Keno and Sarah to the outskirts of town and roughed them both up thoroughly.

Keno sat, hands tied behind his back, wishing someone would give him one of his thin black cigars from his inside pocket. He had asked, several times, but nobody was listening to him. They were grinning and making jokes, watching as Sarah fought and cursed Luke Wilson. Keno could have told her it wouldn't do any good, but he knew Sarah couldn't hear him, either. Nobody seemed to be able to hear him. Maybe it was the blood in his mouth, blood from his broken teeth and lacerated gums, where

Luke Wilson's square-toed boot had emphasized his demand that Keno be quiet when Keno was trying to demand his right to a trial. A thin lariat was draped around his neck and he wanted to tell them it was all wrong, the rope was the wrong size, the knot the wrong kind—everything they were doing was wrong. Everything, from the time the table had tipped and the gun gone off, had been wrong. You never lose the little ones; it's always the big that matter. When your luck has gone sour, all that's left is bad luck, and if it wasn't for bad luck, some days he'd have had no luck at all. If it hadn't gone wrong, he'd have been out the window, down the dusty street and onto the back of a good fast horse. He'd have had a chance, a good chance—and a good chance was all Keno had ever needed to make his way through life. Sarah would have had to sit in jail with the other girls, but not for long, and when they were let out rumor and gossip would tell him where she was and he'd have been able to go and look her up if he felt like it, if he hadn't found someone else. Someone younger, like Sarah used to be, someone who didn't sometimes look at him as if she knew something he didn't, had learned something he hadn't learned, something about himself. But it had gone wrong, and now his hands, that could make a deck of cards do anything he wanted it to do when his luck was good, were tied behind his back. No use making a break for it, the damn rope around his damn neck was tied to the trunk of the damn tree, and even if he could shake it, his knee was shattered. He wouldn't be able to control the horse, wouldn't be able to keep his seat. And even if he could the damn horse was seven hundred and two years old and wouldn't go a mile before it foundered. When it goes bad it goes bad all the way from hell to breakfast. The only person who'd ever really listened to him was Sarah. She'd give him a thin black cigar if she could. If that big horse's ass Wilson wasn't holding her with one hand and slapping her with the other, telling her to shut her evil mouth before he forgot she was a woman and made it a double lesson.

"Your kind aren't wanted," Wilson snarled. "Your kind and your sin and devil worship aren't needed here. You caused the death of a young boy. You led him into temptation and then caused his death and he'll go in front of his Maker with a whore's perfume clinging to his clothes. If he goes to hell, you sent him there."

"Who had the gun?" Sarah shrieked. "You crazy bastard, who had the goddamned gun anyway? YOU killed him!"

Keno shrugged. If anybody would listen he could have told them it didn't matter who had the gun. The boy's luck had run out, that's all. If it hadn't been a gun it would have been a knife or a crazed steer or a piece of loose carpet on the steps or a chicken bone in his throat. When your luck has run out, it has run out, and Keno shrugged again, knowing he'd seen the last of his own.

They hanged Keno while Sarah wept, gagged and screamed. They weren't experts at lynching; in fact they weren't very good at it at all, never having done it before, and Keno didn't die quickly of a broken neck the way he was supposed to do. He swung choking at the end of the lariat, feet thrashing, clothes suddenly wet and stained, smelling of his own wastes as his body rebelled desperately. His eyes bugged out and his tongue protruded, and sickening sounds came from his throat. Two of the posse lost their suppers suddenly and never marched in the army of the righteous again. The others all had second thoughts about swift and sure justice, and a few even wondered if they hadn't been better off ignoring the lower end of town. But those who had second thoughts must have had third thoughts because when Keno was undeniably dead, they smeared melted tar on Sarah, broke open several of their wives' pillows, scattered the feathers all over her, then tied her to a half-broken young horse, whipped it and fired their guns at its head until it broke loose and raced off into the night with Sarah bouncing precariously on top, her skin blistered and hurting, her eyes glazed with terror, only the ropes holding her onto the horse. She looked so funny they all laughed. Except for the two who were still on their knees vomiting.

\* \* \*

26

Anne lay on her belly watching as the family left the farmhouse and rode off in their buggy. They were all dressed up in their best clothes, so she supposed they were going to church. The old dog raced after them for a few minutes, then turned and came back to guard the farm. She waited a while longer, then went to where Dan and Bess were standing and took what was left of the roast chicken from the pillow slip. It was greasy in the heat and she didn't really want it anyway.

She walked toward the farmhouse as if she had just paid for it and signed all the papers, and when the old dog ran toward her, barking, she tossed him a piece of chicken. He stopped barking and swallowed the meat, so she tossed him some more, being sure to keep some with her in case she had to bribe her way back out again.

She had seen them hide the key under the potted geranium on the porch rail, and she very carefully wiped her feet before entering the house. No need letting them know she'd been here.

In the house she moved quickly from room to room until she found what she wanted. The boys' bedroom. One of the boys was smaller than she was, none of his clothes would fit her at all, but the other boy was a year or so older, and she took a pair of overalls, a heavy work shirt and a lighter cotton shirt. With any luck they might not notice. She wished she dared take the new pair of overalls, but they'd know they were missing. As she was leaving, she noticed a hairbrush on the dresser. She doubted if the boys would ever know it was gone, and she swiped that, too.

Anne didn't like the idea of stealing. Martha had read the ten commandments to her, and while she hadn't understood the ones about coveting and adultery, and hadn't for-sure understood about graven images, she had very clearly understood all about stealing, lying and killing. On the other hand, Uncle Andrew had stolen, or as good as stolen, moving into someone else's house, moving in on someone else's farm, buying himself new sturdy boots with money someone else needed for doctoring, and not only had Martha not told the world what a big thief he was, she had cooked his meals, washed his clothes and put up with his bullying. If stealing was all that awful bad, why would Martha let things like that happen? And anyway, who'd know it was her? And if they did know, how would they catch her? And if they did catch her, what could they do to her? And after burning the barn and house, and maybe even Uncle Andrew, what was a pair of overalls, two shirts and a hairbrush?

Just before she left the room, Anne noticed a scuffed pair of work boots shoved far to the back of the closet. The boots had obviously not been worn in a long time. Probably the big boy had outgrown them—the smaller not yet grown to fit them. What was a pair of overalls, two shirts, a hairbrush and a pair of forgotten boots compared to arson and maybe even cooking Uncle Andrew?

The old dog didn't seem at all interested in barking or biting. Maybe he was only supposed to bark and raise a fuss when people came, not when they went. She patted his head, gave him the last of the chicken, then hurried to where Dan and Bess waited. She climbed into the saddle and urged Dan into an easy lope, riding away from the farmhouse, away from the old dog, away from the key she had hidden again under the geranium pot. She hoped the people wouldn't ever know she had been there. She hoped they didn't need the clothes. But they hadn't looked poor. Not really poor. Not like she and Momma had been. Was it worse to steal from really poor people than from people who had good clothes and a buggy to ride to church?

Anne urged Dan on, wishing Bess could run faster. She knew there was no real need for flight. Still, she felt a wish to put as much distance as possible between the farmhouse and herself, between her feelings of guilt and herself. She supposed that in a day or two, with enough miles separating her from the old dog and the geranium pot, she would forget that she had broken another commandment. Stealing, now. Lying, too, because even if she hadn't said anything to anybody, it was a kind of lie to let everyone think she had burned in the cabin, and Dan and Bess had run away in fear. Stealing and lying and maybe even roasting Uncle Andrew. She couldn't make herself think of killing or murdering. Roasting. Cooking. Singeing. Frying. But not those other words.

Dan was sweating and poor old Bess was lathered before Anne could begin to relax. She slowed to a walk, and when Bess quit huffing and puffing, she rode slowly to where she could see a clump of trees, a heavier growth of bush and grass that always meant water. In a country notorious for drought, it was odd that she had yet to go a full day without finding a stream, a creek or at least a trickle of drinkable water. This stream was small, but deep. The water was clean and cold. It left a sharp metallic taste in her mouth and Dan and Bess sucked it in deeply. She even had to back Bess away from it and make her take her time.

"You silly old thing, you know you aren't supposed to guzzle like that. You never learn. How many times have I got to tell you... Dan! You back off for a minute. You're as stupid as she is. Get all bloated up and moan to me about bellyache I suppose." She fussed and muttered, stripped off Dan's saddle and blanket and rubbed him down, laughing when he began butting her gently with his big head. "I know what you want. You want a bath, huh. Getting spoiled. Big tough thing like you wanting your ugly old face washed. Aren't you ashamed of yourself?" But he wasn't. He was getting used to being spoiled, beginning to enjoy being pampered. Anne gave him a piece of stale bread, quickly broke off another piece for Bess, who nudged her insistently, jealously. Then she carefully washed down the horses. They stood happily, their skin quivering, soft whickering noises coming from their loose pink lips. Bess rolled on the grass like a young filly and Dan acted like a big fool for a while, pretending to buck and kick, teasing her and himself, the raw power of his huge body held in check only by the soft voice and happy laughter of a girl so small he could easily crush her body with his metal-shod hooves.

In the saddlebag with the quilt-wrapped treasures was a piece of soap from the tin plate on the counter in the kitchen that had burned the night she let Uncle Andrew know some people can only be shoved so far. Anne took the soap with her downstream, stripped off her torn and filthy rag of a dress and jumped into the water, gasping at the cold. Standing in water past her waist she scrubbed herself vigorously, soaping her skin and her threadbare underwear, washing herself and her clothes at the same time. She dunked herself under the water, soaking her hair, then scrubbed it with the strong soap until she could feel the sweat and sand, dust and grass seed were gone. She rinsed her hair and lathered it again, enjoying the feel of a clean scalp.

She sat on the bank in her underwear, trying to ignore the itching skin of her buttocks as the cotton dried in the late afternoon sun. She muttered and cursed, grunted and winced until the stolen hairbrush had conquered all the tangles. Then she braided her hair into two thick golden pigtails and when her underwear was dry, she stepped into the stolen jeans and the warm thick shirt. She wished she had thought to steal a couple of pairs of socks, too.

Anyone riding by that evening would have seen what appeared to be a young boy eating meat and potato pie, cold ham and crushed cake, drinking creek water and talking constantly to two horses, a middle-aged mare and a strong young stud, both of which followed the slight figure as if they thought they were a couple of faithful dogs.

By midafternoon the next day, they were moving through a prairie dog colony. Anne looked at the pillow slip, grease-stained and grimy, and now nearly empty. The ham was still good, but it was nearly gone, and she wasn't sure she could trust the end of roast pork any longer. She considered carefully, then decided that willing or not, the time had come to begin learning how to make do without the funeral food.

She led the horses away from the prairie dog colony, dismounted and tethered them. Then she walked back with Uncle Andrew's rifle and a handful of shells, and sat waiting.

After a while one of the small animals poked his head up out of his hole, looked around quickly, then ducked back in the hole. Anne didn't move. He stuck his head out again, waited and then began to move out of his burrow. Still she didn't move. She sat ignoring the sweat that trickled into her eyes, ignoring the flies buzzing around her face, waiting until most of the colony were back out of the burrows, searching for food. Then she sighted carefully along the barrel of the rifle and fired at a fat young prairie dog. Before the sound of the shot had died, not a prairie dog was to be seen. Except the wildly thrashing and headless target.

She cut him open with Uncle Andrew's big knife and tried to pretend he was just another chicken to be cleaned before Andrew started shouting. She left the steaming innards for the birds and climbed back up on Dan, wrapping the dead prairie dog in a piece of her old dress which she had washed and kept . . . just in case. It hadn't been much of a dress, but it would keep the flies off the prairie dog. When they finally found water she smeared mud all over the little body, fur and all, and, when the animal was fully covered with thick mud, she dug a small hole, placed the prairie dog in the hole with some more mud over top, smoothed the dirt back in place and built a small fire. She had heard Uncle Andrew and a passing tinker talking about prairie ovens and how in the olden days the Cree and Blackfoot had made camp and cooked. She hoped it wasn't just another bag of hot wind like most of Uncle Andrew's stories had been.

She took the last of the potatoes from her saddlebag and placed them around the fire where they would, hopefully, bake slowly. She'd have to remember to turn them or they'd wind up like they did the last time, raw on one side and burnt on the other. Dan moved uneasily, his ears switching back and forth, and Bess turned to stare up the creek bed, both ears laid back. When Anne rose slowly, Dan tried to stand in front of her.

"It's okay," she muttered, grabbing Uncle Andrew's rifle from the scabbard and jacking a shell into the chamber. She moved cautiously and quietly up the creek, keeping the line of brush between her and whatever it was that had Dan worried. Everyone knew if it was a bear you had to wait until he stood up before aiming at the spot on his chest where the hair was rubbed off by the movement of his powerful front legs. If it was a cat you aimed for the head or hindquarters and if it was a wolf you fired and looked around immediately for others. She hoped it was none of them.

Soft snuffling noises and the cracking of twigs and branches, sniffing and ragged breathing. Anne moved forward, parting the branches carefully. She stared at the strange figure stumbling along the creek bed, slipping on wet rocks, weeping softly. Something black smeared the head and upper body, something white fluttered in the breeze. Anne burst out laughing.

Sarah whirled, slipping on the wet rocks and half falling. The branches parted and a slight figure in overalls and baggy shirt, carrying a huge rifle, with a hat pulled down over the ears, stepped out, laughing. At her.

"What's so funny, little boy?" she demanded haughtily.

"You are," Anne replied, giggling. "What's that stuck all over you?"

"The black," Sarah said carefully, "is tar and the other is feathers."

"What happened?" The child clambered down the bank, carefully pointing the rifle at the sky.

"The self-appointed guardians of public morality is what happened," Sarah snapped, getting to her feet.

"I don't know what you mean," Anne answered.

"I mean the righteous citizens of Feather River showed their Christian indignation when the sheriff shot and killed an eighteen-year-old boy."

"Why'd they take it out on you?"

"Why not?" Sarah sighed. "I was handy."

Anne led her up the cutbank and back toward the camp, grinning to herself as Sarah stumbled in her broken-heeled fancy red dancing shoes, cursed roundly and limped through the grass and weeds.

"You sure are a mess," she commented.

"Oh, shut up!" Sarah snapped, inelegantly snatching the ragged hem of her tattered skirt from a thorn bush.

Sarah collapsed in a heap beside the fire, glaring at both Dan and Bess as if blaming them for something.

"Where's Feather River?" Anne asked.

"Over there. Somewhere. How would I know where the bloody place is; I don't even know where HERE is!"

Anne decided anybody that snarly could sit by the fire and rot for all she cared. She turned the potatoes carefully, added some wood to the fire, and sat leaning against the saddle, waiting.

"You could at least offer me some coffee or something."

"I don't have any."

"What have you got, then?"

"Nothing. What have *you* got?" Anne countered. The sunburned, exhausted woman didn't answer, just stared moodily into the fire, her tar-stiffened hair hanging, the feathers fluttering like the headdress of some heathen chief. When the fire had died down and Anne guessed maybe the meal was ready, she scraped the embers away, poked and dug with a stick until the heat-hardened lump that was, hopefully, going to be supper was exposed.

"What's that?" Sarah snapped suspiciously.

"My oven," Anne answered, trying to juggle the prairie dog out of the depression.

Sarah watched, puzzled, as the tanned young hands grabbed a rock and beat on the baked clay until it split and . . . something . . . was exposed. Something that steamed and smelled enough like something she half remembered that her mouth began to water.

"What is it?" she asked in a less snarly tone of voice.

Anne stared over at the comical figure sitting across the fire from her. In spite of the tar, the feathers, the tattered dress of some kind of shiny material she did not recognize, in spite of the broken-heeled shoes and the blisters, there was something about this woman that made her think of Elizabeth Conroy and the young schoolteacher she had seen in town on one of the few visits she had made with her mother. Somehow she knew this . . . lady . . . might not like prairie dog.

"Big rabbit," she answered shortly, quickly peeling the skin from the body. The fur had come off with the clay, the skin lifted away easily and the meat lay juicy and delicious, teasing them with its scent.

---

33

"Potato," she invited, tossing one over easily. The woman caught it, juggled it from hand to hand, tears springing suddenly to her eyes. "What's wrong?" Anne asked, and when the woman didn't answer Anne reached out, took her hand and turned it palm upward. "I'm sorry, I didn't know," she stammered, staring down at the raw flesh, seeing where the ropes had cut into the frail wrists, wincing inwardly at the stones and gravel imbedded in the skinned palms.

"I fell," Sarah explained inadequately, breaking open the potato and nibbling at it, torn between hunger and a fear the hot potato would hurt her blistered lips.

"Here," Anne handed over one of the hind legs, and Sarah bit into it eagerly.

"It's good," she mumbled, her teeth ripping at the flesh. Anne nodded, and gingerly tasted the big rabbit she knew was prairie dog. It wasn't bad at all.

"Should have used some salt or something," Anne muttered, wiping the juice from her chin. Sarah didn't even nod, she concentrated alternately on the potato and the big rabbit, and when Anne handed over the water canteen, she drank greedily.

"Why'd they get mad at you?" Anne prompted, her mouth full.

So Sarah, between bites and chewing, told about Keno, the young cowboy and Luke Wilson.

"Then they tied me onto a horse," she finished slowly, "and scared the poor thing half to death so he'd run . . . they tied my feet with a rope under his belly and tied my hands to his mane. And he ran until he couldn't run any more . . . then he walked . . . and ran some more . . . and once he tried to rub me off against a tree."

"How'd you get loose?" Anne asked softly.

"I don't know." Sarah yawned. "One minute I was half asleep, the next minute the rope broke and I fell off and landed in the sand."

"Where's the horse now?"

"Oh, how in hell would I know where the bloody horse is! I don't care if I never see him again!"

---

"You will," Anne said, angrily, "when you have to walk." And she rose suddenly, not wanting to share another minute with such a bitchy person. Sarah ignored the insulted child, lay down gingerly, wincing as the ground reminded her of her assortment of cuts and bruises. With her belly full for the first time in days, free of the ropes and the constant painful movement of the half-wild horse, she closed her eyes and was asleep almost immediately.

Anne moved along the creek bed. Unless the horse was a fool, he'd be close to water. Either that or the lady in the tar-and-feathers had walked a long distance in those broken-heeled shoes. And Anne doubted if she'd gone any more than a mile in them. Not far up the creek from where she had found Sarah, Anne came upon the horse. He was too tired to even try to get away from her, or maybe he hoped she could take him to a stall or corral, or maybe he smelled Dan and Bess on her clothes. Whatever his reasons, if horses have reasons, he stood calmly while she walked up to him and took hold of what was left of his halter.

"Not much of a halter," she soothed him with her voice and hands, "but you're not much of a horse, I guess. No saddle, no bridle. I guess they didn't want to waste a penny on either of you. Come on you silly thing, come with Anne, that's a good boy." And talking constantly, softly, she led him back to where Dan and Bess were grazing.

Dan had to put his ears back and bare his teeth and generally demonstrate who was boss around the place, but Bess really didn't seem interested in anything except maybe getting Anne to rub her with a cloth or spoil her with a piece of apple or a bit of cookie. The new horse seemed willing to let Dan give the orders and when Anne offered him a piece of stale bread he took it only because he had already seen the other two horses reaching for it eagerly.

"I'm not sure you'll hang around the way they do, so you're going to get hobbled for tonight," she explained. "Maybe when you're more used to us all you can be left loose like they are. There's lots for you to eat and you can get all the water you want just over there, so don't look at me with big sad eyes because it's for your own good. It's all wolves and bears out there at night and you're lucky you made it this far on your own."

Anne rebuilt the campfire and stored what was left of the prairie dog under a bush. She took her sweaty shirt, the pillow slip and the blood-stained piece of her dress she had wrapped the big rabbit in down to the creek and rinsed them out carefully, then hung them on a bush near the fire. She went back down to the creek and washed her hands and face, tucking her braids securely under her hat again. Then she went back up to the campfire and leaned against the saddle watching the sleeping woman.

It was dusk, almost dark, when Sarah jerked awake suddenly. For a moment she could only stare across the flickering campfire, trying to remember who the slender young boy with the tanned face and the slightly slanted blue eyes was.

"I found the horse," Anne said softly.

"I don't care about the damn horse!" she snapped. "You didn't happen to find any coffee by any chance?"

"Did you lose any coffee," Anne snapped, stung and hurt. For a long moment she glared back at Sarah, and then Sarah shook her head, dropped her eyes, blinking against tears.

"I'm sorry," Sarah said, her voice totally changed. "It's just . . . I went to sleep with you yapping about that damn horse and I wake up and you're still yapping about him."

"Yeah? Well you ought to give a damn about that horse because in case you haven't noticed it . . . lady! . . . those shoes of yours aren't much good for walking!"

"I'm sorry. I said I was sorry."

"That makes it okay, I suppose?" Anne rose suddenly, her face and voice hard, her eyes glaring out from under the too-big hat. "You can be just as bitchy as you want and just as nasty as it suits you to be, and then you just say, 'Oh, I'm sorry,' and that makes everything okay! I do hope you'll forgive me . . . madam . . . I didn't recognize you for the la de dah lady you obviously are. I'm so ignorant all I could see was tar and feathers and blisters and scratches and half-starved and ugly. I couldn't see that underneath all of that was the Queen of bloody England."

Sarah let the tears flow. She didn't care that her nose was running; she didn't care that her eyes were swelling and making her even more comical and ugly.

"I'm sorry," she sobbed.

"Aw, cut it out, will you?" Anne grumbled, heading for her bedroll and taking out her blankets. "That won't do any good. It'll just make you sick." And she lay down, wrapping the blankets around herself, rolling with her back turned to the snivelling Sarah.

Sarah stared at the stubbornly stiff back, tried to think of something to say and couldn't. She began to pick hopelessly at the feathers stuck to the tar on her head. After a few moments Anne rolled over, watching.

"Maybe if you put pork fat on it . . . or butter," she offered.

"You've got butter, I suppose."

"No," Anne admitted, "but . . ."

"Then shut up. If I had butter I could take off this mess. Or if I had kerosene. Or coal oil. Or if I had a store full of clothes. Or a bank full of money. Or . . ."

"Oh shut up," Anne snapped, rolling over again.

"I'm sorry," Sarah said after a long pause. "What's your name anyway?"

"My name's Anne," the child mumbled.

"Sam?" Sarah misunderstood, "Sam who?"

"Sam none of your goddamn business," Anne said clearly, effectively stopping all further conversation.

Sarah glared, then, after a few minutes of nothing to do but stare at the fire, she lay down, again wincing as the rocks and grass dug into her tender bruises. She closed her eyes, shivering slightly in the cooling night air, and went to sleep quickly.

Later that night the child woke up, sitting up and looking around to check the camp. Sarah was sitting, half asleep, shivering by the fire.

"Why aren't you asleep?" Anne demanded.

"I'm cold," Sarah said apologetically.

Anne rose from her blankets, got the warm winter jacket that had belonged to roasted Uncle Andrew and put it around Sarah's shoulders. Then, rather than appear to be making up after the argument, she pulled her hat down further over her eyes and growled, "And I want it back, see?" Sarah nodded, too grateful for the jacket to be able to respond to the surliness. She lay back down on the hard ground, hugging herself in the welcome warmth, her abused and exhausted body demanding more sleep.

# Chapter 3

The sound of the rifle shot brought Sarah awake. She tried to jump to her feet but her muscles were stiff and sore, and when she tried to run, the best she could do was hobble. She was terrified, but the horses seemed undismayed, they were grazing contentedly. "Sam! Sam!" she screamed, "are you all right?" She ran hobbling toward the creek, her feathers fluttering, her torn dancehall dress flapping. "Sam! Sam, are you hurt?"

She slid down the bank, landing almost at Anne's feet. She glared up at the youngster with the big gun and oversize hat.

"Why didn't you answer me?" she demanded.

"I didn't hear you."

"Well, I called!"

"Well, here I am. You okay?"

"I'm fine! Just fine!" She struggled to her feet, glaring.

"Then why don't you get washed up. Breakfast'll be ready in a half hour." The youngster walked away, heavy work boots crunching on the hard rocks of the creekbed.

Sarah moved toward the stream carefully, her bruised and swollen feet hesitating to touch anything. She had taken off her shoes last night and her feet had swelled so much she doubted if she'd ever get the shoes back on again. She walked into the water and though it was bitter cold, it felt good on her sunburned and tar-blistered skin, and she lay back in the water, feeling her body soaking up the moisture. When the cold began to make

39

her teeth chatter, she made her way painfully back up the bank to where the youngster was roasting small pieces of meat over a campfire.

"I found some prairie onions," Anne said, face carefully averted, voice neutral, "and there's sage out there . . . Keep your eyes open for anything like that. It comes in handy."

"What's that?" Sarah asked, eyeing the pieces of meat hanging from a green willow spit.

Anne took a piece, put it in her mouth, chewed slowly. "Well, it looks like meat, it smells like meat, it feels like meat, and, by golly, it tastes like meat." She took another piece. "Boy, it seems like all I've done since I left home is stuff my face. I bet I put on five pounds at least. Must be the fresh air."

Sarah reached out, took a piece of meat, placed it in her mouth and chewed. "You're right," she grinned, "it sure is meat." Their eyes met, and then they were both grinning companionably. "More of that . . . big rabbit?" Sarah asked carefully.

"Nope."

"What is it?"

"Lady," the child spoke carefully, not mockingly, "I really don't think you want to know." Again their eyes met, and Sarah nodded.

"Okay," she said easily, "don't tell me. See if I care. But I don't notice any legs . . ." They both turned away, trying to hide their grins. "Of course," Sarah added, "I don't suppose fish have legs either."

"No, they don't." The child grinned.

"Did you save the rattles?" Sarah asked suddenly, laughing.

"They're good luck," Anne replied calmly.

"Yeah?" Sarah drawled, reaching for another piece of meat. "They didn't do this guy much good."

When they had eaten and Anne had checked the horses, she turned to Sarah, almost hesitantly. "Will you be okay alone here for a while?"

"Alone? Why?"

"I'll be back," Anne said quickly. "I promise! There's wood

for the fire, and I'll leave you the rifle, and there's food . . . some of the . . . big rabbit and . . . fish, wrapped in cloth under the bush there."

"The rifle?" Sarah echoed, feeling frightened.

"You won't need it," the child assured her. "You're the only person I've seen in days and days."

Sarah wanted to ask Sam to stay, but she couldn't.

She sat by the fire trying not to feel abandoned, trying to reassure herself that the boy would never ride off and leave his horse, gun, saddlebags and hatchet. He'll be back, she kept telling herself. Sam said he'd be back, and he'll be back.

She spent the entire day sitting by the campfire, alternately dozing and jerking awake with a start. She warmed up the snake meat and ate some of the big rabbit (or whatever) cold. She drank a lot of water and even found herself talking to the horses. And her eyes constantly scanned the horizon, watching for Sam.

When the youngster hadn't returned by nightfall Sarah gathered a supply of wood. If she kept the fire going all night it might be a beacon to guide Sam back to camp. And it might keep away the bears, wolves, coyotes and, probably, wild Indians and general threats and menaces, any and all of which she half expected to see storm out of the shadows at any minute. She wrapped Sam's big winter jacket around her shoulders and tried to force herself to sleep. Once she even went over to Sam's bedroll and reached out to take a blanket. Then she drew back her hand quickly, guiltily, and returned to sit by the fire. Somehow it seemed a bit much. After all the child had already done for her, it seemed a bit much, and a bit too personal, to use his blankets, too.

Miles away the citizens of Feather River slept soundly in their beds, safe from the dangers of dancing and the evils of drink and loose women. Luke Wilson patrolled the streets, ferreting out all manner of sinful sex, even throwing a rock at Mrs. Franklin's sloe-eyed tabby cat when she arched her back invitingly and a tattered-eared tom crept toward her happily. He

41

was so busy chasing the sex-starved cats he did not notice a small, barefoot figure in overalls and a too-big hat.

Anne moved from shadow to shadow, past the dark and silent saloon, past the hardware store and jail. She caught a glimpse now and again of a rat-faced man who seemed to have a hate going with a couple of cats, but he never looked her way, and, when he dodged down an alley in pursuit of the tattered-eared tom, she slid quickly into the blacksmith shop and came out a few minutes later with a half-filled sack of some kind, a horse blanket she found hanging on a wall, and a large can. No sign of the rat-faced cat hater, and she ran quickly to where she had left Dan waiting with her boots tied together by the laces, hanging from the saddle horn.

First dawn was breaking when she got back to camp. Sarah was asleep by the remnants of a fire, but when Bess whickered a greeting, Sarah snapped awake, her eyes wide with what Anne knew was fear.

"I was worried," Sarah admitted.

"Why?"

"You . . . took so long."

"I said I'd be back." Anne dismounted and moved toward Sarah with a sack and a can. She dropped them, stripped the saddle and bridle from Dan, and patted his rump, then opened the sack and took out a double handful of grain.

"Here, y'ole fools," she urged, spreading the feed where all three horses could nose at it. "Get fat." Then she picked up the can and tossed it to Sarah. "This is for you."

"What is it?"

"Axle grease. All I could find. For your tar."

"Axle grease? Where did you get axle grease?"

"I stole it," the youngster said frankly.

"You aren't supposed to steal!" Sarah protested. "You'll get into trouble."

"Yeah?" Anne reacted to what she thought was criticism. "Well I bet you've done a lot of Not Supposed To's in your life!"

---

They eyed each other warily, each afraid of, but primed for, another argument. "I'm sorry," Sarah admitted.

"That's okay," Anne answered.

They smeared axle grease liberally on Sarah's arms, hands, face and legs, but were halted by the gummy mess that used to be her hair.

"I think we'll have to cut most of it off," Anne said, inwardly glad it wasn't her hair.

"Keno used to say I had the loveliest hair he'd ever seen," Sarah grieved, tears welling.

"Yeah," Anne grunted unsympathetically. "Well, it'll grow back," and the big knife moved quickly, tugging and cutting off the matted hair. "That's more than can be said for Keno," the child added suddenly. Sarah was shocked and insulted, and then amazed as the child suddenly jumped to his feet waving a handful of tar-feathers-hair, and began whooping like an Indian, waving a "scalp" and dancing insanely.

"Stop it!" Sarah snapped. And then she began to laugh. "You fool, what if you make it rain!"

They finished shearing Sarah's head, then spent a long time gently coaxing the tar from her skin, rubbing the axle grease into the burns and blisters. Sometimes Sarah wept with pain, her head bowed and pathetically vulnerable in its nakedness.

"I can stop if you want," Anne offered.

"No," Sarah gritted. "Get it off if you can."

Anne picked at the tar, cursing the mentality that would smear anything hot on somebody's skin, wincing as blisters broke and Sarah made involuntary grunts of pain. Her head, Anne thought, looked like a thin-shelled egg, the kind you have to lift carefully or you'll break it.

"I think that's all of it," she said.

"I don't think I've got any skin left at all."

"Not much you don't," Anne agreed. "I think we should leave most of that grease on for a while or you're gonna get awful sunburn."

"I've already got awful sunburn," Sarah tried to grin, "and

wind burn, and rope burn and sand burn . . . Would you believe, looking at me now, that at one time people said I was beautiful."

"Yeah," Anne said shyly, "I'd believe it." She turned away wondering if she'd be able to joke if it was her with bare patches of skin covered with dark axle grease and her head shorn and nicked. "I got you something."

"Where'd you get that?" Sarah asked, staring at the clothes the child held toward her.

"Offa the clothesline of someone who forgot to take them in last night."

"What if you'd got caught?"

"I wasn't," she grinned. "And you sure can't go much farther in that tarry dress of yours!"

Eagerly Sarah unwrapped the bundle, then stared in shock and disappointment.

"Well, for chrissakes," she exploded. "If you had to go and steal, couldn't you at least steal a *dress?*"

Anne recoiled in shock and hurt, not understanding why Sarah wasn't pleased with the jeans and shirt.

"Are you so stupid you don't know the difference between a man and a woman?" Sarah raged. "What am I supposed to do with . . . this!"

"You can wear it," Anne said hotly. "Either wear it or ram it where the sun don't ever shine!"

"You watch your tongue, young man!"

"What do you want a dress for anyway?" Anne attacked. "So you can maybe go back into town and find yourself another gambler? Maybe wait for your hair to grow back in so you can work in a back room and give him your money? You want *me* to steal you a dress so's you can wind up all tar and feathers again?"

"Damn you!" Sarah snapped, grabbing the child by the shoulders and shaking fiercely. "Don't you talk to me like that!"

The oversize hat fell to the ground, the bright gold pigtails tumbled and hung around the girl's shoulders. Sarah stepped back, surprised.

---

"Now look what you went and done," Anne accused, fighting back her tears. "Now just look what you went and done."

She wept with anger and hurt and because she was sure now that she was no longer "Sam," she would either have to ride off on her own or start taking orders again because, after all, she was just a half-grown girl and so not able to even take care of herself.

Sarah had never had a younger sister or even an older sister for that matter. She couldn't even really remember her parents. Her life had been aunts and cousins, disapproving grandparents and growing resentment until the day she had accepted an invitation to get on the train and leave town with a heavyset middle-aged man who claimed to be a land surveyor. A couple of months later, just before her seventeenth birthday, she woke up in a hotel room in a town the name of which she didn't even know and found the man gone. He left her ten dollars and she still had four dollars of it left when a drover, who was staying overnight in the hotel, asked her if she'd like to join him for supper. She joined him for supper and put her few possessions in his wagon and left town when he did. There were other men, most of them faceless and uninteresting, except that they kept her fed and clothed without asking too much in return. Then, just when she thought she had things in focus, there was Keno. Three years with Keno and the focus was still fuzzy. He had been polite and even gentle, but she never felt she *knew* him. He smilingly allowed her to love him, love him totally, but never even pretended to love her. And when she asked him, "Do you love me, Keno?" he would grin and say, "Honey, I'm here, aren't I" as if that was an answer. For the first few weeks she had been Keno's woman, and then, in some one-cat town or another, he was thrown in jail and his money taken from him. He needed thirty dollars to pay a fine or they were going to send him to jail for a year. The thought of Keno in jail for a year was unthinkable. Keno with his snow-white starched shirts and the tantalizing faint scent of his aftershave lotion in jail? Keno, with his cheeks smooth and freshly scraped and the hair on his chest growing up his throat

45

until he had to trim it so it wouldn't show above his snow white collar, sitting in a smelly jail with stubble on his face, eating pig shit for food and breaking big rocks into little rocks? Not if she could help it. And after that, without either one of them ever saying anything, Keno worked the tables and she worked a back room and turned her money over to him. Anything she wanted, she had, all she had to do was ask. Anything, except, "Yes, I love you, Sarah." Anything except, "Get out of that back room and stay out." Anything except the little bit of life she *really* wanted.

She moved to the stiffly sobbing child and put her arms around the defiant shoulders. "Hey, I'm the one who blubbers, not you." And later, when the sniffles had stopped, she grinned teasingly. "Sam?" she said. "*Sam?*"

"I didn't say Sam. I said Anne and you heard Sam."

"Well, you could have corrected me."

"I figured," the girl said haltingly, "that if you thought I was . . . a guy . . . you'd feel . . . safer and less . . . scared."

"What made you think that?"

"Well," the blue eyes looked carefully down at the dirt, "people figure girls can't look after themselves."

"Hell," Sarah laughed, her voice brittle, "if we don't, who will?" Anne nodded, not really understanding. "You still mad at me?" Sarah teased.

"No. I wasn't mad but . . . I'd done the best I could and . . ."

"And I was being a bitch again."


The sun had warmed the air but the creek water was biting cold. Anne stripped off her overalls and shirt and walked into the water in her underwear, carrying the nub of strong yellow soap. She lathered her cotton garments and reached underneath the wet cloth and soaped her skin energetically.

"You always take a bath in your clothes?"

"Doesn't everyone?" She couldn't even imagine what it was like not to take a bath with your underthings still on. There had been no place private to take a bath for as long as she could remember. Water was heated on the stove and you scrunched down in one of Martha's washtubs and got yourself as clean as you could. Uncle Andrew might be sitting at the table, sipping from his jug or fixing a piece of harness, and you couldn't very well strip to the buff with him there. The bedroom was too small to take the washtub in there. The barn was too far to carry water, and anyway Uncle Andrew might need something in the barn. So you climbed into the tub in your unders and Martha held a towel or a piece of sheet up and you got the whole thing over with as fast as you could.

"What's that thing you're wearing?" she asked, eyeing Sarah's corset.

"All women wear them."

"My mom didn't. All laces and buckles and ... doesn't it hurt?"

"You get used to it. But this one smells, and I don't think I can get used to that!" Sarah began to remove the corset. Anne quickly turned her back, her face flaming, her ears burning.

"What's the matter?" Sarah teased. "Afraid I've got something you haven't got?" Then her soft laughter changed to total shock. "My God," she blurted and Anne whirled, expecting to see Indians or snakes or ... "I didn't even *feel* it." Sarah stared down at the wet bills, the money Keno had snatched from the poker table and stuffed down the back of her dress.

Now that she had some money, Anne knew, Sarah would find some town other than Feather River and buy herself another tight shiny dress with a short hem so her legs showed, and Anne would be alone with Dan and Bess again.

"You figure that wet money is gonna take the place of a bath?" she growled jealously, stalking out of the water and leaving the nub of soap on a flat rock. Sarah watched Anne leaving, staring in puzzlement at the stiff young back walking away from her. Then she quickly put the wet money on the ground with a rock on top of it so the wind wouldn't blow it away, picked up the bar of strong soap, and began to wash, gingerly, her eyes smarting as the laundry soap stung the raw places on her body.

The stolen shirt was too tight and the stolen pants were big enough in the backside to have room for someone else, but the

47

sun didn't beat down on her arms and legs and the wind didn't dry out the scabbed and raw places on her back. The partially trained young horse Anne called "OtherOne" because Dan was a horse. Dan was a horse and "he's the other one." He didn't want to have anything to do with Sarah. Possibly he remembered the frantic days and nights with her tied to his back, because he didn't object when Anne threw the stolen blanket over his back and rode him, but he went into wide-eyed skittish frenzy as soon as Sarah walked toward him.

"He sure doesn't like you," Anne remarked.

"I'm not too fond of him, either."

"Maybe he knows that." Anne shrugged and took the blanket over to Bess and threw it across her broad back. "Don't dig her with your heels and don't pull hard on her head and don't slap at her, or scream at her or be nasty."

"Do I look like the kind of person who would do all that to a skinny old horse?"

"You think she's skinny now you should have seen her a while ago," Anne answered, avoiding the question. "And before you get on her you'd better talk nice to her and scratch her forehead because she doesn't have to let you ride, you know."

"You talk as if she could think!" Sarah mocked, reaching up to scratch disinterestedly between the old mare's eyes.

"How do you know she can't? What have you done for her that she should lug you where you want to go?"

"Isn't she trained?"

"Trained?" Anne laughed harshly. "Sure. Uncle Andrew trained her to drag heavy stuff for him or get kicked and hit. She's not dragging you and if you kick her or hit her I'll do the same to you. If you and I both fell into a big hole that horse would make out just fine. If she falls into a big hole you've got a long way to walk on those sore feet of yours."

"You don't have to get mad!" Sarah protested, wishing she could understand this contradictory young brat who one minute risked getting caught as a thief for you and a minute later bit off your head and spit it on the ground at your feet.

---

48

"I'm not mad. I just think you've got an awful nerve sometimes. OtherOne hates you and you think I'm a fool for being nice to my horse so she doesn't hate me."

Sarah wanted to say that she didn't think the child was a fool at all, but she held her tongue. She led the placid mare to where she could step up on a rock and from there get on the broad bony back. "How can a horse be so rib-showing skinny and still be built like a boat across the back?" she asked idly.

"It's easy," Anne said, looking away quickly. "You just take what ought to be a real big horse and then you give it just enough to keep it from falling over. I hope," she exploded quietly, "I hope that mean-eyed son of a bitch bubbled like bacon!" and she urged Dan to a quick trot, the half-trained young horse following on the tether rope Bess had once used.

"Up, bonerack," Sarah patted the mare's neck, and Bess moved off after Dan, not obeying Sarah as much as keeping up with Anne.

They kept carefully clear of Feather River and moved easily following the setting sun. They camped where there was water because that almost always meant shelter for them and food for the horses. When it rained, as it did one night, they huddled miserably around the fire and wished aloud for either a tent or waterproof slickers. Anne kept them fed with big rabbit and dry-land fish (with and without rattles) that she managed to bring down with Andrew's rifle. Once she aimed at and actually hit a bird, but the rifle bullet blew it apart so totally they couldn't tell if it was a grouse, a pigeon or a penguin.

"My uncle Tom," Sarah remarked, eyeing the splattered bundle of feathers, "told me there were birds out here called Fool Hens. He said that in the last dusk and first dawn you'd see them roosting in trees, spread out side by side on the branches."

"I've seen them," Anne admitted.

"Well, he says if you sneak up on them from the side they won't see you because they never turn their heads, they only look straight in front . . . and he said if you started with the outside one on the lowest branch you could just grab it and if you put

49

one hand over its back so it couldn't flap its wings, and used the other hand to grab its legs and lift it off the branch, the others wouldn't move. The thing can squawk all it wants, that doesn't scare them. But if it flaps or if you pass your hand in front of the others, they'll take off and if one moves they all move. He said if you were careful you could pick a dozen of them off the same tree."

"You think he was talking for real or just joshing? Maybe it's like Uncle Andrew saying if you could get close enough to a sparrow to put salt on its tail you could catch it and keep it for a pet . . ."

"Won't hurt to try."

The first few times they tried they did something wrong and wound up with nothing but a few tail feathers, but finally, one evening, Sarah reached out slowly and before either of them knew what happened, she had a Fool Hen off the branch and in her hands.

"Now I don't know," Anne mused aloud, "whether the story is true or whether we just got so . . . crafty . . . that we made it work!"

"What do you want?" Sarah teased. "A written guarantee? I mean just look at them on the spit! Someone once told me it looks like meat, it smells like meat . . ." and then they were both laughing.

In the evening Sarah would watch Anne talking to the horses, wiping their faces with a damp cloth, cleaning their eyes and the insides of their ears. And one night she surprised even herself by casually throwing her arm over Bess' increasingly glossy neck and speaking to the old mare as if she was a person. Anne noticed immediately, and the smile that flashed was the broadest and happiest Sarah had seen since she had first set eyes on the girl. The half-trained young horse no longer acted up every time she went near him, but he still wasn't eager to have her climb on his back, although now, at least, he would allow her to lift his leg clear of the ground and examine his hooves for rocks.

\* \* \*

50

"We got a letter once," Anne said suddenly. "A man came out from town with it. My mother read it and then she sat in her room for the rest of the day. She looked as if she was crying, but she wasn't."

"What did it say?" Sarah asked idly.

"I don't know," Anne shrugged. "I asked her and she just said something about a piano and lace curtains and then she wouldn't say anything else. We never got another letter."

"Maybe it was from her family?"

"Don't see how it could be," Anne yawned. "A piano and lace curtains means quality. Do I look like any of us were ever quality?"

"You ever read the Bible?" Sarah asked quietly, poking the fire and sending sparks rising to the sky. "Remember how there was only Adam and Eve? And they're the grandparents of all of us. And when all the cousins and second cousins started spreading out and filling up the world, there was the flood and only Noah, his wife, his sons and his daughters-in-law made it through so again we had common grandparents. The King of Persia has the same grandparents you have, if you go back far enough. If he's quality, so are you."

"Yeah," Anne grinned, "but who says the King of Persia has lace curtains and a piano?"

"I don't see why you want to go to whatever the name of that place is!" Anne protested.

"Freshwater," Sarah repeated, sitting sideways on old Bess' back, her bare feet dangling above the long yellow grass.

"Well, I don't see why you want to go there."

"I've got a friend there. She'll help."

"Help who? Help what?"

"Help find work," Sarah said, resisting the impulse to reach out and push Anne off Dan's back.

"You've got money," Anne growled, "lots of money."

"Not enough. It won't last forever and I'll need work."

"Doing what you did before, I guess." And when Sarah ignored her and the silence grew thick, "You didn't always do that, did you?" But Sarah still wouldn't answer. "It was him, wasn't it? That Keno guy?"

"Mind your own goddamn business!" Sarah slapped old Bess on the rump, so startling the old mare that she even managed to pass Dan and stay ahead of him for a few minutes.

They didn't speak to each other until after they had stopped and made camp. Anne had managed, after three abortive attempts, to shoot the head off a rabbit and was skinning it with Uncle Andrew's big knife. Sarah came toward the campfire carrying a rattlesnake on a stick, its head flattened by a large rock she had managed, by good luck rather than good management, to drop on it.

"Want the rattles?" she asked, hoping to repair things.

"Sure," Anne nodded, "maybe they'll bring me more luck than they brought him." Anne too, wanted to repair the rift and deliberately used the weak joke Sarah had made once before.

"You must have quite a collection of rattles by now."

"Yeah, maybe I'll make a necklace or something." She finished skinning the rabbit, then handed the big knife to Sarah who began, inexpertly, to skin the snake.

"Anne . . ." Sarah's voice was suddenly shaky and she was afraid she might even begin to cry. "I'm sorry, but . . . I'm not sure I can take very much more of this. Snake and gopher and . . ." She forced herself to look up, look into the unwavering blue eyes. "I'm sorry. You chose to live like this. I got shoved into it and . . . I'm not really very good at it. I try. But . . ."

The silence grew until she thought she was going to scream and then "Okay," Anne nodded.

"You don't mind?"

"I mind." The small tanned hands busied themselves with the raw meat. "I mind, but . . . Okay."

When they had eaten and were lying by the fire watching the shadows grow as the darkness fell, Sarah tried to explain. There was a chill in the air and the sky looked as if there would soon be geese vee'ing their way south. Sarah pulled the warm jacket tight around her throat and tried to tuck her bare feet under her.

---

When Anne noticed, she moved closer and rearranged the blankets so they were spread over both of them.

"What are you going to do when it's wintertime?" Sarah's voice was soft. Anne had to move even closer to hear her.

"What do you mean?" she asked, admitting she hadn't even begun to think about wintertime.

"There won't be any snakes or gophers. They'll all be in their dens, hibernating. No Fool Hens or prairie dogs, and no grass for Dan and Bess. You'll freeze."

"Maybe not . . ."

"Oh, baby . . . remember last Christmas . . . tell me about last Christmas, at home with your mom . . ."

"Christmas?" Anne's face softened and her eyes shone in the firelight. "Christmas was . . . I didn't have any money to buy anything for Momma, and there wasn't any place in the house where you could go off by yourself and make a surprise, so we talked about it." She grinned suddenly. "Funny, that was when we started really talking to each other, not at each other, you know? I told her there was something I wanted to do for her for a present, but there wasn't any place to go and do it without her knowing, and she said she knew what I meant because she had to wait until I was asleep before she could do some work on what she was doing for me. So we agreed we wouldn't look and if we did, by accident, look, well we just wouldn't *see*. She had this quilt she'd got from her mother when she got married . . . it's in my saddlebag . . . and it was all kind of worn out. And I had a bunch of pieces of cloth I'd saved. Some I scrounged from Elizabeth. She always had lots of pieces of cloth, and she gave me a whole bundle. And where the stitching had come loose, I did new stitching and anywhere the double wedding rings had started to tear or something, I'd make a new piece and fit over it and, like, patch it." Anne half laughed. "I guess a lot of it came out kind of funny colored but . . . she liked it."

"And what was it like? Christmas?"

"Christmas? Well, we killed a chicken we knew wasn't going to be laying much this year, and we had that and some potatoes and a big pot of yellow turnips. We had some cornmeal for bread and Momma made a sort of a pudding out of carrots and stuff. We got up in the morning and gave each other what we'd made, and she had some knit socks for Uncle Andrew." Her eyes widened with memory and her voice was edged with surprise. "And he'd bought some peppermint candy! Peppermint candy and one orange each. I'd forgotten that. Then he put on his socks and he went outside to feed the stock and when he came back in he said his feet were warm even if there was another three inches of snow. Then," her tone hardened, "he sat around in the kitchen drinking from his jug until it was time for him to stuff his face."

"Snow?" Sarah urged softly.

"Yeah, we had snow so deep it was up to my bum and we had to break the ice for the animals to drink. Some nights we slept with sweaters on because the stove would go out."

"And you're going to tough it out on the prairie with a couple of horses, some blankets and this jacket?" There was a long silence.

"My mother told me once that the dumbest thing any person could ever do was cut off their nose to spite their face."

Sarah nodded and patted Anne's shoulder, and the girl turned on her side, reaching back to make sure the blankets were spread over them both. They fell asleep that way, Sarah's arm draped over the girl's waist, and when the wind freshened and the fire burned itself out, they cuddled together under the blankets. When Sarah woke in the morning, Anne was curled against her back, their bodies curved and fitting together perfectly.

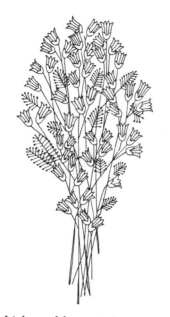

# Chapter 4

Unpainted false-front buildings with small windows of flawed
glass, and when you looked
through them everything danced
and jiggled, shapes were altered
and you saw the same things but
from a different perspective, as
though reality itself was different. Board sidewalks on which
heavily booted feet made loud
echoing noises. An unpaved
street, the dirt pounded hard as
rock in dry weather, churned to
a thick muddy paste in wet weather, and people in faded overalls
and collarless shirts or homemade dresses with long skirts and
high necks, staring at them as they rode into town. A young girl
with long yellow braids, overalls, faded shirt and heavy boots;
a woman in pants and shirt, with a battered hat pulled down
over her head, a woman barefoot and riding a plump old mare
with only a blanket, no saddle or bridle, the mare following
obediently behind a huge young stud and a half-trained young
horse on a tether rope.

They ran the gauntlet of cold eyes, looking neither right nor
left, but, like the Fool Hens, straight ahead, trying to ignore
the obvious suspicion and simple distrust of the people of Freshwater.

"There it is," Sarah said quietly, and they headed to the
hitching post in front of the largest building in town, the dance
hall and saloon. "You wait here," she added, sliding from Bess'
broad back. When Anne fired a hot, suspicious glance she
grinned. "Come on, trust me," she teased, then she headed toward

the swinging doors, leaving Anne to sit up on Dan and pretend she couldn't feel the eyes burning into her back.

Even this early in the day the saloon was crowded, but the girls hadn't yet appeared from their upstairs rooms. Only Belle who stood behind the bar making sure the bartender wiped the spots off all the glasses. Belle with her bleached hair piled high on her head, her face and features hidden behind a carefully applied layer of thick makeup, her eyelids bright green, her lips bright red, her cheeks as rosy as those of a consumption patient. As Sarah threaded her way through the hard-drinking, sweaty crowd, pretending she didn't notice the stares or hear the comments, her nose wrinkled at the strong mixture of smells — the beer suds, whiskey fumes, cigar and cigarette smoke, cheap perfume and sweat. Her toes itched from the sawdust on the floor and she was suddenly reminded that at least half the streams aimed at the spitoons missed their mark by inches and feet.

"Belle?" she asked quietly, tapping the fleshy shoulder. Belle turned, her eyes widening as she recognized the bizarre figure watching her hopefully.

"My God!" she breathed, shocked. "My God, child . . ."

"Belle, I've got problems," Sarah whispered.

"I can see that! *Laura!*" Belle roared, and a moment later Laura hurried down the steps, her dark eyes searching for trouble. She relaxed when she realized nobody had been knifed, there was no fight, no robbery and no rape.

"Take over for me," Belle explained. "Excuse me, gentlemen," she smiled. "Come with me, Sarah," she ordered.

"I've got a friend outside."

"You're lucky."

Anne followed Sarah and the well-padded woman with the mound of bright yellow hair up the stairs and along a hallway. Belle unlocked and opened a door and, with a gesture of her hand, invited them to enter. One wall was window, a broader expanse of glass than any Anne had ever seen in her life, and that alone would have grabbed and held her attention, but in this room even that demonstration of wealth was overshadowed and diminished. The room was dominated by a bed, the biggest bed Anne had ever seen. She couldn't see the sheets or blankets, but the spread was like nothing in her memory. She didn't know enough about material to know if that was silk or satin, but she knew, she *knew*, it had to be one or the other. The chairs were covered with ruffles and cushions, and the floor seemed to be a collection of rugs and carpets. She supposed you could jump up and down and never make a sound. A huge dresser, the top of it covered with bottles and jars, fancy boxes and small cans with flowers and dainty scenes painted on them, and a mind-reeling scent of perfume and powder. She looked down at her heavy stolen boots and wished she could stand three inches off the carpet. Sarah's feet, scratched and dirty, looked even more like intruders, but Sarah herself seemed perfectly at ease in all this display of wealth.

Anne looked around quickly for a place to sit but there seemed to be nothing her travel-stained overalls wouldn't insult. She wanted to leave, to head back out to the street, get on Dan, and ride off trying to put the sight of this room in the back of her mind never to be remembered again, but Sarah had said, "Trust me," and so, finally, her mouth dry, her tongue glued to her teeth, and a tight knot in her belly, she sat down on a dark blue rug that looked as if it, at least, wouldn't be destroyed by the dust and grass seed stuck to her.

Belle clucked and tut-tutted, opened her door and roared orders in a voice that could have been put to good use on any cattle drive. And before Anne had time to really get used to anything, the women Belle called "the girls" were bustling in and out of the room, dressed only in loose or belted wrappers, their faces strangely pale in contrast to Belle's high color and Sarah's and Anne's tans. It took Anne several minutes to figure out why they all looked sick: They were not wearing any makeup at all. Sarah seemed to know some of them and they all seemed to, if not know her, accept her. One or two of them looked curiously at Anne, but after those first glances, each and every one of them ignored her totally.

From the depths of one of the closets they dragged out a tub.

----

In no way did it bear any resemblance at all to Martha's wooden washtubs, and when they began to pour hot water into it, Anne couldn't help thinking they were using more hot water than Martha had been able to use for the weekly wash for three people. When the tub was three-quarters full of steaming water, Belle threw some pinkish crystals in and the room immediately smelled like a rose garden at dusk. The knot in Anne's stomach had begun to move and flutter as if entire nests full of baby birds were getting ready to learn to fly. They began to flop almost frantically when Sarah, with her usual obvious lack of shyness, began to strip off her clothes, eyeing the big tub eagerly.

"Oh, Lord, Sarah," Belle fussed, "you're all over scratches, bruises and marks . . . and your hands!"

"You very politely don't mention my hair!" Sarah tried to grin, but couldn't. She was too aware of her now fuzzy head.

"A wig'll hide that," Belle discounted the ruin, "but your hands! You're going to have to wear gloves, girl, not even a sheepman would want to hold those hands!" She helped Sarah into the tub, nodding happily as Sarah leaned back and sighed the longest sigh Anne had ever heard.

"Oh, it feels good." Sarah moved her arms and legs lazily, the water lapping almost to her chin. "After cold creek water, sand and laundry soap, this is heaven . . ."

"You just soak it up," Belle ordered, scooping clothes from the floor and bustling toward the door. "I'm going to get you some decent clothes. And burn these. They smell!"

Anne knew her face was closing, like a slammed door. Maybe they were dirty and maybe they did smell of horse and campfire smoke, but she'd had to steal to get them.

"Don't burn them!" Sarah said quickly, and not because she had seen Anne's face. "They were a present. But if you could get them washed . . ."

"Washed!" Belle's laughter gurgled from her pouterpigeon chest. "Washed?" she repeated, her face getting redder as the laughter rolled. "Honey, finding someone to wash clothes in this town is like looking for rocking horse shit. You figure there ought to be some somewhere, but . . . I've spent over two hundred dollars on train fare bringing Chinee up from Frisco. The little darlin's no more than get here than they bugger off again. Some yahoo claims he found gold up in the Cariboo. Where there's gold there's jade, and those sweet-smilin' celestial sonsabitches let me buy their train tickets north, then they head even further north without so much as a howdy-do or a fare-thee-well. She leaned against the door, talking nonstop, her voice rising and falling almost musically, and Anne stared, not knowing her mouth was gaping open, or that Sarah's laughter was only partially because of the comic humor of Belle's teasing complaint. "The first little one I brought out here stayed long enough to wash all the sheets and bedding and then he raided my kitchen and took as much food as he could carry, walked to the livery stable with it and rode off on a long-eared jennyass he liberated from its stall. And the second one I brought up stayed just long enough to find out how and where the first one had gone, and, by Jesus, if he wasn't off following him. There's got to be a sign on all the doors in Frisco Chinatown saying Fat Belle Buys Train Tickets. Maybe they're burning incense for me in some heathen temple somewhere because I'm sure I've paid for at least a half dozen Chinee laundrymen to pan gold along some nameless creek up the arsehole of absolutely nowhere. Washing?" And shaking with laughter, she left the room. Anne stared at the closed door, not sure she had seen what she had seen or heard what she had heard.

"Does she always talk like that?"

"Oh, Belle's one of a breed," Sarah laughed softly, lifting her leg from the water and soaping vigorously. "She's in love with the poetry of words and the music of her own voice."

"I never heard anything like it."

"You'll hear a lot more of it."

Anne stared at the rug because every time she tried to look anywhere else, there was a mirror, and reflected in it, the image of Sarah, her skin glistening, soap suds clinging, and always the smell of roses and another smell Anne couldn't identify, a sort of secret-ish smell that dried the inside of her mouth and constricted her throat. Martha had always smelled clean. Clean and very often lavendery. When she was little, Anne liked to sit on her mother's knee and rest her head against the soft cotton front of Martha's housedress and talk softly the way chicks peeped constantly back to the feather-ruffled old hen. But Martha had never smelled like this. Or if she had, Anne had never noticed it.

"You going to have a bath?" Sarah was stepping out of the tub, wrapped in a towel almost as big as a sheet.

"I don't care," Anne muttered, wanting to get into that tub like she had never wanted anything else. At least since she had barbecued Uncle Andrew.

"Climb in," Sarah invited casually. "I'll get Belle to send more hot water."

"Maybe later."

Sarah looked over at the girl sitting against the far wall, staring down between her bulky rough boots at the dark blue carpet beneath her. The capable suntanned hands were clenched together, the fingers white at the knuckle, and the innocently beautiful young face was flushed beet red with a kind of embarrassment and shame that Sarah wasn't sure she herself had ever really felt. Suddenly she remembered Anne's hasty flight when Sarah had begun to remove her corset, and how the girl washed herself regularly but always with the protection of her cotton underwear. The finding of the money had knocked everything else out of her mind and after that she had accepted Anne's behavior the way you accept the strange quirks of anybody you've either lived with a long time or gone through a lot of things with.

She pretended not to be talking about anything in particular, talking to Anne the way Anne talked to Dan and Bess and the half-trained young horse.

"I knew a man once who read books the way other people eat meals, and he told me there are places in the world where women hide behind veils and are ashamed if anybody sees their faces... Are you ashamed of your face?"

"No."

"And he told me that in China women wear their hair so it covers the backs of their necks because they're ashamed to have that part of them seen. Doesn't seem to make much sense to me, does it to you?"

"No."

"You ashamed of your arms?" She reached down, softly touched Anne's tanned arm.

"No." Anne scrambled to her feet, heading for the door.

"*Sam!*" Sarah screamed.

Anne whirled, expecting danger. Sarah dropped her wrapper to the floor and stood naked, arms wide. Anne froze, only her eyes darting frantically. Sarah reflected in mirrors, Sarah naked and not the least ashamed, Sarah in the flesh walking toward her, walking naturally, standing in front of the door to the hallway.

"Maybe you've got something I haven't got," she teased. "Or maybe I'm ugly. Maybe I'm shameful. Maybe we should all cover ourselves with horse blankets . . . never take a bath or go swimming or . . ." Suddenly she jumped on Anne, laughing like a child at a birthday party, her fingers busily undoing buttons, pulling off Anne's shirt. "We could cover ourselves with tar and feathers." She fumbled with the overall snaps, Anne fighting and wriggling, wanting to hit out, slap and kick, not wanting to hurt Sarah, trying to wrestle but not knowing where to put her hands without touching bare flesh.

When she was down to her clean but tired cotton shirt and bloomers there was only one place to go to escape. She couldn't go out in the hallway, there were strangers out there and anyway Sarah stayed between her and the door. She raced for the tub and climbed in.

"Off with the skivvies," Sarah commanded, laughing. Laughing but meaning it.

"No," Anne insisted, face flaming.

"I'll call Belle to help me."

"No!"

"Then . . ."

"Okay. Okay . . ." Anne squirmed in the tub, then, oddly delicate, wrung out her nearly ruined underwear and set both pieces on the side of the tub. Sarah grabbed them.

---

61

"I won't burn them," she promised, "but they've seen their last use."

"I don't have anything else," Anne protested.

"You will have."

Anne leaned back in the tub, the water sloshing around her chin, the scent of roses stronger than before, her skin beginning to feel slippery, her toes wriggling of their own accord. When the door opened and Belle came in with another bucket of hot water, Anne jackknifed her legs, hiding behind her own knees, hunched over, hating her face for the way it flamed. Sarah was again in her wrapper and while Anne's attention was riveted on Belle, who was paying no attention at all to her, Sarah began to loosen the heavy braids that fell to Anne's shoulders.

"Lord," Belle said suddenly, reaching out to touch the long blonde hair. "Lord, look at that child's hair! If even one of my girls had hair like that, I'd be rich enough to retire."

Anne felt as if she wanted to slide under the water and stay there forever. Sarah froze, her fingers still and icy in the child's hair. Belle looked from one to the other, her jaw dropping.

"Lord, I've said the wrong thing," she admitted.

"It's okay," Sarah said in a stiff, cold voice. "We're both tired and . . . touchy."

"No, it's me. I know. I'm tired, too, baby. There was a big uproar here last night and I lost a couple of hours' sleep, and when I get tired I get stupid, real stupid. You forget what I said, honey." She was smiling down at Anne but her eyes were oddly pleading. "Just chalk it up to old Auntie Belle being tired and not too bright to start with. I've got some shampoo here that Laura gave me for my birthday. Here, just duck down in the water a bit and wet your hair and we'll pour on a bit of this . . . all the way from Seattle! That's it. Now you just scrunch shut your eyes so you don't get suds in them and Auntie Belle's gonna get your hair looking like Rumplestiltzkins' gold."

Sarah moved to sit on the edge of the massive bed and watched as the portly woman lowered herself to her knees and, talking gently and softly, began to lather Anne's hair. Sarah liked Belle, liked her sense of humor and her ability to shrug off the moods and tantrums of a house full of working girls, liked the way nobody was ever turned away without a meal and a smile, encouraging words and, if needed, a lead on a job or a ride out of town. For a while, before Keno had got out of jail the second time, when he was sitting behind bars and no amount of money could get him out for at least six months, for a while Sarah had lived with Belle, occupying the favored position Laura now had. Though it wasn't anywhere near the joy of living with Keno, it was far better than anything else she'd known before in her life.

So why did she resent Belle now? Why did she want to tell Belle that she, Sarah, would wash Anne's hair? She knew that Belle had never made any secret of the fact she was dotty about kids. Christmas at the local school was always enhanced by bundles of candy for each child, and if neither the kids nor their parents, nor even the teacher knew where the candy came from, Belle knew. Sarah remembered the night she had asked Belle if she, herself, had ever had any children. Belle had waited long moments before answering and then, with a soft laugh, had said, "Lord, child, nobody who started this life as young and stupid as I did or who stayed in it as long as I have could have avoided that!" She had admitted that at least two decent families had raised children of hers. "I've paid for every bite of food in their mouths and every stitch of clothes on their backs," she said with a pathetic stubborn pride, "but neither of them's ever set eyes on me or knows that their mother is anybody other than the woman who wiped their noses and gave 'em cough syrup. I couldn't do much for my kids, but I done that much." And knowing this, knowing all the needs and hurts that were being met and eased by the simple act of shampooing Anne's hair, why, Sarah wondered, why do I wish she'd get away from that tub. Away from that kid?

Laura brought buckets of lukewarm water to rinse Anne's hair, and provided a warm wrapper. Then, her head covered with a towel, and her wiry body hidden in the folds of the too-large wrapper, Anne sat down with Sarah and stared at the meal Belle had ordered.

"Bread," Sarah breathed. "Look at it!"

"Fried potatoes," Anne crowed. "I haven't had potatoes since about a week after I took off. And eggs . . ."

"I don't really care if I don't see meat for a month," Sarah admitted, "but I may never get my fill of jam."

"You two just stuff yourselves as full as you can, and be sure to drink that whole pitcher of milk. Me and the girls'll get rid of the bathwater and stuff and then we'll leave you alone until you've had a chance to pass out in that bed for a few hours."

"I can't!" Anne blurted.

"And why in hell not?" Belle's voice was definitely cool.

"Dan and Bess and the other guy . . ."

"Who?"

"Her horses," Sarah explained.

"Oh, hell, I'll get one of the guys to take 'em down to the livery. They'll be all right."

"Could you tell him," Anne said hesitantly, "not to try to ride Dan? I mean, Dan doesn't know many people and he doesn't trust anybody but me, and Sarah a little bit, and he hasn't been cut, so he might get awful mean . . ."

"You mean to tell me," Belle exploded, "that a little bitty girl like you has been riding all over the ass-end of creation on a great christly stud? That's the most disgusting thing I ever heard!" Then Belle glared as Sarah exploded in nearly hysterical laughter.

"Oh, he's okay," Anne reassured, stuffing her mouth with fried potato dipped in egg yolk. "He doesn't make much fuss at all as long as old Bess is around, but maybe the guy who takes him to the livery ought to warn the man that if there's mares in time, that he doesn't want covered, he'd better tie Dan up good because he can jump over the moon sometimes."

"Didn't anybody ever tell you," Belle said coldly, "that women and little girls aren't supposed to talk about things like that?" Sarah's laughter bubbled again.

"What's the matter with her?" Anne asked innocently after Belle left, but Sarah could only giggle helplessly and shake her head.

They ate until they couldn't eat any more and then sat staring at what was still left on the table.

"Hope she doesn't throw it out," Anne said. "Sure be a waste if she did." When Sarah didn't answer, she looked over at her. "What's wrong?"

"Nothing." Sarah was beginning to feel very drowsy and almost as if she'd had half a dozen stiff drinks instead of an enormous meal. "I don't know," she added slowly. "You ever feel . . . mixed up? Like part of you was a stranger to the rest of you?"

"Me?" Anne lied bravely. "No."

"You're lucky." Sarah smothered a yawn. "I feel mixed up sometimes. Lots of times, lately. Like today, when Belle said . . . what she said . . . about your hair."

Anne looked away, feeling her face flame again. "Oh, that doesn't matter," she mumbled.

"But it did!" Sarah protested. "It mattered a lot. To me. And part of me is saying 'Belle didn't mean anything by it,' and part of me is saying 'You shut up! Not Anne! She's not like that!' . . . I was . . . insulted . . . and I wanted to say 'Anne is *clean*.'"

"Clean?" Anne laughed, remembering her grimy toenails and dirty clothes.

"Clean." Sarah insisted. "Not like me and Belle. Clean."

Their eyes met across the remnants of their meal.

"You aren't dirty," Anne said quietly.

"That's one of the things that has me mixed up," Sarah confessed. "I didn't even know I felt dirty until she said that."

The silence lengthened until it was no longer uncomfortable but something they both accepted. Sarah rose slowly, feeling her eyelids drooping and her feet increasingly leaden, and moved toward the enormous bed she was remembering in growing anticipation. Anne wiped her mouth again, got up, and moved to the other side of the bed. She crawled under the covers, the damp towel falling from her hair, which spread over the pillow and down onto the collar and shoulder of the oversize wrapper she still wore.

"Boy," she sighed, snuggling down in the bed, "I never had

a bed so soft." She felt the mattress give slightly as Sarah climbed into bed. "At home I had a cot beside the stove until I got too big for it and then I slept with Momma.

"Momma's bed was bigger than a cot," she continued drowsily, "but it wasn't as big as this sucker is. Wasn't this soft, either. Boy, with a bed like this, a person wouldn't ever want to get up again."

"Don't you believe it," Sarah said bitterly.

Anne was still asleep when Sarah wakened a couple of hours later. The table and chairs were gone, the evidence of their meal was gone, and on the vanity top were two wigs, a dark and a fair. A dress, probably one of Laura's, lay over a chair, and on the bench of the vanity was a cloud of silk and lace, several pairs of shoes, different sizes, and a pair of white gloves. Sarah got out of bed quietly, not wishing to disturb the child who slept as if she hadn't closed her eyes in weeks. Then, with fingers surprisingly clumsy and slow, Sarah dressed, applied makeup from the supply on Belle's vanity, and finally, tentatively, she picked up and put on the dark wig. Staring at her reflection in the mirror she saw the woman she hadn't seen since the night Luke Wilson shot the young boy. She smiled happily, her head no longer naked and comical, then went downstairs to join Belle and the others.

Music and laughter, bright colors and noise, all the girls in bright dresses, dancing, drinking and joking with the many men who jammed the saloon. Belle, reigning like a queen from her place at the bar, smiled broadly and waved an invitation, and Sarah moved through the press, hugged Belle gratefully and sipped the drink the bartender, without being asked, handed to her.

"You add tone to this place," Belle approved.

"Only as long as I don't flip my wig," Sarah joked, and Belle's laughter gurgled wetly above the sound of the piano.

Sarah had two drinks, sipping them slowly and watching the activity in the big room. A man who looked enough like Keno to be his twin, and yet looked nothing like him at all, dealt cards at a table against the back wall. The same well-tailored black suit, the same snow-white starched shirt with the ruffled front and black ribbon tie, the same flexible fingers and cunning hands, but different eyes, nose, mouth, hair, eyebrows. She looked away from him, not at all interested in meeting him. She knew before he opened his mouth everything he would ever have to say to her. A hard-faced girl, a short year or two older than Anne, teetered inexpertly on high heels and held onto the arm of a middle-aged rancher, the smile on her lips never coming anywhere near her eyes, moving with a matter-of-fact pretense of eagerness toward the stairs leading to the back room which, Sarah smiled to herself sourly, somehow was never really out back at all, but almost invariably at the top of a flight of stairs. Laura was dancing with a man in his late twenties, laughing happily at something he was saying, and then, as he whirled her smoothly, her eyes, over his shoulder, met for a brief twinkling moment with Belle's, and again the fluid laughter bubbled from Belle's throat. Sarah remembered similar laughter for similar reasons, but it seemed a dim memory, from some time so long ago she could no longer be totally sure the woman in her memory was herself. She shook her head when the bartender offered to refill her glass and, feeling suddenly bone weary and not at all sleepy, she walked toward the stairs alone. Belle watched her leave, then reached over, lifted a bottle from the stock behind the bar, and signaling to Laura, headed up the stairs after Sarah. Laura finished dancing with the smiling dark-haired man, then signaled to Marilyn to replace her, and murmuring an excuse of some kind, she hurried after Belle and Sarah. The man watched her go, puzzled and feeling the first faint stirrings of anger, but Marilyn smiled up at him as if she had been with him all night and he grinned. What the hell . . .

They sat in dim lamplight in Belle's room, speaking in soft voices Anne didn't even hear. She had rolled over when they came in and opened her eyes, but before she wakened enough to focus them, Sarah had said, "Back to sleep, baby," and Anne relaxed and drifted back into the sleep neither she nor Sarah had known she needed.

"Have a drink or two," Belle said quietly, "or three or four, or however goddamn many it's gonna take."

"It's okay," Sarah insisted. "I'll be okay."

"Sure you will, but you'll be more okay if you get it off your chest." And she poured liquor into a water glass and handed it over commandingly.

Before the glass was half empty, Sarah removed the dress and, with a sigh of sheer relief, took off the corset and laid it aside. She sat in Belle's wrapper drinking whiskey and trying to talk away her confusion.

"It wasn't just that he shot the boy," she said once. "It was that he really didn't feel badly about it. He blamed Keno, and in a way it was partly Keno's fault, but . . . that little boy might just as well never have been born for all Luke Wilson cared."

"Yeah, well the world is full of snakes like that," Belle commented.

"Even when I closed my eyes," she said later, "I could see Keno fighting against that rope. I couldn't scream loud enough not to hear the noise he was making, and even when they were pouring that tar on me, even though I could feel my skin blistering, it didn't hurt."

"You're damn lucky they were in a hurry," Belle growled. "If they'd had time enough to do it right you'd have been dead inside of an hour."

"The tar was just barely warm enough to be poured and smeared on," Sarah admitted. "And even then they got nearly as much on themselves as they did on me."

A fight broke out downstairs and Belle lifted her bulk from the chair to go down long enough to calm the antagonists. While she was gone, Laura asked Sarah if she had any plans about staying with Belle and maybe taking up where she'd left off.

"No," Sarah said softly. "Belle told me once that she loved to be loved and needed to be able to let someone love her or at least pretend to, but that she, herself, didn't seem to be able to love anybody. And I've had all I want of people who are willing to let me love them without ever getting involved themselves."

"Yeah," Laura grinned, "but it's better than nothing."

---

"I guess anything is better than nothing," Sarah agreed. She looked at Laura and felt suddenly close to her, not as close as she felt to Anne, but close, and knew however different their backgrounds were, they were similar in all the ways that mattered. "Does she let you work the back room?" she asked softly.

"No." Laura looked down at the amber liquid in her glass, and smiled softly to herself. "I can dance with them, talk with them, circulate with the crowd, get the shy ones to feeling relaxed, but I don't work the back room. And after the joint is closed, every night, before we go to bed, I soak in a tub because she says she can't stand the smell of the place in my hair, or the smell of sweaty men's hands on my skin. And most of the time all she wants to do is cuddle me and stroke my hair and have me rub her back."

"Yeah." Sarah nodded. "She used to get awful backaches."

"Standing so much, I think," Laura agreed. "Leaning against that bar with a big smile on her face even when she's just about going nuts inside her head. In the morning she comes in with coffee. Makes it herself. And she fusses over me all the time. And I like that." She looked at Sarah with a kind of naked honesty Sarah had seldom seen. "I really like that."

"Been with her long?"

"Not long. A few months. I worked the back room before that, and I guess I thought she was just another Queen Bee, you know, and then . . . I got lucky."

They sat in companionable silence for long minutes, each lost in her own private thoughts. Laura refilled their glasses, and leaned back against her chairback, watching the light from the lantern dancing on the ceiling. "I felt embarrassed at first, did you?"

"God, yes!" Sarah admitted with relief. "I was sure I'd wake up one morning with a big mark on my forehead and everybody would know!"

"Yeah. That, too. But I meant the way she sometimes talks." She waited, and when Sarah didn't say anything, Laura took a deep breath and with an obvious effort, tried to explain. "I woke up one morning and she was sitting on the edge of the bed

---

69

with coffee, and I rolled toward her, to cuddle her. She started nuzzling under my arm, licking my skin, and when I tried to pull away she grabbed me, not rough, but, like real insistent."

"Belle can get awful bossy," Sarah agreed.

"And I tried to make a joke about it. Said I probably smelled like a racehorse because, well..." Her face pinked and she looked at the floor, almost shyly. "We'd been...kind of ...active...the night before, and you know how hot and sweaty that gets." When Sarah laughed softly, Laura's blush faded and they grinned at each other. "And Belle, she started talking about how smell was like color, and my neck was pink and my underarms were rose, and my breasts were soft blue." She grinned. "By the time she got to purple I was turned on like a cat in heat. But afterwards, I felt embarrassed."

"It was the curse turned my face beet red," Sarah dared admit. "I'd always felt I ought to maybe go off somewhere and hide. God, my aunts had a real horror of it, burned everything that got stained, even their petticoats if they flooded. And there was Belle acting like it was the most beautiful thing in the world."

"Yeah. That still makes me feel...uncomfortable," Laura agreed. "I guess there are some smells and colors I'm just not ready to enjoy."

"But you love her?" Sarah probed.

"I guess that's what it is. I try to remember what it was like before, and I can see in my mind things that happened, or hear things people said, but I don't seem to be able to remember how I felt about any of it. It's like I wasn't really feeling, or something. And when I try to think about next week, or next month, or whenever she gets tired of me, it's like a big black line has been drawn, and I can't imagine anything at all. I can think ahead to how maybe Belle and I will go to Ottawa together, or maybe we'll go all the way to Montreal, and I can think about how it would be if we could get a place all by ourselves, near a creek, and have some books and maybe a harp I could learn to play. Sometimes I even think about how, when we're old, we'll nag at each other and even if there's no hot touching and tasting,

---

70

we'll still cuddle and . . . it's just when I try to think of not having her in my life everything goes blank."

"Holy Jesus," Sarah breathed.

"Yeah." Laura blinked rapidly. "Holy Jesus, for sure."

"Listen." Sarah leaned forward, intent, reached out and touched Laura's hand gently. "I've never heard of Belle being the one to bring it to an end. Sure, there's been a lot of women in and out of this room, but mostly Belle has tolerated some really inadequate loving in return for the strength and loving she gives. She knew when I moved in that I was just waiting for Keno, and then when he was out, I'd be gone. We both knew that's how it would be."

"She talks about you sometimes," Laura admitted. "I thought I'd really hate you when I finally met you."

"We won't hate each other." Sarah smiled. "We know too much about each other, and we've been to too many of the same places to ever hate each other."

Belle came back muttering about people who thought that just sitting down in a card game meant they'd all win and get rich, and they sat for a while listening to the sound of the piano, faint through the walls Belle had built extra thick because, she said, she didn't want to have to hear any more piano music than necessary. It had been jangling in her ears for most of her life, and all the songs sounded the same.

"They left me to die," Sarah said suddenly. "As if I didn't count. They weren't even angry. It was like . . . like when a dog has been crushed by a wagon wheel and the only thing to do is shoot it so it'll stop yelping and hurting your ears."

"Ah, honey," Belle soothed, feeling helpless.

"I thought she was a boy." Sarah looked over at Anne, sound asleep in the massive bed. "She looked like a boy. Skinny as a beanpole, with this big hat hanging half over her face. Tough and hard and so full of mad and hate I was sure she was a boy." She turned and looked at them, Laura sitting on the carpet, now, leaning against Belle's legs, Belle's hand idly stroking

---

71

Laura's shoulder. "Even if I'd been able to walk it, I couldn't have gone back to Feather River. I didn't even know which direction to head to come here. And I'd never have been able to walk this far."

"Sarah," Belle said firmly, "even with that kid's hat on your head, I think the sun baked your brains."

"No, it didn't. And you don't really believe that anyway, you old farce."

"Don't you start telling me what I believe and don't believe," Belle grinned, "or I'll hire me a man with a whip to take strips off your backside."

"I owe her," Sarah said softly.

"Yeah." Belle heaved herself to her feet. "Well, I've got to get back down there before that perambulating asshole behind the bar starts handing it out free of charge. You get yourself back into that bed and try to sleep off that brain fever you must have, the one that makes you talk like a total idiot."

"What about you?" Sarah yawned. "Where are you going to sleep if I'm in your bed with Anne?"

"Oh, I'll find me a corner somewhere." Belle laughed, and Laura got up off the floor and moved toward the doorway, laughing.

Even with the liquor swirling in her stomach, Sarah couldn't relax and fall asleep. She stared at the ceiling as if there was something written there that she had to read or never know peace, and she lay on her side and stared at Anne, then rolled over and stared at the door. She was lying on her stomach, her face turned toward Anne, wishing she could fall asleep, when Anne opened her eyes, briefly, smiled fuzzily and reached out her tanned, scratched and roughened hand to pat the faint fuzz on Sarah's head. Then her blue eyes closed again and Sarah fell asleep, grinning.

72

# Chapter 5

In the morning Anne and Sarah cooked their own breakfast in the huge kitchen behind the main saloon, while Belle, Laura and the working girls slept behind drawn blinds and drapes. They would rise in midafternoon, when a dark, frowning and muscular Cornishwoman came in to cook for them and then change the bedding and tidy the rooms. "Not that I approve," she would growl, "but I've six young ones to feed and no other way to make an honest living. Not since the fool went and did what he had to do." The fool was her husband, who had been bitten by the gold bug two years earlier and packed to head south to California. Just before he left he told her "a man has to do what a man has to do," and then he got on the train and left her and the children to do whatever they could manage to do to stay alive. However, between the cooking and cleaning, she had no time for doing laundry, and Belle and the girls, with much nagging and swearing, had to do this themselves on what ought to have been their days off.

"Damndest thing I ever heard of," Belle muttered once, fighting with wet sheets. "There's only three to five days a month a working girl can be sure she'll have to herself, and here I am, and there's Hop Sing wherever he is. Gone."

While Anne did the dishes, Sarah dressed in the plainest and most demure dress she could find in Laura's closet and then, mumbling to herself about pinched toes, walked, in shoes borrowed from Clara's closet, while Clara was still asleep, down to the one General Store. Anne had the dishes washed, the table and working space cleaned and the top of the stove bricked clean when Sarah came back with an armload of bundles.

"What is this?" Anne teased. "Christmas come early?"

"You might say that," Sarah smiled, handing half the packages to Anne.

Anne ripped open the wrappings, as excited as if it really was Christmas.

"A dress?"

"You never know when you might need one," Sarah teased. "Open the others," and Anne was relieved to see new jeans, new shirts, new socks, a pair of plain boots and no less than three skivvy shirts and bloomers.

"I never got so much stuff at one time. It must have cost an awful lot . . ."

"No," Sarah said shortly, not wanting to remember where the money had come from or how much it had cost the young cowboy, Keno and herself.

Anne gladly changed from the enormous wrapper to the new clothes, tugging at the boots and then strutting around the room happily.

"Wait'll Dan sees me!" she crowed. "He won't even know who I am. He'll think it's some quality people come to visit him. You want to come with me? I want to check on them."

"Wait until I get dressed in clothes of my own," Sarah grinned. "I'm tired of wearing other people's clothes."

They went out the back door of the saloon and down the alley to the board sidewalk and stopped the first person they met.

"Could you tell me where the livery is?" Anne asked.

"Down the street to the end, and that's it," the old man pointed with a calloused thumb. They smiled their thanks and hurried down the street, Anne's low-heeled boots clicking on the unpainted bleached boards.

"I'll give you a good price for that big stud," the stable owner offered as soon as he knew who they were.

"I wouldn't sell Dan." Anne shook her head determinedly.

"I wouldn't either if he was mine," the man agreed. "Where did you get him?"

"My uncle bought him," Anne said truthfully, "and he gave him to me for my birthday," she lied.

"If he was mine, I wouldn't give him to no bitty girl. He's one big stud!"

He led them around to the back of the building where Dan, Bess and the half-trained young horse were waiting in a corral. All three of them nickered and ran up to the fence, nuzzling Anne and making soft noises, accepting the slices of fresh bread she had brought for them from Belle's kitchen.

"Is, uh, your, uh, father or, uh, brother around?" the livery owner stammered.

"I don't have a brother," she said easily. "And my dad's been dead for a long time. Why?"

"Well, uh, your, uh, uncle, the one who gave you the horse, is, uh, he around?"

"No, my uncle went . . . home," she lied.

"Is this your sister?" the man asked desperately, after much red-faced stammering and four false starts.

"No." Anne was puzzled. "She's my cousin," she added hurriedly.

"Could I speak to you please, miss?" the man asked frantically, and he and Sarah moved away. After another stammered series of false starts, the man finally managed to ask his question. Sarah's laughter rose freely from her throat, and she quickly put up one hand to make sure Belle's borrowed wig didn't slip off her head.

"He wants to know what you'll charge him for stud fee," she laughed, leaning over to whisper in Anne's ear.

"I don't know. What do people usually charge?"

"I'm not very familiar with . . . horses," Sarah giggled, but Anne didn't laugh. She didn't even smile and Sarah's humor died quickly.

"I don't want Dan anywhere near any mare that's got ticks or ringworm," she said sternly. "Nor worms, fleas, or blowfly eggs on her, either."

"No, ma'am," the man promised fervently. "You can be sure he's not gonna be nowheres near no trashy mare like that. I got me a young quarterhorse filly I had brought out from back East and she's just about the nicest little thing you ever saw . . . exceptin' him."

"Where is she?"

"Out of town above five miles. I don't keep her in town because of the bums that come around here sometimes."

"Well," Anne said matter-of-factly, "you're either gonna have to bring her in when it's time, or else you're gonna have to make sure there's some place out there where we can stay for a few days, because there's no way I'm gonna let you lead Dan out of sight. And there's no way he's gonna stay for long without me and Bess, no matter how pretty that mare of yours is. We'll go with him when it's time."

"Yes, ma'am," he said obediently.

They stayed two weeks at Belle's place. Two weeks of fresh bread, potatoes and gravy, cooked vegetables, and preserves for dessert—all the food they had not realized they were missing when they were living on a diet of wild meat. Two weeks of sleeping in a real bed with sheets and a pillow. Two weeks of hot baths and lots of soap. There was only one real confrontation between Belle and Anne, and that came the day Belle found Anne in the back yard, scrubbing sheets on a scrubbing board almost as big as herself. Clouds of steam rose from the huge tubs, clouds of steam that hung in the chilly air and half-obscured the back yard.

"I've been a lot of billy-be-damned things in my life and I've done a lot of others," Belle exploded, "but I never in all my born days stood by and let a girl no bigger'n' a two-minute egg do crap work like that!"

"It's not crap work," Anne said flatly. "It's just work, and I've done it lots of times. I was helping my mom do the wash when I was six years old."

"There's as much difference between helpin' your mom do the

family wash and doin' this as there is between kin and kittens," Belle insisted.

"Water's water and soap's soap and scrubbin's scrubbing and helpin's helpin' and Luella's got cramps awful bad."

"Luella's cramps my ass!" Belle roared. "Luella can just get rid of her cramps. It's her turn to help with the wash, not yours. If that lazy twist hasn't got cramps, it's headache, and if it isn't headache, it's backache, and if it isn't that, it's something else. Let her take her turn like everyone else."

"I don't care," Anne said quietly, remembering Luella's pale face and the bloodless lips of the still figure who looked so much like Martha but without Martha's smile or soft voice, without Martha's gentle movements and warm hugs. If doing Luella's turn at the washtubs would ease the pain of those memories, Anne would do washing daily.

"Belle," Sarah said softly, "for God's sake, you won't get anywhere giving her orders and getting hard-nosed with her. She's as stiff-necked as you are. If you don't let her feel she's paying her own way and earning her keep, she'll just move down into the livery stable and sleep in the stall with Dan."

"That kid," Belle grated, "is as stubborn as a mule."

"Oh, shit," Laura laughed. "In you it's strength of character, in me it's determination, in her it's stubbornness."

"I'm sure not gettin' much help from you!" Belle accused.

"Why should I take your side?" Sarah teased. "I think you're wrong."

"I am *not* wrong," Belle said haughtily. "I may not always be right, but I am never wrong." And she moved back toward the saloon with all the dignity of the Royal Navy under full sail, her brightly colored wrapper billowing around her. Sarah laughed softly, and Anne turned back to the laundry tubs and continued her scrubbing. She liked Belle, and she didn't like arguing with her, but Luella really was sick. Maybe some women could just pretend nothing particular was going on with their bodies, maybe some women could just go about their business without cramps or headaches, but Luella wasn't playing pretend-

---

77

for-sympathy. And even if she was, Anne couldn't take the chance Uncle Andrew had taken. What if she was wrong, as he had been, and how would she live with that.

The big piano in the upstairs parlor was different from the scarred and badly tuned piano in the saloon. The downstairs piano was marked with cigar and cigarette butts, ringed with faded reminders of the numbers of wet glasses placed on it, and gouged with boot heels and spurs. The back was splintered where someone's head had come in violent contact with the wood during a minor dispute, and the sounds that came from it were related to music about the same way mouse turds are related to fresh cheese. The piano upstairs was larger, the lid lifted and there was a special little stick to hold the lid upright. No cigar burns, no water or gin marks, just highly polished wood and deep rich sounds. Anne was fascinated.

"You know how to play it?" she marveled.

"I know how," Laura said, "and I could teach you, too, if you want."

"If I want . . ." Anne breathed, reaching out hesitantly, touching one of the keys. "I always wanted to make some music."

And so, every day for an hour and a half, Anne and Laura sat at the piano, and Anne's strong hard hands struggled with scales.

"My fingers seem so stiff," she complained.

"It's practice," Laura encouraged, "that's all it is. Like learning to ride a horse, or shoot a gun. It looks easy enough when you know how." Anne nodded, and started again from the beginning, brow furrowed, shoulders hunched with concentration. She was practicing grimly when Edna, the hard-faced sixteen-year-old working girl walked in and sat on the edge of the piano bench, hoping to pass the afternoon in idle girlish conversation.

"I might learn to play this," she offered brightly, her voice cutting through Anne's concentration and making her fingers fumble. "I've got lots of time to practice."

"Uh-huh," Anne muttered, starting her scales again.

"Belle thinks I ought to spend some of my time reading some

good books, and I might do that, too. I can read," she said proudly. "Can you?"

"Some," Anne admitted. "The big Bible and the almanac and stuff like that."

"I bet I could even take a course and learn sewing. I could make a lot of extra money doing that."

"You need extra money?" Anne asked quietly.

"Everybody needs money." Edna looked at Anne as if she wasn't quite at home in her head. "Nobody's ever got too much money."

"She doesn't even sew her buttons back on," Anne grumbled to Sarah that night. "And if she's gonna learn how to play the piano, she'd better start soon. She's been here nearly a year and hasn't even started."

"Oh," Sarah dismissed Edna with a casual shrug, "the world is full of places like this with girls like her who talk forever about doing something else and never get around to it. One*day some young cowboy will want more of what she's got than he can afford to buy one night at a time, and he'll ask her to marry him. And she'll do it because she thinks it's easier than this, and inside of four years she'll have three kids and the dirtiest house in a two-day ride."

"But why?" Anne puzzled, staring out of the upstairs window at the night street below and the half-dozen young drovers heading for Belle's place.

"I don't know," Sarah yawned, bored, "but it's something that happens. It's easy to think and dream about making changes, but the changes we make don't always turn out to suit us."

"Then try something else," Anne said, her voice flat and cold. "Just talk, talk, talkin' isn't going to change anything!"

"I hope you have as many answers when you're twenty-six as you do now," Sarah said softly, but Anne didn't hear her, she was watching out the window, grinning, as two well-lubricated trail hands tried to help each other back up onto the board sidewalk out of the mud they'd fallen into when they left the saloon.

---

*  *  *

Anne was getting ready for bed, stripped to the waist, having a sponge bath, standing with one arm raised in an unconsciously graceful arc over her head, washing her underarm with a soapy cloth. Sarah realized with a sort of unwelcome shock that Anne was less and less a gawky little girl every day.

"Belle offered me a full-time job," she said softly. Anne didn't answer at all, just matter-of-factly finished her sponge bath, then sat on the edge of the bed in her clean underwear, brushing her hair. They had moved from Belle's room to a smaller, quieter room under the eaves, far from the sound of the saloon.

"Did you hear me?" Sarah asked quietly. "I said Belle offered me a full-time job."

"I heard."

"And . . ."

"And what?"

"What do you think about the idea?"

"Not much," Anne admitted openly. "But it's got nothing to do with me."

"What do you mean . . . nothing to do with you?"

"Well, if you take the job I won't be here so it won't matter a tinker's damn, will it?"

"You'd leave?" Sarah watched the girl, busily re-braiding her hair.

"Why not? I wasn't in a whorehouse before I met you, so I guess I don't have to be in one after."

"Can you explain why?" Sarah asked, feeling anger rising inside her, wanting to grab Anne and shake her—shake her until her braids loosened and her hair fell down around her shoulders, down over the insolently expressionless face.

The discussion verged on argument for hours, Anne at first refusing to even try to explain her reasons, Sarah stubbornly insisting on hearing the reasons.

"Do you have any idea how much money I can make?" she grated. "If we stayed here through the winter we could leave with more money than you've ever seen in your life."

---

80

"Six dollars and twenty-two cents is probably more money than I ever saw in my life," Anne snapped. "Except for Keno's money and that doesn't count."

"Why doesn't it?"

"Because I never counted it."

"That doesn't make a pinch of sense at all."

"Pinch? I don't give a pinch of goose shit if it makes sense or not. You sound just like Edna. She's gonna learn to play the cockeyed piano, and you're only gonna work until spring . . ."

"Anne," Sarah tried logic, "we can't live on fresh air and sunshine. You need a winter coat, warm socks, and some clothes for school, and . . ."

"Shove school up your nose," Anne flared. "Don't you start trying to make out it's because of *me!* I never said I wanted to go to school. There's nothing I need to know that they're going to teach me! And if I need a winter coat and if someone stole Uncle Andrew's old jacket, then I guess the money I got for Dan's visit to that little mare would buy me as many as I wanted."

Sarah pointed out that there was more than just one jacket being discussed. "Besides which, I could make more in a week than he's going to make in a month."

"You could probably make more in one night than he's going to make in his whole entire life," Anne said coolly.

"Anne!"

"What?" she asked with a cruel, innocent-seeming smile.

"You don't know the first thing about it," Sarah grated.

"I don't?" Anne's smile was twisted and hard. "I spent my life on a farm with toms and tabbys, roosters and hens, and cows that had to be taken down the road to visit the bull. I know all about 'it.' Except," she added, "when it's animals, it's different."

"What's the difference?" Sarah attacked, stung and hurt. "You didn't find 'it' so horrible when you took the money for Dan's stud fee!"

"Dan," Anne said firmly, "is a stud. That's all he's supposed to do. Walk, eat, sleep, shit, be transportation and service mares. He isn't supposed to think."

"And I'm supposed to think, is that it?"

"Unless what Uncle Andrew said was true: that women do their best thinking on their backs and use some other part of them than their brains." When Sarah turned away, Anne pressed her advantage. "My mother told me if you eat with pigs and sleep with pigs and talk to pigs and spend all your time with pigs, you might never be a pig, but you're gonna smell strong from miles away."

"You think Belle and Laura are pigs?"

"Belle and Laura," Anne said flatly, "are only people I know. What they do is their business, not mine. I don't *care* about them. But if you do it, I would care. And I'd feel dirty. And I'd think you were dirty. And I'd hate your guts. And I don't want to hate your guts, so I'd leave first."

"You know you're crazier 'n' hell, don't you?" Sarah yelled, frustrated and angry. "You know you don't make any good sense at all. You're contradicting yourself all over the place and you aren't being at all logical." But Anne didn't answer her. She just got into bed, rolled with her back turned to Sarah and pulled the covers up around her ears. When Sarah finally went to bed, Anne was already asleep and Sarah lay beside her on the small bed, listening to the keening autumn wind pull at the eaves of the house.

Sarah knew Belle would think she was out of her mind, but after a surprisingly short dissertation on the unbelievable stupidity of some people, Belle seemed to accept Sarah's decision— seemed, in fact, to approve, although she probably would have died rather than admit it.

For three dollars on the first day of every month, she rented them the cabin and equipment she'd had built and installed at the end of town directly across from the livery stable.

"Hop Sing, Ah Fong, Mah Boh and them other cheeky buggers who didn't even stay long enough for me to know their names," she grinned, "had everything they needed to make money and were too stupid to use it. It's no use to me at all and you might as well do something with it or the damn stuff'll only either rust away or get stolen."

"Three dollars a month isn't enough," Anne protested.

"For God's sake, how come every time I try to have a talk with you we wind up arguing about money?" Belle snapped and Sarah grabbed Anne's arm and pulled her aside.

"Just accept it gracefully," she warned, "she's done enough for us that the least you can do is accept this as a favor to her."

"That doesn't make any sense!" Anne protested.

"Just shut up," Sarah growled, "and do as you're told!"

Sarah still wanted Anne to go to school, but Anne flatly refused to even consider it until Laura came up with a compromise. Anne wouldn't go to school and sit in a room with a dozen children, but she would, every night after the work was done, read the books Belle and Laura provided, and once a week she would go down to the schoolhouse and write a test prepared by the teacher. Every afternoon she would go to the saloon, enter by the back way so nobody in town would be shocked to see a child going into such a place, and for half an hour, under Laura's sleepy and gentle instruction, Anne would struggle with scales and the simple tunes she was trying to learn to play.

"Waste of time," Belle would grumble, "nobody can learn to play properly if they ruin their hands in boiling hot water. Standin' around in freezin' rain with the wind blowing like hell and chapping her skin. Waste of time to even bother trying." But she would sit for the half hour and nod time, watching happily as Anne struggled with the scales.

They filled the copper boilers at night and banked the stove with coal which they bought by the ton from the large-knuckled Welsh family that had opened a probably illegal coal mine on the land they had originally intended to farm. The sheets and pillow slips from Belle's place were put in the copper boilers with a scoop of the jellylike soap they found in the wash shed. The soap never set although sometimes it froze, and after the linens had simmered in the boilers all night, they were lifted out in the morning and carried to the wash shed. Then, arms stretching and aching, sometimes stumbling, they carried the boilers out to the shed and poured the hot water into the big tubs. While

Sarah cooked breakfast, Anne would stand by the tubs with a plunger and work the soapy water through the sheets. "Just like churning butter, only different," she explained once.

The laundry was left to soak a while longer and Anne and Sarah ate breakfast, then they put their dishes in a pan with some water, set it on the back of the stove, and went out together to lift the steaming sheets from the water and lay them across big wooden tables where any spots or stains were scrubbed with a brush. The sheets cooled rapidly in the chilly air, and then they would each take an end, twist the soapy water from them, and drop them into big tubs of cool water to rinse. By noon all the washing was blowing on the many lines set up in and around the yard. After lunch, Anne would set out with her wagon, delivering the freshly laundered, folded and ironed washing that had been done the day before. At first there was just Belle's laundry to do and deliver, but soon the hotel was sending them sheets and tablecloths from the dining room. Within a month they were having to refuse new orders: There simply weren't enough hours in the day to get all the work done.

When the laundry was delivered, Anne would go to Belle's for her music lesson, then go back home and start bringing in the washing from the lines. She tried to be very quiet about this because Sarah usually lay down for a while after lunch, but somehow Sarah always woke up and insisted on helping. They would fold the sheets neatly, iron the pillow slips and tablecloths, and then start in on the more delicate personal laundry Belle's girls sent them.

Sometimes Sarah would touch a particularly dainty piece of laundry with a sort of wistful remembrance, her red, water-swollen, wind-chapped hands seeming afraid to touch the lace. Sometimes she got a wistful look on her face, but the mood passed and she'd go back to work with a smile.

Supper, and after supper the dishes for the whole day had to be washed, the table and countertop cleaned off, the floor swept and sometimes washed. The water boilers had to be refilled with cold water brought up from the well by a bucket on a rope, and then, and only then, could Anne sit down and feel that the day's work was done. That was when Sarah would pull out the school books. Anne had argued and, at times, even yelled in protest until she realized that Sarah was studying just as hard as she was. When she realized that, Anne began bringing her corrected test papers home, knowing that after she had gone to bed at night, Sarah would cover the answers and write the test herself.

They spent Christmas at Belle's place and for the first time in anybody's memory, Belle closed the upstairs rooms both Christmas Eve and Christmas night. The poker game was suspended and the standard free lunch of hard-boiled eggs and cold fried sausage was enlarged until half the back wall was taken up with a buffet table of roast chicken, beef, lamb and all the bread, potatoes and gravy a person could eat. Anne and Sarah provided a haunch of venison from a buck Sarah had seen out behind the wash lines, and even the dour Cornish woman who'd muttered sullenly while doing the cooking, thawed enough to join them for a glass of wine, and after her third, loudly declared that, by God, the woman has more brains than I have. If I'd been half as smart as her I'd have had the washing business. "But," she added dourly, "nobody would have rented me the tubs and all that have been sitting idle for how long."

"I couldn't stand to lose you," Belle laughed. "Who'd do the cleaning and cooking for me?"

"I would," Laura offered, and everyone laughed at her joke.

There were gifts to everyone from everyone else, bottles of perfume and small bars of fancy soap. Belle gave Sarah a collection of creams and lotions for her hands and face and Sarah gave Belle the kitten that had shown up two weeks earlier, skinny and sick and more dead than alive. Now it was healthy and fat and loved to climb and cuddle. Belle stared at it as if she wasn't sure what to do with it.

"Every cat house," Sarah said gravely, "ought to have at least one honest-to-God cat." And Belle began to laugh until Anne thought for sure she'd choke. Belle named the cat "Sarah," and everyone agreed that within six months they'd probably be up to their knees in kittens. Anne couldn't believe the numbers of shirts, socks, and underwear she got. Laura gave her a box of hair ribbons and several sheets of music. Belle gave her some new storybooks and they both exclaimed with delight over the comfortable but plain slippers she had bought for them.

"These feel good," Belle announced, taking off her fancy shoes and sliding her feet into the warm slippers. "By God, I don't know why I didn't get me a pair like this years ago." Anne smiled happily.

She and Sarah exchanged gifts in private after the noisy party at Belle's was over and they had walked back in the bitter cold, their boots crunching on the frozen snow.

"Where did you get it?" Sarah breathed.

"It's not new," Anne admitted. "I couldn't get a new one, but Jake said this was the best used one he had, and he helped me fix it up."

"It's lovely."

"I was thinking maybe to get you a sidesaddle," Anne continued, "because that's what ladies have, but nobody around here has even heard of one, let alone seen one."

"Saw one," Sarah corrected automatically, then hugged Anne tightly. "Now open yours." Anne stared down at the warm winter jacket, bright red gloves and toque. All new. She wanted to say thank you, and couldn't. All she could do was nod and blink rapidly.

"You were right," Sarah tried to sound as if she was joking, and she turned her back, pretending the hot chocolate she was making needed her full attention, "there's more than one way to get a good winter coat."

New Year's Eve the saloon was jammed, the out-of-tune piano was valiantly trying to be heard over the din of jokes and laughter, and the bartender was red-faced and sweating, and cursing the inexperience of the five extra part-time assistants Belle had hired to handle the crowd. Anne sat quietly, halfway up the stairs, pressed against the banister, avoiding as best she could the constant traffic of busy working girls and half-drunken grinning men. Any money Belle might have lost by not staying open at Christmas, she more than made up for New Year's Eve. Anne enjoyed the music, enjoyed watching the dancing, and ate until she had to admit she couldn't swallow another bite of food. At midnight, everybody singing and cheering, she pounded on an old water bucket until the bottom fell out, then kissed Belle, Laura, and Sarah, and wished everyone else a year of the best. After that, it was all downhill for her: The cigar smoke burned her eyes, the jokes seemed old and stale, the noise more frantic, the laughter forced and harsh.

"I'm just about ready to go home," she hinted to Sarah.

"Okay," Sarah smiled, her eyes shiny, her face lightly filmed with sweat.

"You ready?" Anne pressed.

"No," Sarah laughed, "but you can find your way home okay."

"Sure," Anne agreed, nodding slowly. "You'll be okay?"

"Oh," Sarah laughed again, sipping thirstily from her glass, "oh, I'll be just fine."

"Okay," Anne nodded again, got her jacket and toque, and slipped through the back door to the alley. The snow crunched underfoot, the stars hung low in the icy mid-winter sky, and her breath plumed around her face. She turned from the alley to the board sidewalk, her boots clicking steadily on the thin film of ice, the sound of laughter and the badly tuned piano fading behind her. Halfway down the street, a figure lurched from a doorway and a hand reached out to grab her arm.

"Hey," the voice slurred, "you wanna celebrate New Year with me?"

"No," she said shortly, pulling her arm free.

"Don't be like that," the man coaxed, reaching again.

"Okay," she said agreeably, smiling up at him. He smiled back, and she stepped forward quickly, slamming her boot hard on his instep, bringing up her other knee and driving it viciously into his crotch. He gasped, gagged and slumped to the ground. Anne ran down the street, past the big brightly lit house where the manager of the hardware store and his wife were having a party. People were already leaving the party, and she knew that inside an hour and a half, husbands who hadn't been able to find an excuse to sneak away earlier, would leave the beds where their wives slept peacefully and slip down to Belle's for something other than weak punch and dainty sandwiches.

She waited for two hours, but Sarah didn't come home, so Anne checked the water tubs, added some water to one, banked the fire, and went to bed with the warm bricks wrapped in a towel. She tried to stay awake, but her eyes, irritated by the cigar smoke in the saloon, felt itchy, and no matter how hard she blinked, they wouldn't stay open. Finally, she fell into a restless sleep, missing the warmth of Sarah's body beside hers. She slept late, and wakened unwillingly, the bed beside her still empty.

She had eaten breakfast, done the dishes, tidied the kitchen and started the first of the laundry before Sarah came home. One look told Anne there was no use saying much. She just turned back to the sheet on the scrub table, and took her feelings out on it, rubbing the brush savagely against the already clean cotton sheet.

"Never mind that," Sarah slurred. "It's a day off."

"Might as well get it done," Anne said evenly.

"I'm not workin'," Sarah laughed. "I'm gonna have a party."

"You do that," Anne agreed, her voice flat. The brush bit into the sheet even harder.

When she went into the cabin several hours later, Sarah was stretched sideways across the bed, her clothes a rumpled heap on the floor, her face flushed, her lips parted, breathing heavily through her mouth.

"Chrissakes," Anne muttered. With some difficulty, she got Sarah under the covers and went to the oven to get the bricks. She tucked the bricks under the covers, hoping Sarah hadn't caught a chill, and stoked the stove before making herself a thick sandwich and a cup of tea. Anne ate to the gentle sound of Sarah's deep snores, then stacked the dishes and went outside to attack the laundry again. When she went into the house to cook supper, Sarah was still snoring, mouth open, face clammy white and beaded with sweat.

"Come on," Anne insisted. "It'll do you good."

88

"Gonna make me sick," Sarah moaned.

"Just eat it, will you? If you're sick, you're sick. It'll just mean you've got somethin' in your stomach that isn't good for you."

"I don't want it," Sarah protested, but she swallowed obediently when Anne spooned the soup into her. She managed to finish the bowl of soup, but only picked at her supper, staring woefully from red-rimmed eyes.

"You look so goddamn healthy," she groaned, finally, putting her plate on the floor and flopping back to the pillow, wincing as her head objected to all the sudden movement.

"Merry nights make sorrowful mornings," Anne quoted piously. "Except it isn't morning. It's nearly bedtime again."

"Good," Sarah announced. "You should have let me sleep right through."

"You'd have been awake halfway through the night, waking me up because you were hungry or something," Anne argued.

"Oh, God, Annie, don't bitch at me. I'm dying!"

"You aren't dying," Anne said. "You're hung over. And it's your own goddamn fault."

"I'm not hung over. I'm *sick*," Sarah insisted.

"Hung over," Anne snapped, "and no damn wonder."

"Oh, okay, get it over with," Sarah invited, martyred. "Tell me I made an ass of myself."

"Did you?"

"No. All I did was dance and sing and have a few drinks."

"Then you should be able to sleep tonight. A clean conscience makes a good pillow."

"Where did you learn all those awful sayings?" But Anne wouldn't answer. She turned away, and, with much disapproving clatter, did the dishes and filled the wood box. Then she refilled the tubs, stuffed the stove with wood, and, still angry, jealous and punitive, and more than a bit tired, she got ready for bed and climbed in. It was hard to stay angry with Sarah when the bed was so much warmer and cozier than it had been the previous night, with only two flannel-wrapped bricks for company.

"Annie?" Sarah whispered.

"What?"

---

89

"You mad?"

"Me? Mad?" Anne mocked. "Why would I be mad?"

"'Cause I didn't come home last night."

"You're a big girl, I guess." Anne tried to shrug, but found it wasn't easy when you're lying down.

"You sure?"

"Sure what?"

"Sure you're not mad?"

"What have I got to be mad about?" Anne yawned. "After all, we went to a party together, and I came home alone, while you got drunk and made a fool of yourself."

"I *knew* it!" Sarah sat upright, then moaned and reached for her head. "I *knew* you were mad!"

"Me?" Anne rolled onto her side and faked another yawn. "Why would I be mad?"

"You've ruined New Year's," Sarah said tearfully. "The whole year is starting out wrong. I'm sick and you don't care. And you're mad and picking a fight."

"I'm not picking a fight," Anne contradicted carefully. "You're the one won't let me go to sleep. I let *you* sleep when you wanted to."

"Oh, you're just hateful!" Sarah snapped, lying down carefully and turning so her back was to Anne. They lay back-to-back until sleep claimed them both. Then, sometime in the middle of the night, one of them rolled over and threw an arm around the other, and they slept more comfortably and soundly.

In the morning, Sarah got out of bed first and had the fire roaring and breakfast cooking before Anne stirred.

"Well, sleepyhead," Sarah teased, but her eyes were anxious.

"Did you go into one of the rooms with a man?" Anne demanded, sitting upright.

"Why?" Sarah asked, back stiff.

"Because if you did I don't want to hear about it," Anne flared.

"Then why ask?"

"I don't know," Anne admitted. "But you didn't come home!"

"Well, I'm home now," Sarah evaded, "and I'll give you breakfast in bed if you promise to stop glaring at me."

"Coax me," Anne grinned, flopping back onto the pillows and sniffing appreciatively.

They were working at the washtables, scrubbing sheets with stiff brushes, Anne cursing the men who lay down on hotel beds without taking off their dirty clothes. The snow on the ground had melted down to dirty-colored patches. The worst of winter's grip was over, and the spring mud was thick and clinging to their boots. Sarah took a sheet to the clothes line and in the minute her back was turned, Anne saw a bedraggled figure duck around the corner of the house. Clothing torn, feet bare, covered with mud and with a large cut on his face, he froze when he saw her, then stood as if the world was about to come to an end. At the same time she heard the sound of rapidly approaching horses. Without thinking, she lifted an empty washtub, turned it upside down, and motioned. He dove under the barrel, curled himself as small as possible, and Anne lowered the edge to the ground, returning to her scrubbing just as a posse led by Luke Wilson, himself, rounded the side of the house.

Sarah heard them coming and half stepped from behind the billowing sheets, then hid herself again, keeping the sheets between her and Luke Wilson. She reached up to be sure her head was completely covered by the scarf she had tied around her short hair.

"Is your mother home?" Luke Wilson asked.

"No, sir." Anne knew who he was, because Sarah had described him perfectly. "There's nobody here but me and my cousin."

"You see a man come by here today?"

"A man?" Anne echoed. "No, sir. There's no men come around here. Except, sometimes, Jake the liveryman."

"Six foot, shabby dressed, cut on his face here..." Luke Wilson described the man under the washtub.

"No, sir," Anne repeated. "That's not Jake the liveryman."

91

"What about you?" Luke Wilson asked suddenly, riding over and moving a sheet aside so he could talk to the girl's cousin.

"Haven't seen anybody at all. Except her..."

Luke Wilson nodded, urged his horse away from the wash line, not wanting to soil the spotless white sheets. Then he turned back, frowning slightly. "Don't I know you?"

"Me?" Sarah gasped.

"Yes, ma'am," he lifted his hat politely. "Haven't we met?"

"I don't think so," she replied, coldly, turning away.

"I didn't mean it like that, ma'am," he apologized. "I'm not a man to insult a decent hard-working lady. But I seldom forget a face..." The young woman kept her back turned to him and went about her business hanging up sheets, the young girl glaring at him, as well she might. "I'm sorry, ladies." He nodded. "My men and I won't bother you again." And he rode off quickly.

"That's him," Sarah gasped.

"I know," Anne said just as the washtub moved and the raggedy man crawled out from underneath.

"Oh, shit!" Sarah gasped. "He'll be back for sure, now!"

# Chapter 6

There was no way they could send the raggedy pilgrim away with Luke Wilson on the prowl. It would have been sending him to his death. They fed him, gave him dry clothes and a tub of hot water in which to scrub off the dirt, mud and dried blood. There wasn't a pair of boots would fit him, but he pulled on thick woolen socks and wrapped strips of what had been a shirt around the socks in a vain attempt to keep them clean and dry. Then he crawled underneath the house, under the stove where it was a bit warmer and dryer than anywhere else, and wrapping himself in a feed sack, he wolfed down the food they had given him and fell asleep.

They put the laundry on the delivery wagon and set off down the street, trying to behave as if it was just another day like any other. Sarah pushed through the back door of Belle's place first, Anne following, the huge pile of clean sheets obscuring her vision. She bumped into Sarah, opened her mouth to protest, and was shocked when Sarah's elbow dove into her ribs. Anne gasped, frozen with insult.

"What makes you think she'd be here?" she heard Belle ask easily.

"Well, I figure," whined Uncle Andrew, "that this is the only thing she'd be trained or equipped to do." Anne's kneecaps danced up and down, her legs trembled, the weight of the sheets on her outstretched arms seemed to multiply every second and her tongue stuck to the roof of her mouth. She backed slowly into the kitchen, hoping nobody would pay attention to her.

"She can barely read and write," Andrew continued, "so she isn't likely to get a job in a bank or a store." He giggled foolishly. "And while she can cook, she can't cook good enough to get paid for it. There's only one thing a girl like her can get paid for. And I figured, what with this being the closest establishment of its kind, that she'd make for here."

"You seen anybody like that?" Belle demanded.

"Like what?" Sarah sounded disinterested, almost bored.

"Young girl, about so high," Andrew described. "Long blonde hair, blue eyes. No idea what kind of clothes she's wearin', but she's likely riding a big black blooded stud name o' Dan."

"Shouldn't be hard to find her." Sarah dismissed the problem. "I'll leave these on the bar, and the Chinaman can leave the others in the kitchen, okay?"

"That's fine," Belle agreed. "How come she left home?" she questioned Andrew.

"An ungrateful child," he whined piously, "is like unto a serpent's fang. And that ungrateful child has bit me deep. That horse is worth a lot of money."

"Have a drink," Belle offered.

"I have to tell you, ma'am," Andrew tried to sound poor but honest, "I don't have any money for buying drinks."

"I didn't say *buy* a drink." Belle's laughter gurgled into a wheeze. She coughed several times and continued, "I said *have* a drink. You were telling me about that runaway neighbor kid of yours."

"Stepdaughter," Andrew corrected, then he coughed as the raw whiskey burned his throat. "Her momma died from worryin' over her, and then the little vixen stole my blooded stud and took off with him. Stole every penny I had, too," he finished, and this time it was the lie, not the whiskey that made him cough.

"I'll kill him," Anne raged in a whisper, setting the sheets down on the big pine table in the cathouse kitchen.

"Just get the hell out of here," Sarah hissed. "Take the laundry to Jake . . . the next place that bastard heads is gonna be the livery!"

---

Anne ducked out of the back door of the cathouse, grabbed the wagon and hurried off down the alley and up the street. All she had for Jake were two pairs of clean overalls, a clean union suit and two clean shirts, but she had to pass the hotel to get to the livery, and she might just as well make one trip as two.

"He was here already," the hotel clerk greeted her. "Mean lookin' bastard with a face like an asshole that needs wipin'. I didn't know what to do with him, so I sent him down to Belle's place. I didn't want him goin' near the livery. He'd'a seen Dan for sure. You better move that horse, Annie."

"It's not *his* horse," Anne protested. "It was my dad's farm, my dad's crop and my mom and I did the work that raised the money that bought Dan."

"I believe you," the clerk said softly, "and you might find two other men in the territory who do, too. But you'll never find a dozen. And that's what you need for a jury."

"Oh, Jesus," Anne gasped.

"Well," the clerk winked, "with Him and three reliable witnesses, you might have a chance. Otherwise, you'd better get rid of that stud!"

"Where's your dirty laundry?" she asked, her voice shaking.

"Right here. But you aren't going to take time to do the laundry, are you?" he gaped.

"I don't know what I'm gonna do," Anne said honestly, "and until I know what to do, I might just as well keep on doin' what I've been doin' while I figure somethin' out. Help me pile it on the wagon?"

She hurried up the street with the half-loaded wagon bumping behind her, watching anxiously for any sign of Luke Wilson, his posse or mad Uncle Andrew.

"I gotta hide Dan," she blurted.

"What for?" Jake asked, so she told him, briefly, and when he had heard about the gall sores on old Bess' back, and the inadequate diet both animals had been given, he shook his head firmly. "No way he can have them back," he decided. "But we'd be damn fools to try to move that stud in broad daylight. I'll go open the door to the shed out back and you coax him in.

---

Maybe if I give him a real bellyfull of oats and a few apples, he'll stay inside without makin' any noise."

Dan didn't want to leave the spring sunshine and the fresh grass for the dark interior of the shed, but Anne coaxed him, and Jake bribed him, and finally the big stud pranced inside and buried his nose in a bucket of oats. "The whole town knows about Dan," Anne mourned. "Sooner or later, someone is gonna let the cat out of the bag."

"Just keep your fingers crossed that cat don't leave the bag before it's dark enough for the stud to leave the shed." Jake tried to reassure her with a smile, but his face was pale and his eyes nervous.

Uncle Andrew was sitting at a table talking over a bottle of whiskey with Laura, who was smiling, leaning forward. Her elbow on the table, her head resting on her hand, her creamy bosom rising and falling with each breath, her eyes fixed on Andrew's face, she was the picture of absorbed interest. From time to time, Belle raised herself from the pine table in the kitchen, and checked through the crack in the door, and once she signaled to the bartender, who nodded and uncapped another bottle and took it to the table.

"It was the bones," Andrew confided, lifting the shot glass of amber liquid and swallowing happily.

"What bones?" Laura smiled.

"That's just it." His Adam's apple bobbed in his scrawny throat. "There weren't any. Do a fat old mare who ought to have been compost years ago, and a fine big blooded stud burn in a barn, there ought to be some bones. Skulls. Teeth. Then there were the hens."

"Hens don't have teeth," Laura protested, patting his hand.

"No," he agreed, pouring himself another drink, "and they don't carry their egg boxes out under a tree, neither. Nor turn the cow loose in the garden."

"I don't suppose they do." She smiled, lashes fluttering.

"Do a saddle and bridle burn?" he continued. "There's got to be metal left in the ashes. But there wasn't. Nor no axe head nor rifle barrel, nor . . ." He hiccuped suddenly. "'Scuse me," he

---

blurted, burping. "Took me a few days to figure it out. I was," he explained, "a bit shook thinking that wayward vixen had perished. But the flames of earth were of her doing, so she avoided them. It's the flames of hell will bring her to her just reward. But first," he hiccuped again, "I gotta find my horse."

"Are you a religious man?" Laura poured Andrew another drink. "Your reference to the flames of hell is . . . rather . . . evangelical."

"I wasn't always," he assured her blearily. "There was a time I rolled in the mire of sin and lusted and fornicated like any unrepentant devil worshipper. But a man has a lot of time to think when he's sittin' in the rain in his long johns and one boot, and I've seen the error of my ways. I am washed in the blood of the lamb, sanctified by his love, saved from the fiery pit of damnation, born again to righteousness and truth."

"Indeed." Laura smiled again.

"Indeed," he nodded. "In deed, in thought and in full deep intention. I have looked on my past life and found it unsatisfactory."

"Haven't we all," she agreed.

"Train up a child in the way in which she is to go," Andrew misquoted, "and when she is older, she shall not depart from it."

"I'll drink to that." Laura lifted her glass. Andrew smiled, lifted his own and drank. Deeply.


"Looks to me," Belle said quietly, "like you're caught between a rock and a hard place. You've got that asshole out there steamin' after Anne and Dan, and that fanatic shitface of a marshal about to tumble to where he's seen you before. And then, of course, there's the small matter of the pilgrim asleep under your house."

"We could send him on his way," Sarah suggested.

"Doesn't matter if he stays or goes," Belle contradicted. "That Luke Wilson doesn't ever forget a face. Sooner or later something is going to click and he'll be back."

"But we haven't done anything wrong!" Sarah protested.

"Honey, you've committed the worst sin in his book. You

---

97

lived! He'd go behind the walls of a convent and drag out Mother Superior if he thought he had reason. He's hung strange crops on trees in every place he's ever been. The crazy bastard really believes he is the arm of God, and Justice on Earth."

"Why doesn't somebody shoot him?" Anne suggested.

"People have tried. Luke says they've never managed because God has His hand over him. Sometimes it makes you wonder."

"If he and Uncle Andrew get together," Anne mourned, "dyin' will seem like a nice way to end what they cook up between them."

"If that sosspot drinks much more, he'll pass out for a week," Belle predicted.

"What will we do?" Sarah moaned.

It was the Cornishwoman who came up with the solution. She had been preparing supper and pouring coffee for the three at the table, listening to every word. "I'll send me daughters down there," she said suddenly, "then if yon fanatic goes back he'll see two entirely different women. That'll hold him for a while. And if Belle will rent me the tubs and boilers and cabin for the same price as you've been paying, I'll give you a wagon I've got and some harness I don't need. In exchange for your customers, you see."

"Hang on," Belle said firmly. "A wagon and harness is fine, but who pulls the damned thing?"

"You want my horses, too?" the Cornishwoman glared. "Those are good drays!"

"Won't do you any good just standing around eating," Belle dickered. "You haven't used them in a year and a half. And that wagon is something else you haven't used. It's just sitting behind your barn. Soaking wet. And if you aren't using the horse and wagon, you sure as hell aren't using the harness; but they've been using their customers, and building up the business."

"Oh, let's not argue about things like money," Sarah said nervously.

"Why in hell not?" Anne snapped. "What's wrong with talking about money? She's got stuff she doesn't have any use for, we've got stuff she does have use for. What's wrong with settling things?"

"What about my cooking?" Belle demanded. "It's a great idea, but it leaves me with a house full of hungry working girls."

"Laura said she'd do the cooking," Anne said. "She doesn't like what she's doing now half as much as she likes cooking."

"Yeah?" Belle grinned suddenly. "I didn't know that. I don't much like what she's been doing, either."

It all happened so fast that neither Anne nor Sarah could keep track of what was going on. The Cornishwoman went home, and Anne and Sarah went back to the cabin to pack their things. "We'd be better off," Anne grumbled, "just climbing up on Dan and OtherOne and riding like hell."

"We've got too much stuff," Sarah protested.

"We could leave it behind," Anne grumbled. But she didn't really want to leave her books, her ribbons, her changes of underwear, socks and clothes. When you don't have anything, it's easy to walk away quickly, but the roots you sometimes develop slow you down and it hurts to pull them up again.

The Cornishwoman arrived with a sturdy wooden wagon, and a faded but serviceable canvas top stretched over metal hoops, the heavy harness well preserved and oiled, and two strong young dray mares, Sunny and Babe, champing eagerly at their bits.

"That's worth more than our laundry business," Sarah said firmly, and, while Anne glared disapprovingly, Sarah counted six months' rent into the Cornishwoman's tough hand, then smiled warmly. "Good luck," Sarah offered.

"My luck'll be what I make it," the Cornishwoman answered frankly, "but you're the ones going to need help from the Old Ones. That marshal and that ferretty-faced fellow are prime examples of the kind the Old Cold sends after us. Don't trust either of 'em, ever."

"What was she talking about?" Anne whispered later.

"I don't know," Sarah answered nervously, "but even if I didn't understand it, it made good sense at the time."

They packed their things on the wagon and drove back to

Belle's. Sarah went inside to say good-bye to her friends, and Anne continued up the street to the livery stable to saddle Dan and OtherOne and put a lead rope on old Bess.

"Annie," Jake said fervently, "you can be sure I'm not gonna tell Luke Wilson nothin' at all. Nor your uncle, neither. And you take care of yourself. If you ever get yourself in a bind you can't get yourself out of, you send me a letter. I'll go down to Belle's and get someone to read it to me, and if there's anything I can do . . . anything at all . . . you consider it as good as done."

"Thanks, Jake." Anne hesitated, then threw her arms around him and kissed his bristly cheek. The liveryman stiffened, went deep red, then hugged her fiercely, clumsily.

"Goddamn," he muttered, finally pulling away, "it's a hell of a life when a wonder like you can't live in peace."

Jake went with her back to Belle's place. Word had spread like secret fire. The Welsh woman whose sons ran a probably illegal coal mine on the homestead they had filed and proven, was there with a cage in which several puzzled hens sat peering nearsightedly at the confusion. Jake and the raggedy pilgrim fastened the cage to the back of the covered wagon while the Welsh woman said for the fourth time that as soon as they'd heard Luke Wilson was in the area two of her boys had headed into the coal mine with sticks of dynamite, vowing if the marshal went in after them they'd take the miserable English bastard with them if they had to, but they wouldn't come out to be taken alive. Nobody asked why Luke Wilson might want the laughing, singing young giants; it wasn't polite to ask questions. Pilgrim thanked everyone for their donations; a pair of boots from Belle, a pair of boots left behind by a cowboy who got drunk and had to be carried home by his almost-as-drunken friends, none of whom noticed the unconscious rider was barefoot. The boots were used and stiff, but better than nothing. Uncle Andrew's old jacket, unused since Anne and Sarah had arrived in town, fit Pilgrim fairly well, and after he'd eaten the enormous meal prepared for him he was ready to drive the wagon anywhere. Anywhere Luke Wilson wasn't!

Snores from under the table in the bar kept them all aware

of Uncle Andrew. He lay on the tobacco-stained sawdust, a half-grin on his face, eyes shut, mouth open, a slight film of sweat on his face.

"Bastard'll sleep for three days," Belle predicted. "Whenever anyone tries to out-drink Laura, we've got 'em for the better part of a week. Three days snoring, two days puking and whining." She chortled quietly, watching with unabashed pride as Laura packed food into a hamper and supervised the loading of sacks of supplies from the General Store, where the proprietor, smiling happily, was rewarded for his inconvenience by two of the working girls whose attentions more than made up for the wholesale price Belle had convinced him was fair. Several other small businessmen, customers of Belle's, acquaintances of Anne and Sarah, handed them small farewell gifts: a big cookpot, a warm quilt, a bottle of all-purpose digestive aid medicine made primarily of cascara and peppermint. Belle poured several drinks, everyone shook hands and said repeatedly what rotten luck it was that they had to leave, and Jake sat glaring at the comatose form of the man Anne discovered she was relieved to learn hadn't sizzled like bacon when the cabin flamed.

They waited until the town was dark and then they went outside, to the wagon. Nobody cried, although Anne was afraid she was going to. She cuddled Belle, cuddled Laura, and accepted the money the working girls had collected for her and Sarah. Sarah cuddled Laura, then hung onto Belle, both of them fighting tears.

"You take care of yourself, yourselves, and each other," Belle warned, "and write me a letter."

"You look out for Luke Wilson," Sarah begged.

"Honey, this place is closed until that mean-eyed motherless bastard is gone."

For all that they had been amazingly busy, the majority of the townspeople had noticed nothing. Perhaps they didn't want to notice anything. When Luke Wilson was in the area, you were better off seeing, hearing, noticing and knowing Nothing At All.

"What if he follows the wagontracks?" Anne blurted.

"So you delivered some laundry," Belle soothed. "No law against delivering laundry. And no law says I have to know what you did after that. You'll drop off the face of the earth. Inside of a week or two you'll catch up with a wagon train. The whole goddamn country's heading West!"

"Except for the jamtarts," Laura teased. "All the jamtarts got off the wagons in the East."

"I wish I could leave Bess with you," Anne whispered, snuggling close to the warm perfumed bulk of the woman she had thought she could never learn to love, "but she'd only fret."

"Don't worry, honey. Don't worry about Bess, or me, or Laura, or any of us. You just take care of Sarah. And for God's sake remind her to use cream every day or she'll look like a lizardskin inside of a week!"

"No she won't." The cold triumphant voice came from the darkness. They whirled, their fear already recognizing the darker shape in the shadows. Luke Wilson stepped out into the faint light, his huge hogleg pointed right at Sarah. "She won't look like nothin' inside of a week," and a thin snicker escaped his tight lips.

Anne dove between his legs, landed painfully on the dirt, rolled into the dark gloom between the buildings and scurried out of sight. Luke Wilson didn't even flicker his eyes. He was staring at Sarah with the same fixed interest a snake shows to a young chick. "I thought I'd seen you someplace before," he smirked.

"I haven't done anything wrong!" Sarah protested.

"Then why you in such an all-fired hurry?" he mocked. "The guilty flee when no man pursueth, like it says in the good book."

"It also says in the good book," Belle said firmly, "'Let he who is without sin cast the first stone.'"

Without even looking at her, Luke Wilson swung his free fist. His leather glove banged against the side of her head, and big Belle fell to the ground.

"You bastard!" Laura screamed, running to cradle Belle's head. "You rotten cocksucker!"

"You, too, lady," he grated. "I'll send the pair of you to answer

---

102

for your sins. And you, my friend," he barely glanced at Pilgrim who was standing white faced and frozen with fear, "you've seen the last of everything, too. Inside!"

Anne waited in the shadows across the street, her heart racing, as Luke Wilson herded her friends back inside the saloon. Several men she had never seen before, men who had attached themselves to Luke's crazed crusade, moved inside to back up the lunatic lawman in his move to clean up Freshwater, as he had cleaned up Feather River, Small Butte, Twin Bluffs and towns whose names nobody either knew or remembered. The customers of the saloon backed against the wall, hands in clear sight, making sure the guardians of morality wouldn't mistake their intentions, making sure it was obvious none of them had a gun.

"I'm gonna burn you out." Luke grinned.

"You been tryin' for a long time," Belle admitted, fingering the huge blue swelling along her jawline.

Luke Wilson looked at her, and his guts churned. She was everything he detested. Everything he'd ever found slimy and untouchable. The only good woman he'd ever known was his mother, a strict and righteous woman who made sure he changed his clothes, washed from head to foot, and moved his bowels every day until a week after his fourteenth birthday, when she'd seen him off on his first cattle drive. He'd been scared, but he hadn't shown it. He stood quietly beside his mother, staring at the deeply tanned, wiry men on the tough prairie ponies, wishing his father had been like that instead of the soft-stepping seldom-speaking faded mouse he was: A man who blinked his watery eyes constantly, as if surprised at what life had put on his plate, a man who never argued with anyone, least of all his wife. If his father had been like those men, his mother wouldn't have had to be the breadwinner. But his father wasn't like them, and nothing could be done about that except for Luke to be sure, for the rest of his life, he wasn't the milksop his father was. When it was time to go, Luke's mother shook his hand, almost formally, and gave him two dollars and a new knife. "You be sure to read the Bible at least once a day," she ordered and he nodded. The last sight of her he had she was standing as straight

---

as a lodgepole pine, her hands folded calmly across the front of her skirt, watching him ride off.

He never met another woman like her. But he'd seen plenty of this other kind. The kind who smiled and twitched their backsides and turned good men into simpering fools.

It was all in the Bible. All you had to do was look for it. Eve tempting Adam with the sin she'd learned from the serpent. Eve, the mother of all of these women, a slut who'd fornicated with a serpent, who'd lay down in the grass and spread herself wide and let that snake crawl right inside her, crawl inside, and writhe with pleasure, then crawl out again with her inside smell forever on his skin. All you had to do was pick up a snake and you could smell it on your fingers, and even horses and dogs had sense enough to shy away when they smelled the thick odor coming from a nest of serpents.

Luke Wilson had never lain with a woman. The weakness of his flesh was something he had spent his life overcoming. Sometimes, when the evil in him grew until neither a cold swim nor a hot coal held against his leg would dispel it, he would deliberately, teeth gritted, lie curled on his side, his gloved hand between his legs, squeezing and hating himself until the juices of sin burst from him and landed in the leaves he'd carefully spread. The Bible said a man was not to waste his seed upon the ground, and Luke was careful he never did. But it didn't say you couldn't spill the sin slime onto leaves. Like draining pus from a boil.

The smell of whiskey was thick in the room, and his nose wrinkled, his gorge rose. Women and whiskey were two of the devil's prime weapons, and the cards on the table in the rear of the room were another tool to twist the minds of good men. Men made in the image of God Himself, turned away from righteousness by the devil-worshiping evil these women flaunted. Luke knew the taste of whiskey. He knew from personal experience what whiskey could do to you.

Late night and the bone-tired boy had waved at his relief and ridden away from the restless herd, already feeling the comfort of his bedroll, anticipating the quick slide from raw weariness to sweet sleep. He stripped his gear from the remuda horse, hobbled it and carried his saddle to where he had spread his bedroll before going on nighthawk watch. Without even removing his boots, he slid into his blankets, his head resting against his saddle, his eyes fluttering shut. He sighed, and turned over, and became aware of the soft stirring and fast breathing coming from behind the wagon. The sounds increased, and even though he had never heard them, they made him feel uneasy, restless, and too keyed-up to get to sleep. As if some part of him he didn't know recognized the rhythm of the rustling, the increasing hoarseness of the breathing. He sat up, alert and uneasy. And then the foreman, the man Luke most wished his father had been like, rose from his bedroll and came to sit next to Luke, grinning in the faint rosy light from the embers of the fire. "You know what's happenin'?" he asked conspiratorially. Luke shook his head, admitting his ignorance. "Here," the foreman grinned again, "I'll show you. Come with me." And Luke had gone with him, trusting him, wanting to prove himself, wanting to be like his hero.

When the foreman told him to strip naked, Luke felt the first twinge of fear and shame, and the foreman laughed softly and handed over the small jug. "Take half a dozen big gulps," he urged. And Luke had. Because the foreman was everything Luke wanted to be. The whiskey had burned his throat and made his eyes water, and he almost gagged on it, but he forced it down, and they sat behind the wagon, watching the two cowboys rolling on the blanket under the stars, their pale untanned bodies glowing in the moonlight, their faces, arms and hands almost as dark as the shadows. When the foreman passed the small jug again, Luke drank thirstily, and when the foreman again urged him to remove his clothes, it seemed silly not to, and Luke stripped, enjoying the feel of the night breeze on his skin, suddenly aware for the first time of the body hair sprouting where none had been before. When the foreman reached out and touched him, Luke had enjoyed it.

The cowboys watched as Luke knelt and used his mouth the way the foreman instructed him. Leaning against the wagon, his powerful hands clutching Luke's shaggy hair, the foreman jerked rhythmically, then arched his back and lunged, and Luke was gagging, trying to pull his head back, trying to free his throat, but the strong hands on his head wouldn't let him, and the seeds of sin had entered him then, flowed down his gullet to his guts to fester in him forever. The two cowboys watched it all and when the foreman sagged, covered with sweat, one of the cowboys grabbed Luke and forced him to bend over and hold his own ankles, telling him it would make him puke up the stuff that was burning his throat. But he didn't puke, and then the burning was at the base of his spine and he was flailing, trying to get away, trying not to cry like a little baby, feeling the whiskey fumes swirling around behind his eyes, and even half drunk and all scared he knew all three of them had infected him, front and back, top and bottom, and he couldn't fight them because of the whiskey. He couldn't even keep his own body from enjoying it, couldn't even push away the face of the grinning freckle-faced foreman.

Luke woke up in his own blankets with a head that ached almost as bad as his arse, and he knew he was soiled and would have to redeem himself. He never again touched whiskey, he never again went out behind the wagon, and he never forgot that if there had been women around, his hero wouldn't have even looked at him twice. And his hate festered as the sin festered. Once he had seen a cowpuncher straining against the hindquarters of a bewildered, frantic and securely tied heifer, arching into her the way Luke knew the foreman had arched into him, and when the cowpoke strolled off, grinning and doing up his pants, Luke pulled his new gun and shot the heifer in the head.

By the time the cattledrive was over, Luke Wilson had observed most of the sins the devil used to tempt man away from his God, and he knew, as surely as he knew his name, that he would spend his life fighting evil and corruption, fighting what he knew he carried inside himself.

"He's twelve bricks short a full load," Laura whispered, watching the madness dance deep in the lawman's eyes.

"He means," Belle said flatly, "to kill every damn one of us."

"Shut your mouth," Luke Wilson said flatly, again slapping Belle alongside the head. She just nodded, wiping away the blood that trickled from the corner of her mouth. Ignoring the sneers and muttered insults, Laura hugged Belle, kissed the torn lip, her hand soothing the huge bruise that distorted the soft pale face.

"Did I ever tell you," Belle whispered, "you're the best thing that ever came into the mess that's been my life?"

Anne crept from shadow to shadow, the way the cats had done the night she went into Feather River to steal clothes and axle grease for Sarah. Through the big front window of the saloon she could see Luke Wilson and his gun, aimed at her friends, huddled together in a helpless group. The posse members had their guns out, too, some aimed at Sarah and the others, some aimed at the customers along the back wall. Laura was cuddling Belle, and Luke Wilson was laughing, his back to the window, the light from the huge chandelier above him glinting on his badge and his gun.

Anne reached out, slid the rifle from the scabbard, spoke softly to Dan so he wouldn't get frightened and took careful aim. Right between the shoulder blades, a bit to the left and the bullet would rip through rib bone right into the cold shriveled prune that was Luke Wilson's heart. But she couldn't do it. She couldn't gently squeeze the trigger and send lead and bone chips to ravage his flesh. It was different than just spreading kerosene, lighting a piece of paper, and riding off, leaving the rest up to chance and luck. Sweat beaded her forehead and the barrel of the gun wavered and she knew if she didn't do something, Sarah would die. As sure as there was shit in a goose, it was up to her to make the lucky break that would be the only chance they had. She swung up on Dan's back, and urged him across the street, so he could have some distance.

Luke Wilson was giving orders when the front window of the saloon burst into fine dust and the huge black stud leaped into the saloon. He half whirled, trying to bring his gun to bear on the figure with the rifle, but Laura kicked at his knee and the rifle boomed loud and the huge chandelier plummeted from the

---

ceiling and fell over his shoulders, pinning his arms to his sides, knocking his gun to the floor. Belle had it before it could bounce, and she aimed it unwaveringly at the posse.

"I want to see all your fingers," she grated, "pointin' at heaven. And if you're short one finger, you're dead." They dropped their guns, suddenly white-faced, their arms jerking as if on wires, hands to the roof. Bad enough that a fat bleached blonde with a face full of bruises should be pointing a six-gun, but behind her a mean-faced girl with eyes as cold as the glacier in the mountains beyond town was staring matter-of-factly down the barrel of one hell of an efficient-looking rifle.

"Bartender," Anne said quietly, "wipe the shit from yourself and get some rope."

"Yes, ma'am," he breathed with relief, coming from behind the bar and moving swiftly.

"The rest of you," she nodded at the customers, "can either make yourselves useful or shift ass outta here."

Nobody left. They helped tie up the posse members and watched, not quite daring to grin, as Belle and Laura and the working girls stripped Luke Wilson of his clothes.

"Aw, ain't he cute," one of the girls giggled.

"He's got real nice legs," another teased. "But best of all's his bum. He's got a round little bum looks like a punkin restin' on a flat board."

"No, it's not the legs or the bum," a third said judiciously. "He's got a pecker on him as big as most men's forearms."

"God'll get you for this!" Luke roared.

"No She won't," Belle answered. "She's too busy laughin' like hell at the sight of you tryin' to kill that stiffer to pay any mind to the rest of us. Set him up on the piano, boys, where we can all see what's gonna win. I personally," she drawled, "have got ten bucks says that guy's gonna lose and that stiffer's gonna grow like corn after a rain." They stood Luke Wilson on the piano and laughed while the working girls patted his rump, tickled his knackers, and made sure Belle won her bet.

"Whore of Babylon," Luke groaned, knees sagging, watching his come smear on the piano top.

"This ain't Babylon," Belle chortled, "it's Freshwater, and you just won me some money."

"You okay?" Anne slid from the saddle, and hugged Sarah tight.

"I'm fine," Sarah gasped. "But let's get the hell out of this place before something unbelievable happens!"

The chandelier was removed, and Luke was sitting tied to a chair on top of the piano, his face flushed, his eyes glittering. Belle grabbed his hair, forced his head back, and poured some more white wine down his throat. He moaned in protest.

"It ain't whiskey!" she barked.

"Too much," he gasped.

"You can't ever get too much wine," Belle snorted. "Don't it say right in the Bible, 'Take a little wine for the sake of thy stomach'? Well, don't it?"

"Yes," he admitted.

"And if a little is good, a bit more is better, ain't that logical?"

"Yes."

"And it says, 'Look not on the wine of the grape when it is red,' don't it?"

"Yes."

"Well, this ain't red. It's white. Have some more." And again she poured the wine down his throat.

"Make you a little deal," she said suddenly.

"What?" He was suspicious, his head lolling loosely.

"Well, you see yourself as white and me as black, right?"

"Right."

"And you see it all as a contest, right?"

"Right."

"And you're a sport, aren't you?"

"Right," he hiccuped slightly.

"Okay, Luke old boy, I'll make you a deal. If you can win the contest, I'll close up shop forever and take alla these girls with me and go West and open a convent dedicated to the rehabilitation of all fallen women and working girls."

"You mean it?"

---

"I said, didn't I?"

"What's the contest?" he hedged.

"And if you lose, you stop this pernicious persecution and work for me as cook, housekeeper, and general fancy man."

"Not windows," he argued, "I don't do windows."

"Okay."

"What's the contest?" He nodded for her to hold the bottle so he could drink more white wine.

"We strip down," Belle grinned, "and if you don't get randy, you win, and if you do, I win. You've got an edge," she pointed out quickly, "because you've already blown the worst of your wad."

"That's true," he countered, "but you're at home and I'm in a strange place."

"Oh, no you goddamn don't!" Laura flared, stamping her foot.

"What?" Belle blinked.

"If you climb up on that piano and start gettin' it on with that hairy-bellied bastard, that's *it!*" Laura raged. "I'm not havin' nothin' to do with you ever again!"

"Ah, honey, what difference would it make?" Belle was honestly puzzled. "It's just a contest."

"Not a fair one," Laura argued. "You touch him and he'll go nuts. You kiss him and he'd take on a herd of goats."

"Oh, go on." Sheila yawned. "She's not *that* good."

"What do you know about it?" Laura raged.

"Nothin'," Belle put in quickly. "She don't know nothin'."

"She better not," Laura threatened, "because I'm not dedicatin' the rest of my life to anybody that trashes around with back room women or furry-assed cowboys."

"What d'ya mean, the rest of your life?" Belle burped. "Who asked for the rest 'a your life?"

"Just shut up," Laura snapped.

"Kiss my ass, lady!" Belle was indignant.

"Oh, any time," Laura grinned. "As long as no steerhumper was there first!"

"I," Luke Wilson said with as much dignity as he could muster, "have never humped a steer in my life."

---

"I'll take your place," Carol offered.

"You!" Sharon laughed. "Hell, what kind of contest would that be?"

"Oh, yeah?"

"Easy," Belle took another dainty sip of wine. "Let Luke decide for hisself, then."

"Oh," Luke weaved on his chair and a foolish grin flickered across his face, "I ain't choosy. I can lick any one of 'em." It was six months before he understood why they had all roared with sudden laughter. And by then he was so adept at cooking, cleaning and being a banjo-strumming sweet song-singing fancy man, he didn't care one damn bit.

Uncle Andrew slept in the wet smelly sawdust. Slept through the crash when Dan leaped through the big front window, slept through the crash of the rifle, the descent of the chandelier, the piano-come episode and the one-hour carefully refereed contest between Luke and Carol. He slept through the noisy party that celebrated the hasty exit of the wagon and the three fugitives.

"You don't have to go, now," Belle suggested. "He's not going to win this contest."

"There's still Uncle Andrew," Sarah said grimly. "If he can't get Luke Wilson to help him, he'll do it alone. And he'd shoot Anne if he thought it would get him that horse back. Shoot her from behind in the dark of night."

"Not if she shoots him first," Laura protested.

"I'm not taking that chance," Sarah said. Her eyes locked with Laura's. "Would you take that chance if it was Belle he was after?"

"I'd slit his scrawny throat here and now, while he's passed out, if I thought he'd even think about making a move against her," Laura gritted.

"Well, I can't slit his throat," Sarah replied, "so I'm putting miles between him and Anne."

When Andrew woke up, head splitting, belly heaving, four days later, he groaned for two days over the escape of his stud and the favored position Luke Wilson filled. "If it hadn't been for that last drink," he assured himself, "I could'a been fancy man around here."

"Yeah," Belle howled with laughter. "On top of all your other talents, you're one hell of a comedian, too."

"I'll get 'em," Andrew promised. "I'll get 'em and get my horse back. If I have to follow them to hell, I'll get 'em."

"Here." Laura handed him a glass. "Have a drink before you leave."

"Thanks." His eyes lit up, his face creased in a shifty grin, his dirt-encrusted hand with the thick rimed nails reached for the glass, and he licked his lips eagerly.

"Bloody mooch," Belle muttered, knowing it would be at least another week before Andrew took off after the fugitives.

# Chapter 7

They headed out of town, Pilgrim driving the wagon, Sarah sitting beside him, Anne riding Dan. OtherOne, no longer the half-wild fury Sarah had been tied to, but a well-mannered, trained saddle horse, and Bess followed. They were tethered to the tail gate of the wagon, Bess staring at the crate of chickens securely lashed to the weathered wood. Down the only street in town, and out across the parallel ruts that meandered in a less than straight line across the grasslands, past the ranches and homesteads, past patches of late snow, through large slicks of mud, heading west, heading west so slowly Anne was impatient and ready to scream.

"If we didn't have this dumb wagon," she blurted, "we'd make some decent time."

"He won't be lookin' for us for a while," Pilgrim said quietly, "and once he starts lookin', won't matter how far we've traveled. I've seen fanatics before."

"Then why not," Anne was disgusted, "just sit on your ass and wait for the mad bastard to catch up to us?"

"Oh, I don't intend to make it easy for him." Pilgrim tried to smile.

Dan wanted to run. He tossed his head and made soft teasing noises, trying to coax Anne into a midnight race, but she talked to him and soothed him, promising him that very soon they'd come to a place where he could burn off his excess energy. Bess just plodded happily behind the wagon, her huge bulk made even huger by the unborn foal inside her.

"Sure hope Belle and the others are going to be all right," Anne muttered.

"Don't worry about Belle," Sarah reassured her. "She's made out fine so far in life and she'll make out okay in spite of that screwball."

They stopped at dawn long enough to unpack some cold food. When Anne gave each of the horses a small measure of grain, Pilgrim eyed her speculatively.

"We might need that grain before we get where we're going."

"We might," she answered coolly, "but you can be damn sure we'll need the horses even more." She gave each of them a good drink out of her battered black hat, and spent a few minutes fussing over and talking to the dray horses, checking that their harness did not rub, drying the sweat from their bodies with a piece of soft cloth.

"We can chew our food while we're riding," Pilgrim reminded.

"Yeah, but they can't," she answered.

"Maybe we ought to get something straight right now!" He stood up, towering over them both. "I'm driving this wagon!"

"Pilgrim," Anne said softly, "you might be driving a wagon, but you don't even own them boots you're standin' in. You've got my jacket keepin' out the cold and your mouth is full of our food. If you want to leave right now, start walkin', but those horses are getting another five minutes to finish what they're doing. Which is eating. Which is what you're doing!"

"Anne, please..." Sarah soothed. "He only meant..."

"He can talk," Anne answered. "But they can't."

Sarah got off the wagon and walked behind a small bush and before she got back again the horses had finished eating, Anne's temper had cooled and Pilgrim's threatened dignity was again intact.

"Let's go," he said firmly.

"Okay," Anne agreed, swinging up on Dan again, and riding

to the front of the wagon, then on to ride alongside the heads of the dray horses. When Pilgrim lifted the reins to urge them forward she leaned over, patted the big head. "Come on, baby," she said, as the reins slapped on the broad back. The horses moved forward, Anne talking softly.

The wagon creaked and groaned and twice Pilgrim stopped and smeared thick black grease on the axle and muttered to himself about people who just store a wagon in a shed and think that's all they have to do to it. Sarah got tired of the hard wagon seat and, reassured by Anne that OtherOne was now a well-trained horse, swung up on his back.

"I don't know," she laughed uneasily, "the only experience I've had with him has been . . . unwelcome."

"Oh, give him a chance," Anne teased. "We all make mistakes."

"But I'm more used to that quiet little gray gelding Jake let me use."

"Yeah, but look at it this way," Anne grinned. "You've got one hell of a good saddle this time." And Sarah laughed softly.

OtherOne behaved himself like a gentleman but as soon as he and Dan moved away from the tail gate of the wagon, Bess began to fuss up, tossing her head and lashing out clumsily with her hind legs.

"Spoiled old thing," Anne muttered, returning to loosen the tether rope and let the fat old mare plod after her friends.

"You sure she won't wander off?" Pilgrim said, scowling.

"Do birds chirp?" Anne laughed, and he grinned suddenly.

"Do snakes have armpits?" he countered.

"Is the Pope Catholic?"

"Are lemons sour?" he offered and tension between them eased.

By late afternoon Sarah was tired, Anne was looking for an excuse to stop and Pilgrim, slouched on the seat, was beginning to think his backbone had been driven up into his skull.

"We're going to have to stop soon," Anne suggested.

"Not yet," Pilgrim said reluctantly.

"I would."

"You been this way before?" he asked coolly.

"No."

"Well, I have." And he urged the weary horses on without explanation. An hour and a half later they came to a river fording, and Pilgrim stopped, jumped off the wagon and began to unhitch the horses.

"You want to get them a good measure of grain?" he asked Anne. "Then we'll light a fire, have a proper meal, let them rest up while we eat, then we cross the river. With rested horses."

"Good idea," Anne nodded. "I guess you know what you're doing."

"Sometimes," he grinned, "but not always."

They took advantage of the break, cooking a hot meal, boiling a pot of coffee, unhitching the drays and letting them eat and drink their fill, then tethering them to graze and roll in the fresh grass. While Sarah was busy with the meal, Anne checked over the animals, wiped them down with a cloth, gave them grain and a dried apple treat. Pilgrim made sure the load on the wagon was properly distributed and secured. They lifted the crate of hens down and set it on the grass, and the half-frantic birds calmed down immediately, pulling at the first green shoots poking through their cage.

"Be great," Anne eyed the river wistfully, "to have a quick wash and a change of clothes, but that water looks too cold for swimming."

"Yeah?" Pilgrim teased. "Then how you figure to get to the other side?"

"I hadn't thought of that," she admitted with a small laugh.

"Well, what I figured," he said around a mouthful of food, "was, if you ladies aren't too shy, I could strip down to my one-piece and take 'em across that way, then on the other side I can hang my one-piece to dry and put on the pants and shirt."

"The man," Sarah grinned, "is capable of reason."

"Sometimes." He nodded.

"You gonna push them all night again?" Anne asked, her face carefully blank.

---

"No. We rest them an hour or so more here, then ford the river and push like hell until nightfall. Then we make an early camp, get a good rest, and head off at first light. We ought to pick up sign of the wagon train before tomorrow afternoon. If not tomorrow, next day."

Anne finished her meal, rinsed the dishes in the river, then went over to make a fuss over the dray horses and try to get them to look more kindly on Dan, OtherOne and Bess. The older mare, Babe, was willing enough to be friends but the younger mare, Sunny, wasn't going to rush into anything. She and OtherOne spent a lot of their time glaring at each other, ears laid back, long yellow teeth showing.

"They look like that mean-faced jasper who was hot on your trail," Anne laughed.

"I hope he rides around in circles until his backside splits and he falls off either side of his horse!" Sarah exploded.

"Oh, I don't know," Anne drawled, "I wasn't all that fond of that town anyway. I'd rather be going somewhere else anyway."

"The whole idea of Going," Pilgrim laughed, "is to Get Somewhere. And if we don't get over that river . . ."

The river was deep and swift and at one point it looked as if the drays were going to lose the struggle. Pilgrim stood up in the wagon, slapping the reins and urging them forward. But they didn't know his ways very well and had never really worked together before, and things were just not happening the way they should. Anne urged Dan forward, ready to jump off if she had to and swim hanging onto his tail. As they passed the frightened drays she began to coax them loudly, urging them to pull together. The heavy drays, not knowing what else to do, followed the voice they heard when they were fed grain and apples, followed the voice they heard when they were patted and rubbed dry.

"Come on, baby," she urged. "'Atta girl, haul it over."

"Take 'em over, little lady," Pilgrim yelled, his face creased in a wide grin. They surged up the bank on the far side, the wagon spilling water from its sides, dripping to the muddy ground and running back into the river in a dark brown trickle.

"Check the load," Pilgrim ordered, reaching for his dry clothes and boots.

"Everything looks okay," Sarah announced several minutes later. "The wagon bed is a bit wet, but everything else seems fine."

"Good old Babe," Anne congratulated the big dray mare, "she was a good old Babe."

"If you're through cuddlin' them animals, we can get moving," Pilgrim teased, walking back and hanging his wet underwear from the tail gate of the wagon.

"Just a minute," Anne promised, hurrying under the sagging canvas top and stripping off her wet clothes. She pulled on dry clothes and socks, got her boots from where they were hanging from the hoops holding up the canvas, and as the wagon started to move on, she shoved her feet into her boots and whistled for Dan.

They stopped before dark and settled the animals for the night. Sarah lifted the crate of dry but still half-hysterical chickens from the tail gate of the wagon, set the crate on the ground and dropped a handful of grain in for the hens. She used a metal pie plate to give them drinking water although, as Anne said, they probably had more than their share going across the river. They had a good supper and then all went to bed early, the dray horses tethered, the other three wandering loose.

"No need to post guard," Anne assured Pilgrim. "If anybody comes too close to us, old Dan'll give us plenty of warning. He'll probably run 'em off before we even get our eyes open!"

The wagon was roughly divided into two sleeping areas, Anne and Sarah on one end, Pilgrim at the other with a couple of quilts and a thin pillow. How long he had gone without sleep was evident in the way his eyes snapped shut as soon as he lowered his head. Anne and Sarah took longer to fall asleep — about half a minute longer.

The next day was a repetition of everything that had gone on before, except that the fordings were easier, the country crossed by streams rather than rivers. Anne remembered the waterholes she had found when she was on horseback and wondered if what had been a blessing would now begin to seem to be a bother. The chickens, certainly, were not going to appreciate a fording at least once a day. But then she remembered how many of her water finds had been little more than mudholes and when she remembered how much more water would be required now, she looked at the big barrels hanging from the wagon and reminded herself that at every possible opportunity, she would check and refill them.

They caught up with the rumored wagon train the night of the second day. They pulled up beside the lead wagon, and Pilgrim dismounted while Anne stared at the wagons, drawn in a circle as if expecting imminent Indian attack, and tried to convince herself that she was looking forward to having company.

The wagon master was young and tough, and when he asked Pilgrim's name, obviously assumed that he was talking to Mr. Pilgrim and that the other two were Mrs. Pilgrim and baby Pilgrim. Nobody bothered to correct him. Whatever Pilgrim's real name, all it had brought him was trouble, and neither Anne nor Sarah wanted to try to explain to these good people how it was that three unrelated people slept in the same wagon at night.

"Personally," Sarah teased later, "I take it as a bit of an insult that he thinks I'm old enough to have a daughter as old as you."

"Maybe we can say I'm big for my age," Anne soothed.

"As far as I'm concerned," Pilgrim offered, "I got the best of the deal."

"And that," Sarah snapped, "is all you're gonna get, too!"

After a few days with the wagon train, Pilgrim began to squirm under some of the glances he got from both men and women.

"They think there's somethin' wrong with me," he grumbled, "sittin' up on the wagon safe as a baby while you two ride. None of the other women are ridin'. Only the men are ridin'. Women sit on the wagons."

"What good would it do for all of us to sit on the wagon?"

Anne asked, honestly puzzled. "Besides, how'm I gonna find any meat up on that thing?"

"I could do the hunting," Pilgrim offered.

"With what?" Anne asked. "You don't have a gun."

"I could use yours," he said flatly.

"No," she said, her eyes suddenly narrowing, "you couldn't. Because I'm not gonna loan it to you. And if I did, you're never gonna catch any wild meat on foot."

"There's horses," he was challenging her now, and they both knew it.

"It took me six months to get OtherOne to let Sarah sit on his back, I doubt if he's gonna accept you in a hurry. And old Bess isn't fit to ride at the best of times. Right now she's got all she can do to carry that foal inside her."

"There's Dan."

"That's right," she smiled coldly. "And if you ever try to ride him I'll use a rifle on you. And if I miss you, Dan'll knock your brains out on a rock. He don't let anybody but me ride him, and above all he hates men."

"So I sit up on the wagon like a milky-mouth baby, is that it?"

"No," Anne said flatly. "You don't have to do that. You can start walkin' any time you feel like it." She walked off, knowing it wasn't over, there would be other times.

They moved west slowly, the wheels of the wagons biting deep into the prairie, cutting the roots of the buffalo grass, leaving a bare double-rutted scar twisting behind them, a path other restless or desperate people could follow to the free land somewhere beyond the mountains.

They were washing clothes at a creek, pounding the stiff pants with flat rocks, rubbing the sweat and dirt stains from the faded shirts, when one of the women asked why it was neither Sarah nor Anne ever wore skirts. "It doesn't seem right," she said almost hesitantly.

"The truth is," Sarah spoke softly, her eyes fixed on the wet clothes in the gurgling water of the creek, "Mr. Pilgrim doesn't believe that it's ... right ... for us to pretend that things are as they always have been. I mean, we're all living very close together, without the usual civilized privacies, and, well, Mr. Pilgrim feels that it isn't quite ... ladylike ... for Anne and myself to be in skirts."

Anne turned away, not sure she could keep herself from smiling. The woman misinterpreted the move as shyness or embarrassment at the outlandish ideas of her father. "It's impossible to get in and out of a wagon with ... well, decorum ... in a skirt," Sarah continued, rubbing at the clothes again, "and with water a possible problem ... you know how hard it is to keep one's skirts from trailing in the mud ..." She sat back on her haunches and looked at the other women, one at a time. "As for us doing the riding and hunting ... Mr. Pilgrim feels that we've just got to face facts. Many brave men don't survive the dangers of the trail." The women nodded, each of them admitting to a fear that lurked just out of sight all the time. "We've passed several graves already," Sarah continued, "and where would we be if something should happen? God forbid. If we didn't know anything about riding or hunting, we'd be a burden to the entire wagon train. You know only those who can keep up can travel with the others, and a wagon out here on its own is ..." Her voice trailed away meaningfully. There was a long silence, and then the women went back to their washing, each busy with new thoughts.

"Why did you say that?" Pilgrim protested. "Every man in the train thinks I'm some kind of lunatic already. Those women'll all go back with that wild story, and by tomorrow morning everyone will know for sure there's something weird about me."

"What did you want her to say?" Anne defended. "That you sit up on the wagon because you don't even own a horse?" Pilgrim glared at her.

"You shouldn't have brought that up," Sarah scolded gently, some time later, when she and Anne were alone. "You know it hurts his pride."

"Too bad about his pride," Anne snapped, stung that Sarah

would side with Pilgrim. "He's just tryin' to grumble and grouse until he gets one of our horses. Once he's on, you'll never get him off again, and inside of two days he'll be talkin about *his* horse."

"No, he won't," Sarah laughed.

"You think not? That's prob'ly because you never met my Uncle Andrew!"

Anne didn't like the casual way the animals were treated, but when the entire wagon train had the same attitude, there didn't seem to be much she could see to do about it other than to make sure everyone saw how she treated her own stock and how much better they looked and worked than the other animals. One family in particular bothered her. A man, traveling without a wife, with what seemed to be an absolute horde of dirty children, all of them with runny noses, none of them with shoes or clean clothes.

"His animals look like boneracks," she muttered into her supper. "They're all over sores and blowflies, and he spends all his time yellin' at them or hittin' at them with his whip."

"You mind your own business," Pilgrim warned, his voice cold.

"Someone should tell him," she protested.

"It's a man's own business how he treats his wife, his family and his stock," Pilgrim insisted hotly.

"Says who?" Anne flared, but she knew she wasn't going to argue with Pilgrim about it, not yet.

That night, Sarah had again cooked too much. And, again that night, she invited the skinny children over to help "clean up." Anne sat on the ground, leaning against the wheel of the wagon, watching a sharp-faced, skinny girl who reminded her of . . . someone . . . wiping stew traces from her plate with a thick slice of bread.

"You're gonna wind up hungry yourself," she muttered.

"Better than letting them starve," Sarah answered softly.

"Let him worry about them."

"He doesn't worry about them, that's the problem."

"Not our problem," Anne growled.

"You fret and fuss over some worthless horses," Sarah snapped, "and you'd let those little kids go hungry."

"If they can't learn how to feed themselves," Anne stood quickly, face flaming, temper snapping, "then they might just as well starve sooner as later. You gotta learn to feed yourself!" She stalked off into the darkness.

She was leaning against a rock, watching Dan standing head to tail with old Bess, softly swishing flies away from her nose with his long tail, when the thin-faced, skinny girl came up quietly and sat down beside her. Anne decided to ignore her, but the scrawny ten-year-old refused to be ignored.

"Why don't you like me?" the child demanded.

"I never said I didn't like you," Anne evaded.

"But you don't."

"I never said that," she repeated.

"Well, you look at me like you don't."

"You're outta your mind," Anne muttered, refusing to look at the girl. The girl jacknifed her scabby knees, rested her chin on them, and stared at the horses, sitting in silence. When Anne got up and walked back to the wagon to go to sleep, the strange silent child was still sitting, staring at old Bess, as if waiting with her for something.

Old Bess' foal was born in the midst of a rainstorm and Anne muttered and cursed to hide her fear, accusing the fat old mare of having picked the most absolutely wretched night of the year as the night to have Anne out of bed and worrying.

"Worrying over nothing," Pilgrim grumbled, but he helped stretch the spare tarpaulin from the side of the wagon to a pair of hastily cut poles stuck into the mud. The old mare waited patiently under this makeshift cover, her sides knotting and pushing, her eyes wide as she labored.

"What are you doing?" Anne demanded of the soaking wet, strange-eyed skinny girl standing in the rain.

"Waiting," the girl said quietly, shivering.

"Waiting for what?" But Anne knew, and after a long silence

123

she turned away, feeling somehow ashamed of herself. "Might as well get under the tarp," she relented, "unless you're too stupid to come in out of the rain."

The child moved quickly, gratefully, and hunkered patiently, the flesh on her arms goose-pimpled.

"Here," Anne said curtly, handing over a dry sweater, "or you'll be half-dead with pneumonia."

"Thank you," the child smiled, slipping on the warm sweater, her eyes fixed on the old mare.

Just when Anne was certain she was going to have to grease up her arm and reach in to help, the way the livery man had described, the mare grunted and strained and the glistening bag of water began to emerge.

"Look," Anne breathed in wonder. "You can see the hooves and legs . . ."

And then the old mare was on her feet, cleaning her baby, and for the first time in years there was something that meant more to Bess than Anne did.

"Think I should be jealous?" Anne laughed, reaching out carefully.

"Don't touch it," Pilgrim warned.

"Hey, Bess, hey, my pretty old girl, what did you find in the rain? Look, Sarah, she's trying to stand up already! Oh, what a clever little girl you are. That's it, up you get, that's a baby . . ."

They watched in wonder as the long-legged foal struggled to her feet.

"She sure looks like her daddy," Pilgrim remarked, "but she's gonna be bulky, like her momma."

"Look, Sarah, she knows exactly where to go for her breakfast!"

"That's something we could all use," Sarah admitted, moving to put fresh wood on the campfire. The scrawny girl pulled the warm sweater off, and handed it to Anne.

"I'll go now," she said quietly.

"Might as well stay for breakfast," Anne said gruffly. "You must be as cold and hungry as the rest of us."

"Thank you," the little girl said, squatting again, and staring at the little filly nuzzling her mother, wobbling on long shaky legs.

Anne wanted to stay where they were for a few days but Pilgrim insisted they had to move on with the wagon train.

"But the baby isn't going to be able to keep up!" Anne protested.

"She will. Wild horses do it. That's why she can get on her feet so fast after being born."

Sarah suggested the compromise, and though Pilgrim scoffed, he gave in, and the tail gate of the wagon was lowered, the chickens were repositioned and for the first part of the day, at least, little BelleTwo rode on Anne's lap, old Bess reaching out with her soft muzzle, sniffing her baby, sniffing Anne, and whickering softly. Even Dan seemed intrigued and trotted behind the wagon like a huge dog, ready to slash out at anything or anybody who came near his daughter.

Dan was the subject of a heated discussion the day after BelleTwo was born. Several of the men had ridden alongside the wagon, staring at the foal, then at her fat, swaybacked mother, then at the proudly prancing young stud.

"You watch," Pilgrim grinned, "they're gonna be back soon to ask about usin' him for stud. That filly is going to be as fine a piece of horse flesh as any of them ever saw, and they're all figuring if she came outta that ugly old tub, what they'd get out of their own mares is gonna be pretty special, too."

"Dan's not goin' near any scabby mare!" Anne flared. "If they want him for stud, they better do something to improve their stock first."

"You can't tell a man that!" Pilgrim retorted angrily. "It's none of your business how he treats his horses or his women."

"It is when they want me to agree to using Dan for stud," Anne countered.

"Well, they won't ask *you!*" Pilgrim roared. "No decent man'll talk about a thing like that with a half-grown kid like you."

"Well, it sure isn't up to you!" she argued, almost shaking with fury. The discussion raged hotly until Sarah intervened and suggested Anne might agree to let Pilgrim pretend he made the decisions, if Pilgrim would agree to find a way to let the hopeful applicants know that no fleas, ticks or blowflies would be tolerated.

"Don't give a thunderin' hoot how many mares you've got in season," Pilgrim said firmly, "all I got to do is tell Anne to ride that big bugger off into the hills and follow along outta smell and sniff range, and he'll be all right."

"I don't see why we have to pay stud fee! We're all part of this wagon train together," the man protested.

"Yeah? Well, if he steps in a gopher hole and busts his leg, are you gonna all chip in so's we can buy us another like him?" Pilgrim countered.

"You're a hard man, Pilgrim."

"And you're tryin' to take advantage. You want to improve your stock but you don't want to pay for it. That's a blooded stud and you know it!"

"Doesn't seem right to take advantage of a natural situation," the wagon master insisted. "It's not like he wouldn't want to!"

"Okay." Pilgrim grinned. "We'll just let him run loose and cover every mare he wants, but we get the offspring."

"Not likely!" a farmer flared.

"Okay, then, you cheap stubble-jumping tit-puller!" Pilgrim roared. "If you want better foals than you got mares, you reach into them tatty pockets of yours and pay stud fee. Or your mares will still be empty when you get where you're going."

Privately Anne wasn't sure even she could have kept Dan away from the mares, but she wasn't going to let anybody, least of all the wagon master or the raggedy man get anything for nothing. Not from her and not from her horse!

"They're just all such a bunch of raggedyass do-nothings," she whispered to Sarah one night. "They aren't going to have it any better when they get where they're going."

"They might," Sarah soothed. "By the time they get to the end of this trip they'll be so glad to get home . . ."

"Wish we could just ride off, like we did before," Anne muttered. "Then you wouldn't be workin' extra, fussin' over them and feedin' them . . ."

"Anne," Sarah whispered reproachfully, "they're babies."

"Raggedyass do-nothings."

"I was pretty raggedyass when I met you," Sarah reminded her.

"Yeah, but you weren't stupid!" Anne rolled on her side, closing her eyes stubbornly. "Not then, anyway."

# Chapter 8

Noone of the women had been at the meeting. The men hunkered around a small campfire with the wagon master, nodding, listening, occasionally asking questions. Then they rose, dusted off their grimy pants and went back to the wagons to tell the women what had been decided.

"It'd be a lot easier to go around it," Anne said flatly.

"It gets worse before it gets better," Pilgrim explained. "It'd take at least two extra days."

"What's two extra days," Anne pressed. "It's better'n having one of the horses slip and bust a leg."

"Wagon master says we go over it."

"What's two days alongside a good horse or a wagonload of stuff?" she insisted, staring off at the massive shale slope that seemed to dare them to find a way up and over it.

"They had their meeting," Pilgrim said stubbornly, "and it's been decided."

"Bunch of raggedyass know-nothings," she snorted, as stubborn as he. "Do it the wrong way every time."

"The wagon master . . ." Pilgrim started.

"The wagon master," Anne interrupted, "hasn't ever been this way before. He said so himself."

Pilgrim shrugged. It was true. The four previous trips the young man had led had swung far to the south, avoiding this area completely. But the growing resentment of the ranchers and cattlemen because the wagon wheels ruined the prairie, and their suspicion that a number of missing calves and steers had found their way into the ever-hungry bellies of the emigrants, plus loud and bitter threats against anyone found cutting or crossing fence lines, had forced this detour and brought them to the threatening ridge of sharp shale.

"Well," he turned away, "we're doin' it."

They spent the night in the shadow of the massive obstacle, and in the morning, after a hurried and half-cooked breakfast, they lashed everything tightly, preparing for the ordeal.

"Time they get the first three wagons up there," Anne muttered, "we could'a gone twice around the bottom. Four steps forward, three and half back!"

"I'm not riding a wagon up that!" Sarah agreed. "We'll lead Babe and Sunny up. If anything goes wrong, I want to be able to run!"

"Just keep Dan away from the mares today," Pilgrim grumbled. "Some of the men were sayin' they don't think it's right the women and kids should see him primed up and prancin'."

"Too bad," Anne snapped. "They want his foals, they put up with his foolishness. You don't get the one without the other."

She turned away, still in a foul mood, and started to saddle OtherOne. "You sure you'd rather walk?" she asked Sarah.

"I'd rather fly over the top," Sarah laughed, "but since I don't know how to do that, I'll walk. The idea of falling off a wagon or a sliding horse doesn't thrill me."

"Coward." Anne grinned, her bad humor disappearing.

Pilgrim and Sarah walked at the heads of the patient drays, Bess and BelleTwo tagged along behind the wagon, and Dan followed freely, shaking his head, prancing and trying to entice a young mare to follow him for a brisk run. The slow-moving wagons picked their way carefully across the rocks, toiling upward, the burning midsummer sun reflecting back from the shale, drying the sweat on the horses' bodies and turning the surface of the shale face into a blistering oven.

Ahead of them the raggedyass man and his runny-nosed brood of kids were having a terrible time. The kids sat in the wagon, stunned and miserable in the heat. The half-starved horses were trying, their hooves sending up a spray of shale, but the wagon was barely moving and the gap between it and the wagon in front was widening.

The raggedyass man stood up, cursing, waving his whip, yelling at the horses and adding to the confusion, but doing nothing that in any way improved the situation. Anne was tired of his noise, tired of his constant ineffectuality and tired of the way he abused his animals. She was just about ready to ride over and tell him the time of day when Pilgrim loosed his hold on Sunny's gear, and jogged ahead, his boots kicking aside loose pieces of shale.

"Hey, neighbor," he grinned companionably, "how be it we work together on this."

"Lazy bloody things!" the red-faced, frustrated man raged.

"It's a pretty ugly slope," Pilgrim soothed. "Why don't we try lightening the load? Maybe the kids could wait to one side and when we're at the top they can join us. They look pretty tired of all the bouncing," and again he grinned, already lifting down the youngest who immediately scampered away from the wagon. Sarah loosened her hold on Babe's gear and headed after him, and Anne, muttering to herself about the way some people's uselessness made more work for other people, moved OtherOne to a place at Babe's head, talking softly to the huge mare, leaning in the saddle to stroke the glistening hide and the heavy muscles beneath.

"Hey, my Babe," she soothed. "Wait your turn. That's my Babe." The massive mare relaxed, shaking her head, making her harness jingle softly.

"Okay, neighbor," Pilgrim grinned, "let's you and me get this load to the top." And the skinny man swallowed his anger and insult, cracked his whip defiantly, and the tired boneracks leaned into their harness, straining up the slope.

Anne didn't think the few pounds less made the difference. The tribe of scrawny kids didn't weigh enough to slow down a pheasant, let alone a team of horses, however abused and weakened they might be. It was Pilgrim's calm direction, the cessation of noise and confusing orders, the absence of the stinging whip.

The rattletrap wagon lurched ahead slowly, Sarah and the sallow kids tagging along, walking slowly, easily accompanying the wagon up the slope.

"Okay, Babe," Anne said, nudging OtherOne with her knees, "let's go. Get this thing rolling or we'll be here forever. Come on, Babe, come on, Sunny, lean into it." Babe and Sunny did just that, they leaned into their well-oiled harness and moved forward steadily, their large shod hooves striking sparks off the shale, clattering up the slope, sending bits of flat black rock skittering behind them, rolling faster downhill than the horses and wagon were moving uphill, loosening other rocks and taking them, too. "Keep that up," Anne coaxed, "and you'll flatten this hill all by yourselves. That's the way."

Ahead of them the boneracks strained and lunged, and in spite of Pilgrim's calming presence, they began to panic. The raggedyass man was immediately on his feet, screeching with futile rage, cracking his whip, adding to the confusion and hysteria. Nobody was ever sure exactly what happened first, whether a horse fell and the harness snapped, or whether the harness snapped first and then the horse fell. But everyone agreed the jerry-built wagon started to roll back down the hill and everyone agreed that after one ineffectual grab at the faulty brake, the raggedy man leaped clear, rolling to one side, leaving the wagon without any hope of control or direction, careening crazily.

"*Sarah!*" Anne screamed, digging her heels into OtherOne's flanks and sending him across the shale to where Sarah, trying to get out of the way of the wildly careening wagon, trying to get the terrified children out of the way, had fallen to the ground.

"*Annie!*" Pilgrim roared, lunging for OtherOne's bridle and missing totally, falling almost under the feet of Babe and Sunny. Unsure what to do in all the uproar, the huge drays stood stock still, while Pilgrim scrambled unhurt out from under them.

Anne leaned over, ready to scoop Sarah out of the path of the wagon. The front wheel of the unbraked cart hit a rock and the wagon veered. Sarah screamed as the wooden catapult slammed OtherOne broadside, knocking him flat and sending

Anne flying through the air to land in a bloody heap on the sharp rocks.

Pilgrim raced past the wrecked wagon, his boots stepping unconcernedly on bits and scraps of poor possessions, his huge hands reaching out to check for broken bones. Sarah pushed him aside and grabbed Anne, holding her close, cuddling her, weeping.

"Bastard!" Anne struggled to her feet, pushing past both Sarah and Pilgrim. "The raggedyass son of a bitch killed my horse!" She staggered, ignoring the blood coursing from her cut scalp, pushing aside the hands that reached to help, raving with rage and grief. "You filthy flea-infested bastard, you'd gag a maggot with your uselessness. You've killed my horse!"

But OtherOne wasn't dead. He lay on his side, unable to rise on fractured legs. The horrible sound of his screams slicing through the air, horrifying the onlookers more than the accident itself had. His eyes were bugged with terror and pain and there was blood in large pools on the ground around him. A splintered piece of wood protruded from his side.

"He's all bust up, Pilgrim," Anne sobbed helplessly.

"Come on, Annie," Pilgrim soothed, taking her arm, trying to lead her away.

"He's my horse!" she protested.

"Sarah," Pilgrim begged, "get her away from here."

"Anne," Sarah shook Anne gently, "let people *do* something for you."

"I can do it myself," Anne insisted.

"I know you can. They know you can. But don't be so prickly all the time, honey. Let people give something to you. There's a big difference between scratching your ass and ripping out great bleeding hunks. Come with me. Nobody else can do anything with Dan."

OtherOne's screams tore into their ears. Many of the women were weeping; the children were all hysterical and some of the men looked ill. Pilgrim reached down and took the rifle from the scabbard on the saddle still on the thrashing horse. The sharp sound of the rifle shot stilled the dreadful noises, and the silence after was broken only by the whickering of Bess, trying to calm BelleTwo, and by Dan's snorting and whickering as he bucked and tossed, half-crazed with fear and the thick smell of blood.

"You cheap son of a bitch!" Anne's voice rang in the stillness, and the emigrants looked away guiltily, knowing she was right. The raggedy man stared at her, uncomprehending. "Look at this harness," she raged. "They must'a used it on the ark. Two bits here and two bits there. Two-bit wagon and two-bit driver. Too cheap to get good gear, too lazy to fix this, and too ignorant to know what a useless piece of shit you really are." And when his eyes flicked away from hers, she was reminded of Uncle Andrew when he didn't want to look at the truth. "You're so goddamn cheap you cost me a good horse, goddamn near split my head wide open, and nearly killed Sarah and your own stinkin' kids! You raggedyass people are going to two-bit me to death!"

"Sarah," Pilgrim said quietly, "get her away from here if you have to drag her."

"I'm not goin' anywhere," Anne screamed impotently. "I'm buryin' my horse. You'd have buried those festerin' little pukes," she pointed at the pale-faced weeping children, "and they aren't worth as much as he was!"

"You got any idea how big a hole you'd have to dig?" Pilgrim said, brutally. Anne stared at him, shocked into silence. "You got any idea how long it'd take? He'd be swole in the heat and stinkin' and you wouldn't have it more than started."

"I figured," she said dully, turning away. The strange-eyed, hard-faced girl was staring at her father with an expressionless face. Then she, too, turned away and walked to where Bess and BelleTwo were stamping their feet nervously.

Anne held Dan's head against her chest, her fingers gripping his heavy mane, her eyes brimming with tears.

"Anne," Sarah urged gently, "it's time to go."

"I feel crappy," Anne whispered. "I keep thinking how glad I am that Dan was . . . calvicating . . ." Her lip quivered and her voice shook. "If he hadn't been, I'd'a been riding him and it would'a been him . . . and that's like sayin' OtherOne didn't count . . ."

Sarah didn't say "it's natural" or "well, after all, Dan has been with you longer" or any of the things people say when they're trying to help, the things people say that only make it all seem worse. "I know OtherOne counted," she said softly, "but you're right. It would have been horrible . . . more horrible . . . if it had been Dan."

Pilgrim securely blocked the wheels of the wagon, unhitched the drays, and moved them to where the body of OtherOne lay in the hot sun. He stripped the gear from the young horse, quickly rigged a harness and Sunny and Babe dragged OtherOne clear of the proposed route of the wagon train. Anne tried hard not to hear the slithering, clattering of the shale, tried hard not to picture what the sharp rocks and friction were doing to the sleek coat she had so often brushed. The raggedyass man picked around helplessly in the remains of his wagon, as if waiting for Pilgrim to tell him what to do next. His oldest daughter stared at him, the younger kids sat slumped in the heat, exhausted by fear and horror, waiting for someone to do something.

"It was agreed," the wagon master said defensively, his face reddening, "that anyone who couldn't keep up got left behind."

"Behind?" the raggedy man echoed foolishly.

"We can't stay here," the wagon master pointed out the obvious.

"What do I do?"

"Go back. Nothing else to do."

"Back? To what? And how?"

"You'd have to walk now anyway," the wagon master said flatly. "Might as well walk back as try to travel with us."

"You can't!" Sarah blurted. "You can't expect those kids to walk all the way back!"

"Can't expect 'em to walk over the mountains, either, ma'am," the wagon master shrugged. "They're closer to a town than they are to where they said they wanted to go."

Sarah stormed angrily at the wagon master, but he wasn't

touched, and finally just walked off, leaving her still ranting. It was then she decided the children should be loaded into their wagon.

"That's one hell of a load for a wagon," Pilgrim protested.

"Hell of a load?" Sarah mocked. "Four or five little kids? They don't weigh anything."

"And their clothes," Pilgrim snapped, "and their gear . . ."

"Their clothes?" Sarah laughed bitterly. "Their clothes are on their backs. And their gear is scattered all over this hellhole."

"Yeah, but . . ."

"And the drays aren't going to get tired," Sarah argued. "And if they do, we can use their horses as relief."

"Those goddamn boneracks couldn't shift this wagon two feet supposin' it was on a downhill slope with a hurricane blowing from behind!" he roared.

"Anne?" Sarah appealed hopefully.

"I don't give a tinker's damn what happens to them," Anne growled, hating the raggedyass man so much she even hated his children. "What makes you think it's up to you to save the world, anyway?"

"Okay," Sarah shrugged. "Leave them here to bake in the sun without food or water. Maybe before we go we can tar and feather them, too?"

"Goddamn," Anne sighed. "You sure know how to use that as a weapon."

Sarah moved triumphantly to lift the youngest into the wagon.

"Oh, no you don't!" Anne exploded. "Not one of those little buggers is gettin' within five feet of our bedding until those creepy crawlies've been taken outta their hair! I'm not scratchin' like a damn dog because of them."

"That's a lie!" the raggedy man protested feebly.

"Lie my aching ass," Anne snarled. "Those kids are lousy! They stink, and so do you."

It was true. The whole family had a stale, unwashed smell, and the children did have things crawling in their hair. Pilgrim tried to point out that most of the people in the wagon train had fleas and lice, but Anne wasn't impressed with that argument.

"We don't. But we will if them damn kids sit near the bedding."

"But my stuff!" the raggedy man protested. "You aren't going to just leave it here."

"It isn't worth botherin' about," Anne glared at him. "But if you want it, you salvage what you can and make yourself a sledge and drag it along behind."

"A sledge!" Pilgrim was appalled.

"Why not? The Indians use sleds, or travois, or sledges. Let this sad-assed freak do the same."

"That's not the way a white man travels," the raggedyass man shrieked.

"Then sit on your ass in the sun and bake to death and to hell with you," she said coldly. "Because your fleas aren't riding in my bedroll."

She walked to Dan, led him to a big rock, climbed on it and jumped on his back without saddle or bridle. Riding defiantly to the drays she whistled once, and the big horses leaned into their harness and followed her up the shale, leaving the cluster of confused and arguing people standing in a group surrounded by trash and refuse from the broken wagon.

Sarah hurried after the wagon, the children following her, and after a moment Pilgrim raced after her. The raggedy man stood unable to put two and two together for a moment, then he hurriedly began to pile some of the fluttering remnants onto a broken wagon side.

"Anne," Sarah trotted alongside, looking up at the angry girl atop the huge stud, "Anne, you're being mean."

"Me? Did I bring 'em on this trip? Did I come without food for 'em? Did I not bother to wash them until they were creepin' with bugs?"

"They're just children!"

"That's not my fault, either."

"Goddamm it Annie, you stop this!" Pilgrim demanded.

"Listen, you," Anne turned to him, her face white with fury, "you got nothing at all to say about anything. Everything you own is on your back, and you're free to take it an' head in any direction you want. You've been sitting on our wagon eating our food for months now, thinking we needed you or something. Well, we don't need no driver on this wagon, Babe and Sunny'll follow me anywhere I go. So your opinion doesn't count for a fart in a windstorm and it never did. This is between me and Sarah."

"Anne, please."

"Which one you want, Babe or Sunny?" Anne demanded.

"Anne!"

"Front half of the wagon or back?" she insisted.

"Anne, please." Sarah fought tears.

"For that matter," Anne continued coldly, "you can keep the whole damn wagon, and I'll rig a travois for myself."

"Anne. There's no need for this."

"I don't *need* you!" Anne exploded. "I can ride off just fine, me 'n' Dan 'n' Bess 'n' BelleTwo, and Babe. We'll do just fine. You'll last about a week and a half."

"That's right." Sarah stopped chasing after Anne and Dan. "And if that's how you feel, good-bye and to hell with you."

"What!" Anne's eyes widened with surprise.

"I said good-bye and to hell with you," Sarah repeated. "I thought we had some kind of friendship, some kind of partnership. But you're willing to just ride off, knowing I can't make it on my own, so I must have been wrong."

"Then *leave* them flea-infested snot-nosed weak-kneed brats with their old man, get on the wagon, and let's get the hell away from this pack of stubble-jumping plow-whacking sodbusters!" Anne exploded.

"It's breaking your heart to leave OtherOne out there," Sarah sobbed. "How can you ask me to leave these kids? He's at least dead."

"Oh, for chrissakes," Anne muttered. "Just keep the stinkin' little slime away from the blankets!"

And Anne refused to relent any further. She urged Babe and Sunny up the face of the shale slope, watched the terrible confusion and near suicidal descent the other wagons were trying to make on the other side, and then defiantly unhitched the drays, moved them to the back of the wagon, and, using several sections of rope and some crazy-looking knots, managed to harness them to the back axle.

"What are you doing?" the wagon master demanded angrily.

"I'm not fightin' the brake all the way down the hill," she snarled. "If it gives out, my horses are in trouble. I've already lost a good horse listening to your bullshit. From now on, I'll do it my own way." And she rode past him, ignoring him completely.

She tied a rope to the tongue of the wagon; the other end she tied loosely around Dan's neck. "Easy, boy," she soothed, "easy." The nervous stud moved gingerly, hating the tug at his neck but obeying her voice. The wagon moved forward, began to roll down the hill, and Babe and Sunny dug in their hooves, leaned backward instinctively, slowing the wagon almost to a halt. Anne untied the rope, coiled it neatly, and tossed it into the wagon. "Easy, Babe," she crooned, "easy, Sunny. Up, that's it, up." Foot by foot, the wagon moved down the slope, the tongue lashed to the springless seat. The wagon master watched, almost hoping the haywire and jacknife rig would break. But when it was safely at the bottom of the murderous bank, and Anne was moving Babe and Sunny to their usual place, the wagon master shrugged, turned his back on her, and went back to his job of bringing wagons down the shale, the proper way—horses first.

Anne had been camped beside the small stream for almost an hour before the next wagons arrived, and it was several hours before the raggedyass man and his bonerack-drawn sledge caught up with them. Sarah and the worn-out children were walking ahead of him. Pilgrim limped along disgustedly behind, his blistered feet objecting with every step.

"Smells good," the watery-eyed man tried to smile.

"Smells just fine," Anne said coldly. "And if you want to taste any of it, you get busy."

"But we've barely eaten all day!" he whined, his ferret face flushing with disappointment and insult.

"And if you don't wash that stinking mess you call bedding, and get them damn kids cleaned up, you won't eat tonight, either!" she promised.

---

"Anne..." Sarah sighed.

"Have a cup of coffee," Anne suggested.

"I ought to..." Sarah hesitated.

"You ought to sit down and mind your own damn business for once today!"

"But the kids..."

"Let their father look after them."

In the end, it was the older girl who stripped the younger kids and stood them, shivering and whining protest, in the stream, scrubbing them with the strong yellow soap Anne handed her.

"Could have at least heated the water," Pilgrim snapped.

"You want it hot, you heat it," Anne said calmly.

"You," he said distinctly, "are a pain in the ass." But he grabbed the stinking pile of rags the family called bedding and carried it to a large ants' nest. He knocked the top off the nest, laid the bedding over the teeming mass of angry ants, and came back, satisfied. "The ants'll find every flea, louse, nit and egg," he promised, "and by morning them blankets'll be cleaner than they've ever been."

"They'll still stink," she insisted.

"He'll wash 'em before we leave," Sarah said quickly, "and we can spread them over the canvas to dry in the sun."

"I can't get the bugs washed out of their hair." The skinny face looked up at Anne, not pleading. The strange eyes held her gaze firmly.

"Cut it, then."

"Anne!" Sarah gasped.

"You lived," Anne reminded her. Sarah nodded and moved for the scissors in the box of household articles.

"Did ya get fleas in the sweater ya loaned me?" the girl demanded suddenly.

"Yes," Anne said flatly.

"I'm sorry," the child replied stiffly. "I thought everyone had 'em."

The children were sitting at the fire, their shorn heads finally clean, wearing a strange collection of Anne's and Sarah's shirts and sweaters, filling their faces hungrily, when their father finally came wandering back with their few tattered clothes dripping water. He draped the clothes over the wagon wheels and hurried to the fire, reaching for a plate.

"No you don't!" Sarah's anger and frustration burst loose. "You get yourself washed clean."

"That crik's freezin' cold!" he protested.

"The kids got clean in it. You get clean in it. Or else you find your own supper, sleep downwind of the wagon, and walk all day tomorrow."

"Who are you to talk to me like that?"

"And wash them stinkin' clothes, too," Anne added.

"I got nothin' else to wear."

"Then wrap yourself in a blanket, dammit!" Pilgrim roared. "If I can do it, you can do it. I don't blame your kids. They're too young to know any better, but you got no damn excuse at all." Pilgrim half rose, his fist already clenching. The rabbit-faced man hurried to the creek to wash, pinning both women with glances of pure hate.

Anne was appalled at how much the children ate. She watched them swallowing without even chewing their food properly, watched the way their pale eyes flicked constantly, looking to see if there was more food, if there was more bread, if there was . . .

"You're gonna be sick," she warned.

"No I won't," the little boy said flatly, stuffing his face.

"What's your name?" Anne asked suddenly.

"Ruth," the strange-eyed girl replied shyly.

"You always the one takes care of them kids?"

"Someone has to," the girl answered, her eyes fixed on the spot where her shivering father was being shorn almost bald by a grim-faced Pilgrim. The raggedy man stared at the pot of stew, worried the ravenous kids would empty it before he was ready to eat.

They slept that night in uncomfortable closeness, Anne and Sarah jammed together with the clean, shorn and happily stuffed children; Pilgrim and the raggedy man sharing the space at the front of the wagon. In the morning, without having to be told,

Ruth sent the younger ones searching for firewood, while she moved to help feed and water the stock. After a substantial breakfast, they moved off, Anne riding Dan, looking occasionally at Sarah who had the smallest child on her lap, trying hard not to look back where Bess and BelleTwo were following with the two boneracks, trying hard not to look back where OtherOne wasn't.

Pilgrim and the raggedyass man, who said his name was John Smithers, had a lot to talk about on the wagon seat together.

"Smithy," Smithers grinned. "I was a smithy for a while." Anne looked at his scrawny arms and privately wondered.

"But," he sighed philosophically, "there were already two good smiths back home so I turned to farming. But I guess there was already too many good farmers, and I wasn't all that good . . . Then, when my wife died, well, it just seemed like a good idea to head out. Wasn't much sense sticking it out there."

"Might be room for a good smithy out West."

"Need an anvil and a forge, I guess," John Smithers sighed. "And I don't have either."

"Shouldn't be impossible to rig something up," Pilgrim encouraged, and for an hour or so they discussed ways of improvising and making do.

"Of course," Pilgrim mused aloud, "if people worked together instead of always being in competition. Like, someone runs the farm, someone else runs the smithy, maybe set up a mill, too. Everyone else is gonna be busy growin' corn and wheat. Someone ought to make cornmeal and flour . . . people are going to want bread, aren't they?"

"You mean like a . . . commune, sort of?"

"Sort of. Like a big family. Everyone sticks together until everyone else is on their feet."

"A man needs a family," John agreed. "There's too much work to do alone."

"And the women," Anne said quietly, "can look after the kids, do the cooking and washing, and keep house . . ."

"Like a family," John agreed, nodding.

Day by day they moved across the prairie, and day by day

their food supplies dwindled. The children ate almost constantly, filling out and losing their lost and listless look. John looked less scrawny and was beginning to make noises as if he thought he was in charge of the trek.

"No," Anne said quietly, "you will not ride Dan. And no, you will not use my rifle. And no, you will not use my skinning knife because you aren't going to need it to skin anything unless you run it down on foot and rip its throat out with your teeth."

"Anne!" Sarah was shocked.

"I thought this was a sort of a commune," John protested.

"That was your idea," Anne snapped. "How come sharing and commune is always such a great idea to those who don't have damn-all to share? You want to ride a horse, ride one of your boneracks, but don't you go anywhere near Dan. Or my saddle. Or my rifle. Or anything else that's mine. If I want you to have it or use it, I'll offer, but don't you bother askin'!"

"One of these days I'm gonna slap your cheeky face," he promised, grabbing Sarah's saddle and throwing it on the back of one of his own work horses.

"You try," Anne promised, and John knew she meant it, "and the last thing you'll ever hear is a bullet splattin' into your gut!"

"Honey," Sarah ventured later when she and Anne were cooking supper, "why are you so hard-nosed to him?"

"John?" Anne shrugged. "I guess he just reminds me too much of Uncle Andrew. He doesn't even ask the way people ask; he asks in a way that's supposed to make you feel bad if you say no."

"Maybe we should all share . . ."

"Share what? He's got his stinkin' ass on your saddle; what's he got that you can use? And how do you know if he *had* something he'd let you use it? I bet you'd have to sign a paper before he'd let you use his privy!"

"He's had a hard life," Sarah insisted.

"How do you know that? Because he told you? The son of a bitch sits on that wagon seat and talks about being a smithy; but when the axle needed greasing, where was he? All of a sudden for the first time in a week he had to check his horses.

---

When was the last time he did damn-all about his own kids? You're looking after them!"

"I don't mind," Sarah said faintly.

"Yeah? Well it's a good thing you don't!" And Anne refused to say anything more about it. She just slapped the hands of the youngest child who was reaching for a piece of bannock, and told all the children to gather more firewood and bring more water. "Make yourselves useful," she ordered, and they scattered like quail, willingly working, once they had pointed out to them what required doing.

Anne had the growing suspicion that even the young wagon master didn't really know where they were. Every night he walked away from the ring of wagons, away from the firelight, and stared up at the stars, checking the direction of their route so carefully that after a few nights even Sarah began to wonder. Every day Anne rode off on Dan and returned with wild meat, and tried to ignore the anger she felt at being considered responsible for feeding people she didn't even want in her life.

She was gutting several large hares when Dan nickered softly. Anne rolled, her darkly tanned hand closing around her rifle, her eyes scanning for signs of danger. Across the prairie, not following the ruts of the wagon train, several Red River carts moved easily, their ungreased wheels squeaking, the half-wild mustangs pulling them dancing and tossing their heads. Anne relaxed, finished skinning her rabbits, and waited as the outriders moved toward her, arms raised in greeting. Even before she saw the smiles on their faces, she knew she had nothing to fear from them.

They looked down at her, tanned faces grinning, then they looked at Dan and whistled admiringly.

"*Vôtre?*" one of them asked.

"Mine," she agreed.

"*Pas couper,*" he nodded approvingly.

"What?" she asked.

"*Anglais?*" the speaker queried.

"I don't know what you're saying," she blurted.

"He says," one of them ventured hesitatingly, "your 'orse is not cut. He likes it dat your 'orse is not cut. He wants to know if you are English."

"Me?" Anne laughed. "No. I'm not English. I was born here." The young man grinned, translated, and the dark-skinned men all laughed approvingly.

"Us, too," the young one nodded. "We belong 'ere, too."

The people in the wagon train didn't feel comfortable around the métis.

"Half-wild," one woman sniffed disapprovingly. "They're more Indian than human."

"Yeah?" Sarah snapped. "You didn't mind eating their buffalo meat." And the woman's face reddened slightly.

"Their women got no shame," Smithers growled.

"What would you know about shame?" Anne glared. "You got no pride. You need pride of some kind to feel shame."

The métis recognized the feelings of the wagoners and camped separately. That evening, when the stock was watered and fed and the dishes cleaned and put away, Anne and Sarah walked over to visit. Ruth followed them at a safe distance, the filly, BelleTwo, trailing after her like a puppy.

A man and two of the laughing women played fiddles, several of the boys and girls twanged jaw harps and everyone danced. Dressed in a comfortable and sensible mixture of Indian and ordinary clothes, their feathers, ribbons and beadwork breaking the monotony of dark pants and shirts, their feet covered in soft moccasins, they danced and sang, laughed and urged the visitors to drink another cup of tea made from the leaves of wild peppermint and comfrey plants, to eat another slice of dried pemmican.

"What's your name?" Anne asked frankly. "I'm Anne."

"Exovede," the young man answered quickly. "My frens call me Exovede."

"You speak good English," Sarah complimented. "I wish I could remember some of the French I thought I'd learned."

"English," Exovede agreed, "and Cree and Blackfoot, and Peigan and some Nez Percé."

"How'd you learn?" Anne asked, awed.

"I listen'," he chuckled, "an' soon it makes sense. Except some things." His smile faded. "There are some things make no sense to me at all. Not the words—the ideas."

"Yeah," Anne agreed. "Some people got weird and crazy ideas."

"Crazy," he grinned, "is no problem. Some of the nices' people I know are crazy. It's power makes no sense to me." And he laughed softly. "I t'ink maybe I should try to understan' power." Then he jumped up, laughing, and began to dance with the others, his smile flashing in the firelight.

"They're like butterflies," Anne whispered, walking back to the wagon. "They flutter and dance and move around without ever really settling down in one place."

In the morning, after breakfast, the métis prepared to go their separate way. They discussed route and direction with the wagon master, and he heaved a sigh of relief, but didn't offer to shake hands with any of the men or women, and was obviously happy to see them leave.

"We can get supplies at the trading post," the wagon master told the assembled travelers. "Spend a few days resting the stock, then push on through the pass. We'll be out of the mountains before first snowfall." And he managed his first smile in days.

A week later the wagon train camped outside a small trading post-almost-town. When the camp was established and the stock turned loose to graze, Anne whistled for Dan. "Want to ride into town with me?" she offered Sarah. "Dan'll carry two easy."

"What about the kids?" John snapped.

"They're yours, aren't they?"

"I got business in town. Someone has to watch the kids."

"I don't mind," Sarah said quietly.

"I do!" Anne snapped, reaching down and taking Sarah's wrist. Sarah half smiled and moved quickly to join Anne on Dan's back. Dan snorted and pranced but made no real objection.

"And I gotta walk?" John grated.

"You damn better," Anne smiled, "because if you put your ass on Bess, I'll blow you right off her back. It's not five minutes to the gate, and if you and your goddamn kids can't make it together, you're a sadder pack than I thought you were."

"You're gettin awfully owly, aren't you?" Pilgrim growled.

"You wait and see how goddamn owly I can get," she promised, as Dan moved off easily toward the gate.

She knew John and Pilgrim were going to mutter together once she was gone. They'd banded together a lot lately, just little things, like both of them refusing to take a bath in cold water even though standing downwind of either of them was becoming a test of endurance. "You can't expect men to work and not sweat," Pilgrim had argued.

"Yeah. Well you can wash it off before it chokes everyone," she defended, but they refused to get washed until Sarah had heated the big pot of water.

"I really don't mind the kids," Sarah said quietly.

"Oh, I know you don't," Anne snapped, "I don't either, really. It's the way that raggedyass bum *expects* things!"

"Still, it's not fair to them to make them feel they're a bother."

"Why not?" Anne countered. "They are. And they ought to be *his* bother."

"But that's not their fault!" Sarah snapped.

They looked around the trading post without buying anything, then walked off, followed by Dan, to discuss what they needed.

"How much money have you got?" Sarah asked.

"I don't know for sure," Anne admitted, reaching under her shirt and bringing out her money bag, which hung from around her neck on a leather thong. "Here . . ."

"I don't want it," Sarah laughed. "I just want to be sure how much we've got. We need a lot of things. It's going to be expensive . . ."

"What would that bum do if you didn't have money?" Anne asked very quietly. "Even if his wagon hadn't bust open and everything, how did he figure to get far without anything?"

"I don't know," Sarah admitted. "Maybe he thought God would provide."

"Yeah? Well . . . do me a favor . . . let's just buy a bittybit of stuff, just enough for a day or two."

"Why?"

"So we aren't living in each other's pockets for at least a couple of days," Anne evaded. "The more we put in that wagon, the less room there is for sleeping."

Sarah was puzzled, but she went along with Anne's idea and they bought cornmeal, rice and, since there was no coffee, tea. Sarah bought some dried peas and dried beans, and Anne, moved by an impulse she would never understand, bought ten cents' worth of peppermint candy for the kids. Then they rode home on Dan, and Sarah started planning supper. Anne had managed to bag several rabbits the day before, and soon the nose-tempting scent of stew drifted from the large pot. Less than an hour later, the children ran toward them laughing.

"I knew it," Anne teased. "They can smell food a mile away. Downwind. With runny noses and head colds," but she welcomed them and promised them all that, if they ate up all their supper, there would be candy. "Not that there's much chance of you not eating," she teased.

"Daddy and Pilgrim'll be along soon," the oldest girl said dourly. "They got business."

And Daddy and Pilgrim showed up an hour or two later with a jug of business in John's hand, and another jug divided between them and carried in their bellies.

"Did you buy any coffee?" Anne asked casually.

"No," John laughed. "We knew you'd buy that."

"Any food at all?" Sarah asked coolly.

"No. We knew you'd buy that, too," he mocked.

"But you had money for moonshine," Sarah flared.

"Well," John hee-hawed, "we knew damn-sure you wouldn't buy that!" He reached into the stew pot with his fingers to lift out the last piece of meat. Anne's boot shot forward, dumping the stew into the fire.

"Why'd you do that?" John roared.

"I'm sorry," Anne smiled widely. "I guess I tripped."

"You did it on purpose," he accused.

---

148

"Me?" Her eyes widened. "I'm just a little girl. Why would I do a thing like that?" She walked away slowly, heading back to town. After a moment, Sarah joined her, leaving the children to the care of their father.

"You come back here," John roared, and when they ignored him, he rushed over to where Dan was grazing, still saddled, and hurled himself on Dan's back, kicking the big stud's flanks, slapping him with the reins. Dan very calmly bucked twice and sent John flying headfirst into the dirt. Then Dan trotted off after Sarah and Anne, both of whom were howling with laughter. John got up, snarled at his children to shut up, then sat down with Pilgrim and began sipping on the contents of the jug. The children put themselves to bed, mouths stuffed with candy, trying not to laugh as they remembered their father flying through the air.

"You knew," Sarah accused.

"I didn't *know*," Anne said firmly. "I just figured that nobody, not even someone as useless as him, would set out without some kind of money. I figured he'd be the kind to eat all your food and drink all your coffee and talk about communes and sharing and then come up with money for something useless that only he could enjoy."

"He shared with Pilgrim."

"Yeah?" Anne laughed. "Well, I saw Belle slip that man some money . . . for a jacket, she said . . . but then he got Uncle Andrew's so . . ."

"Cheap bastards," Sarah breathed, and Anne burst out laughing.

The middle-aged white man with the young Indian wife had more than a dozen horses in a corral behind his trading post. He eyed Dan longingly, then came over to stand beside the big stud, and finally ask, "Can I touch him?"

"Sure," Anne grinned. "He's not mean." And, as she had expected, after much roundabout questioning, he got around to what he wanted to talk about.

"Your father around?" he hemmed.

"Got no father," she answered.

"Oh, well . . . maybe you got a brother?" he hawed.

"No, sir," she laughed, "and if you're getting ready to ask about stud service . . . he's mine. You got to ask me."

"Oh," he said, and his young wife laughed.

"I got some no's, though," Anne warned. "No mares with ticks, fleas, blowflies or canker . . ."

"Of course not!" he flared, insulted. "My horses are cleaner'n some people I could name."

"I believe you," Sarah said quietly.

They left Dan in the corral with several mares, left the saddle and bridle in the trader's shed, and walked back to the wagon. The smell of moonshine was so heavy in the wagon they took their quilts and slept on the ground, staring up at the stars.

"Besides," Sarah explained, blushing, "a man gets dumb ideas when he's been drinking."

"He'd only get them the once," Anne promised, and Sarah remembered the big skinning knife and how expertly the girl could use it.

The week they were camped by the trading post was a week of tension. They were supposed to be resting the animals, repairing harness, and stocking up for the next leg of the journey, but they spent a lot of their time wrangling. Pilgrim and John expected to be forgiven their drinking bout and were both insulted and hostile when neither Sarah nor Anne would look lightly on the episode.

"It wasn't the drinking," Sarah explained patiently, "it was the sneaky backbiting low-down way you went about it. You didn't even make sure your kids were fed before you were spending money on a jug."

"I knew you'd feed them," he protested.

"Yeah? Well don't ever *know* that again," she snapped. "If it's no skin off your ass if they go hungry, it's no skin off mine, either."

"What are you going to do about supplies?" Pilgrim demanded on the fourth day.

"Do? What should I do?"

"Well, we're going to need a hell of a lot to make it over the mountains!"

"Fine. Figure out what you need and get it. He can figure out what he needs for him and the kids. We know what we'll need. Then, if you still want to share, everybody will put their supplies together."

"You're a cheap bitch!" he snarled. "We do all the work!"

"Work?" Anne was almost hysterical with rage. "Work? You sit on your ass while the horses follow *me*. You don't cook. You don't wash clothes. You don't even wash your stinking selves! The kids collect firewood, I do the hunting and Sarah has to mother the whole lot of you. Work?"

"We'll wash, we'll wash," he mumbled, insulted and hurt.

Anne went down to the trading post and spent an hour talking seriously with the middle-aged man. Then she came back, invited Sarah to go for a ride on Dan, and they rode off together, leaving Pilgrim and John with the children.

"You like the idea of keeping house while John has a smithy and Pilgrim has a mill?" she asked.

"It might work," Sarah said cautiously.

"I lived on a grub-dirt farm." Anne looked off at the hills, purple in the evening light. "And I'm not about to do that again. They say it will be share and share alike, but I bet it'll be just what it's been since they joined up; getting a jug instead of getting food, expecting you to look after the kids, expecting us to make sure there's food. They'll just say that what they do is work, and what we do isn't."

"It doesn't have to be that way." Sarah's voice was soft.

"No, it doesn't. But I bet it will be." When Sarah didn't answer, Anne let the silence grow and then turned to look down at the trading post.

"Remember the Red River carts the métis had?" she prodded. "Well, those people got a couple. Old Bess could haul that cart from here to hell and back and not even work up a good sweat. Sunny or Babe would have even less trouble. And they've got a young mare, funny-lookin', but pretty. Got spots on her bum.

---

151

For ten dollars we can have the cart, the mare and a big sack of rice."

"Dan's been there all week," Sarah frowned. "He must have covered a half dozen mares. What about stud fee?"

"Oh," Anne grinned, "that's counted in the deal, too. I gave them a really sweet offer. A bit of friendship never hurts," she teased. "They were real receptive."

"You might be losing money," Sarah grinned.

"Well," Anne laughed, "Dan don't mind. And he's been eating his head off on their grain the whole week. Besides, a year from now, when those mares start foaling, we won't be here to count, anyway. And," she added, "they threw in some cartridges, and a pair of moccasins, and some other considerations."

"What about the children?"

"What about them? They aren't mine."

"Anne!" Sarah protested. "That's cold!"

"Is it?" Anne's young face was hard. "I told you the raggedyass will two-bit you to death if you let him. He's hoping you'll think of those kids every time he pulls a smart stunt. Pretty soon it'll be one smart stunt after another and them kids hanging around your neck like rocks."

"Those kids," Sarah corrected.

"I ain't takin' them," Anne said flatly. "They aren't my responsibility. They're his, and their own. If he can't look after 'em, they'll have to look after themselves. I ain't takin' no responsibility that ain't mine. I got," she growled, "more of the damn stuff than I can easy handle as it is."

Anne didn't like the way John Smithers made her feel. As if the things she was protesting about were so small and picky that only a very nasty person would object. She knew there was no way she was going to be able to explain to him why it was she wasn't about to feel responsible for his children, why it was she wasn't going to allow Dan and Bess in the hands of someone who would let his own stock become boneracks. How could she explain she'd see the casual and careless way he handled his own gear and she wasn't about to have the rifle treated that way. Most of all, she resented the way he automatically assumed that he ought to be listened to rather than her, he ought to be more respected, even catered to, that he ought to be able to treat others with cavalier disregard for their feelings just because he was a man, and older. She wished she didn't find herself counting the number of meals he ate without either paying for them or earning them. She wished she didn't begrudge having to shoot extra rabbits for him and his children. She didn't begrudge hunting for the children as much as she had; they were friendly and willing to help if someone just took the time to tell them what to do. It was him she begrudged having to do for: He expected he could sit in the shade and do nothing all day and still have his meals prepared for him.

And Pilgrim was beginning to think that he, too, ought to be catered to once in a while. Instead of rinsing out his own shirt he'd just drop it with the pile of clothes Anne and Sarah were washing, drop it without a please and pick it up later, washed and dried, and put it on without a thank you. And that type of thing stuck sideways in Anne's craw, too.

Then there was the smithy. And the mill. And the farm. And the thought of her and Sarah doing for John's four kids what Martha had sickened trying to do for one child and one man. Sometimes Anne thought that the hate Martha had never been able to express, the bitterness she had never dared voice, had eaten away inside her until the hole was so big her life drained out of it.

She rolled over and lay on her back, staring and hearing the constant tooth-grinding of the middle boy, a sound that obviously meant he had pinworms.

Down where the animals were tethered for the night came the soft mumbling noises old Bess made to BelleTwo when the baby was nursing. Anne rolled on her side and tried to close her eyes, but sleep escaped her until long into the night.

In the morning, while they were still sitting around the campfire, she spoke her piece.

"I've got some things I'd like to say, and when I'm finished, if anyone has anything to say, I'll listen," she said quietly. "Half of damn near everything in that wagon belongs to me, because

Auntie Belle gave the stuff to Sarah and me, and we traded our customers for the wagon. But if I take half of everything that's mine, those raggedyass kids won't make it very far."

"You're leaving, then," Sarah said softly.

"Yes." Anne's voice was firm and quiet. "I figure I had everything I needed almost a year ago, and I'm better off now than I was then because I'm not running any more, I'm just going."

"You mean you figure to just take as much food and stuff as you want and leave us?" Pilgrim was shocked.

"You're the one told me to always think logical." She smiled, not resenting him half as much as she had. "And logically, I can take damn near anything I want. And you," she stared levelly at John, "you owe us one good saddle horse."

"He wasn't yours anyway," John snapped. "He was hers and she hasn't been half as hard-nosed about things as you!"

"She just sorta got . . . stuck . . . with him," Anne answered, without any sign of anger or dislike, "and he'd've wandered off if I hadn't found him and taken him back to camp." Sarah nodded agreement and Anne continued. "But I always thought of OtherOne as hers so it's her you owe a good saddle horse to, not me. All I'm taking is what's mine."

"Don't talk nonsense," John said angrily. "You'll wind up bones by the trail. You're just a little bitty girl and you'll do what you're told."

"Not by you," she answered, her face hard, "and not by anybody who looks and sounds like you. You want to worry about a kid, worry about your own. Your boy has pinworms. You'd better give him some raw garlic."

"Don't sass me." He jumped to his feet, ready to slap her.

"Mister," she said with a sweet smile, "I already burned a cabin, a barn and a feed shed. It wouldn't take but two minutes to burn you, too."

She walked off toward the trading post, Sarah running after her.

"Anne . . ." Sarah pleaded.

"Sarah." Anne was nearly crying. "Don't let them raggedyass bums know how much money you got or they'll use it to buy a

---

154

plow to hitch you to." She turned away again. "You hang on to what you got because, sure as hell, by wintertime you're gonna need it."

"Half of it's yours," Sarah protested.

"No," Anne answered, walking away determinedly. "You'll need it more than I do."

Within an hour she was heading off across the prairie, heading toward the beckoning mountains. Instead of the Red River cart, she had two sturdy pack horses, and on them, an easy burden for the tough animals, was everything in the world she owned. Everything except the shirts and underwear she had left with the children.

"Hey, Dan," she chuckled, "you get your mind back on your business and never mind those mares. You're back to work, you old fool."

"Ought to have just tied her down until she got over it and smartened up," John raged. "She ought to be tanned until she calms down and learns to cook and sew like a proper girl. No girl of mine," he warned, "is going to run wild like that."

"Well," Pilgrim growled, "someone's gonna have to run damn wild damn fast to do the work I was countin' on her doing!"

Anne rode easily and quickly and without stopping for a break, heading away from the raggedyass man and a wagonload of responsibility she hadn't brought on herself—riding away from things she couldn't explain to herself, things she couldn't even put name to or understand.

That night she ate a cold supper, tethered the pack horses and let Dan and Bess forage freely, knowing BelleTwo wasn't going to go far from her mother. She took dried apple from her saddlebags and gave each animal a treat, talking to them softly, coaxing the pack horses and getting them used to the sound of her voice, the touch of her hands. Then she rolled herself in her bedroll and after no more than one or two hours, fell asleep. Just before dawn Dan began to kick up a fuss and Bess nickered loudly and stood between BelleTwo and whatever was approaching. The pack horses, upset by the noise, pulled on their tethers and whickered uneasily. Anne rolled from her bedding, grabbing the rifle, coming awake immediately.

"Baby?" Sarah's voice cut through the cool dawn. "Are you here? Don't shoot me."

"*Sarah!*" Anne yelled, running from behind the cover she had chosen.

Sarah sprang from the mare with the spotted rump, and she and Anne embraced tightly, laughing, crying and talking all at once.

"He said he was going to get supplies," Sarah blurted, "and he said he was going to get some material . . . That I could sew clothes for the kids instead of just sitting on the wagon bench. 'Make yourself useful,' that's what he said."

"Told you!" Anne crowed.

"They've got it all planned. They're going to be rich. They're going to be up to their backsides in horseshoes and cornmeal. But not me!" Then her smile faded and she looked deeply into Anne's eyes. "It wouldn't be any fun without you, baby. I might as well be back at Belle's as doing what they had in mind."

Anne stirred the embers, added wood and, in minutes, had a small fire going and breakfast started.

Anne looked up from the fire, almost trembling with joy. Sarah was sitting across from her, leaning against a tree, the fine lines around her eyes that had begun to develop recently were already fading. "He had money all the time, you know." Sarah grinned. "Even after you left, he didn't buy supplies. It was as if he was waitin' until I didn't have any money left."

"Sure," Anne agreed. "Then you'd be stuck."

"So when the kids came asking for food I said, 'Go ask your father.' And he came asking why they hadn't had dinner. I said probably because he hadn't made it. He called me a lazy slut." Her voice hardened. "And that's when he said he was going to buy material and I could sew while riding my own goddamn wagon. Make myself useful!"

Anne waited, knowing Sarah hadn't finished, knowing she

had to talk it out at her own speed. When breakfast was ready, she handed a loaded plate to Sarah, then filled her own and went to sit next to her friend, smiling contentedly.

"They had business with the wagon master," Sarah said around a mouthful of food. "So they went for a couple more jugs. Can't do business without jugs. As soon as they left the trading post, I went down, saw your friend, then went back to the wagon and packed the stuff I figured I'd need."

"They'll be cussing a blue streak by now," Anne giggled.

"They've got nothing to complain about. They've got a good wagon, a good team. John's horses are almost in good shape, so they have backup if it's needed, and they've got more and better gear than they had before."

"You've got nothing to feel guilty about," Anne insisted. "Pilgrim had nothing and John next to nothing before, and now they're both sitting pretty."

Dan's ears straightened, then laid back against his head. Anne put her plate on the ground, froze for a minute, then dove for the rifle, levering a shell into place, and aiming at where Dan's eyes were fixed.

"Don't shoot," came a small voice.

"Ruthie!" Sarah called.

"I should'a known it," Anne flared. "Soon as you cook food, one of them goddamn kids shows up!"

Ruthie rode into the clearing on Babe, leading Sunny on a soft tether.

"How did you find us?" Sarah asked.

"I followed you," Ruth said steadily. "I knew you were going to take off as soon as I saw you comin' from the tradin' post with that spotty-rump mare."

"Did you tell your dad?" Anne asked suddenly.

"No." Ruth's lip curled scornfully. "I'm not stupid! I cooked some grub for the others and then told 'em I was going for a ride. By the time he got back, they'd be asleep and he'd be too drunk to notice anything." She grinned suddenly, her strange eyes sparkling. "Bet he's waking up right about now. Bet he's gonna be madder 'n hell."

"Lord God," Sarah sighed, and began to laugh to herself.

"I don't see what's so damn funny." Anne tried not to grin, filling a plate with food and handing it to Ruth. "Now we got a religious fanatic with a gun maybe chasin' after us, not to mention a bereaved father with a gripe, and my Uncle Andrew."

"He won't chase," Ruth said, her mouth stuffed. "He'll be mad because he got fooled, but he'll be glad I'm gone. He never liked me, anyway. He never liked none of us."

"What about the others?" Sarah asked, hesitantly.

"They'll make out," Ruth said calmly.

"Oh, it's going to be wonderful," Anne crowed. "Pilgrim's gonna be doin' all the work, and the raggedyass bastard is gonna be sittin' talkin' about bein' a blacksmith and havin' a mill and fartin' wonders and shittin' miracles. And in ten years one or all of them kids is gonna be sneakin' around at night with a jug of kerosene and a can of matches!"

# Chapter 9

They had been riding toward the dust cloud for three days when they first noticed the glinting in the hot prairie sun. Puzzled, they urged the horses forward, and within hours stared down at the twin rails stretching west ahead of them.

"Well, where did that come from?" Anne asked stupidly.

"It's a train track," Ruth explained. "I saw it back home."

"I know it's a train track!" Anne answered. "But what's it doing here?"

They followed the track, drawing ever closer to the cloud of dust, and that afternoon they passed the first grave. Less than a mile further, they passed another, larger one. Neither grave had a marker, just a mound of raw earth under the relentless prairie sun, a mound of dry earth whipped by the prairie wind.

The following morning they rode past the cloud of dust. Skinny little men with strange yellow skin, sharply slanted eyes, dust-caked pigtails and heavily calloused hands looked briefly at the three women and seven horses, then turned back to their back-breaking labor. Burly white men with whips, like the one the raggedyass man had used on his horses, strolled up and down the toiling column shouting orders, cursing and using their whips. When they noticed the women they grinned, and only their own awareness of the scarcity of women and the unspoken code of gallantry kept them from calling out to them.

"I never saw people like that," Anne whispered.

"Me, neither," Ruth agreed.

"Remember Belle talking about the Chinee?" Sarah reminded. "Well, that's them."

"She said they'd all gone after gold!" Anne protested.

"These must be some others."

They rode clear of the dust, away from the slaving little men and the noise their huge hammers made on the spikes and rails. Looking back, Anne wondered how men so small and obviously ill-fed could work so hard with such heavy sledges. As if to underline her unspoken question, one of the Chinese suddenly folded at the knees and fell in the dust. The foreman, cracking his whip at the others, stepped over the fallen man and left him face down where he fell.

"Don't even think about it," Sarah warned.

"But . . ." Anne protested.

"Don't you go back there!" Sarah insisted. "It's no place for a woman!"

Their water bags were half empty, and they made dry camp that afternoon, not daring to push the horses too hard, not certain when they would next find water. Anne gave each of the horses equal amounts to drink, wishing she could give them more, but not daring to in case they ran out completely before they found more. They ate cold food and lay on the dry yellow grass, hearing the faint sound of hammerheads on spikes. They could not know the man who fell lay in the heat the rest of the day, then was dragged by his countrymen to the crowded, stifling tent that was their only protection from dust and rain, heat and cold. They could not know the water he was finally given to drink was wasted on him. They would never know he died in the middle of the night and was buried in an unmarked grave with two other nameless men. It would be years before anyone learned that for every mile of track a Chinese slave was buried. It would be even more years before anyone cared.

Dan whickered uneasily, and Anne grabbed her rifle, rolling clear of her blankets, tensed and alert.

"You better step forward," she hissed tensely, "or I'm gonna start shootin'." The small shadow stepped closer to the fire and stood, head hanging, waiting with neither fear nor anger.

"It's one of the Chinamen," Ruth said sleepily, sitting up and staring.

"What are you doing sneaking around here?" Anne demanded. The man just looked at her, still waiting.

"He probably doesn't speak English," Sarah decided.

"What do you want?" Anne asked.

"If he doesn't understand you, how can he answer?" Sarah mocked. "And if you'd been getting treated like he was getting treated, what would *you* want."

"Gone," Anne admitted.

They gave the man as much food as they could spare and a drink of water, and Anne handed him a blanket, and shrugged.

"Wish I could do better by you, mister," she apologized, "but much as I'd like to help you, I'm not going to leave myself on the short end of the stick."

He stared at her with his funny slanted eyes, then, to their amazement, he bowed deeply.

"Take care of yourself," Sarah blurted, and the scrawny man with the whip-scarred back faded into the shadows and was gone again.

Twice more that night Dan nickered uneasily, but nobody else came near the camp. In the morning, they were awake and preparing to leave when a man with a whip and two sneezing dogs approached camp.

"Do something for you?" Anne asked, sliding the rifle from the scabbard and holding it easily.

"Seen a Chinaman come this way?" he asked.

"A what?" Anne pretended stupidity.

"Those lazy little things you saw yesterday," the man tried to smile. "They're Chinamen. Some of them took off last night."

"Didn't look lazy to me," Anne growled. "Looked like they were doing two men's work each."

"They move a lot," the man explained, "but they don't do much."

"Neither did you when that one fell."

"Oh." He managed a smile. "They do that all the time. Pretendin' to be sick so they can get some time off. Laziest people you ever saw."

"Why'd you hire them, then?" Sarah asked reasonably.

"I didn't!" the man laughed. "The company brings them in. Ships 'em in by boat. Soon's they've got this line built, they'll get a free trip home again. But they keep runnin' away," he ended.

"Can't help you," Anne said flatly.

"Used to be," the foreman sighed, "you could chase 'em down with a good dog. Now . . . crafty little devils spread pepper on their trail. Can't trust 'em," he explained. "They're the sneakiest people I ever met. You can be standin' right next to one and then he's gone. *Poof*, like that. Never saw the like," and he turned back, tugging on the leashes, leading his watery-eyed dogs back toward the plume of dust.

"I don't like that man," Ruth decided.

"Guess the Chinamen don't, either," Anne agreed.

They found water by midmorning, refilled their water bags, let the horses drink all they could hold, then headed off again, riding easily and talking seldom. Behind them the plume diminished, but Anne felt as if she could still hear the steady sound of hammers on spikes.

"Look," Ruth's excited voice pulled Anne out of her reverie. "There's that little guy!"

He didn't look around, he didn't slow down or speed up, he just kept putting one determined foot in front of the other, heading away from the road gang, away from the whips.

"Hey, mister," Ruth grinned down at him. "You want a drink of water?" She held out her water jug, and the small man bowed before taking a drink. Then he carefully replaced the stopper, handed back the jug, and bowed again.

"He could ride Sunny," Sarah suggested.

"Or he could walk," Anne contradicted.

"Just for a day or so."

"Why would I want to do that? If he rides with us, you're

gonna want he should eat with us. Next thing you know, he'll be handing you some cloth so you can make him a pair of trousers in your spare time." But she knew Sarah would have her own way. Somehow Sarah always managed to get her own way.

For six days the silent little man with the slanty eyes and the long black pigtail sat on top of Sunny, riding with them. He watched as Anne rode off by herself and returned with wild meat, and he nodded to himself, and moved unbidden to start the fire, feed the stock, and, after they had eaten, he put the big cooking pot on the fire to warm water for the dishes. He helped Anne, Ruth and Sarah gather wild onions, sage, wild peppers, and even found and introduced them to things none had ever before tried eating, things that proved to be delicious.

"It's just grass," Anne protested, staring out at the small lake, and the thick reeds growing in it. But the little man was persistent and demanding in his own silent way. Finally Anne shrugged, dismounted, removed her boots, rolled up her pants and followed him into the water. He spread the spare tarp on the surface of the shallow lake, bent the reeds over and shook them. A shower of small black grains fell to the tarp and his face creased in a happy smile.

"Grass seed?" Anne demanded, but he ignored her and continued gathering his crop. That night she stared doubtfully at the meal he had cooked, and she tasted hesitantly, and then only because Sarah was setting a firm example.

"It's a lot like rice," Sarah decided.

"Grass seed," Anne insisted.

"Wild rice," Sarah corrected, firmly.

"Grass seed," Anne argued. "And nobody is ever going to call it wild rice or spend any time at all gathering it. Unless," she added, forking it into her mouth eagerly, "they're as hard up and hungry as we are."

Every day Ruth took the rifle and practiced shooting it, and soon she was adept at knocking the heads off prairie dogs and gophers. The little yellow man smiled, but never tried to speak. He got his meaning across without words. The night they ate the boiled rice he spread the tarp on the ground, divided the dark grains into four piles, then looked at each of them and pointed at a pile of rice. Then he sat back and waited. Finally Sarah nodded, rose, went to the wagon and came back with a large and a small cotton sack. Into the large one she put three portions of rice, into the smaller one the final portion. The little man nodded, reached out, took his bag with his share, and tucked it under his shirt. The next day, while Ruth practiced with the rifle and Anne and Sarah rested with the horses, the little man went back to the lake and returned with his sack full to the brim and their sack three-quarters full.

"Guess he doesn't figure to travel with us forever," Anne remarked, and Sarah turned her head away to hide a smile.

The afternoon of the sixth day he pointed suddenly, his face creasing in a wide grin. He pointed, and his voice tinkled like silver bells.

"I'll be damned," Anne laughed. "He can talk after all!"

"They can all talk," Sarah added, "the whole bunch of 'em."

The skinny little man slid from his perch on top of Sunny and ran to meet the three excited friends rushing toward him.

"They all look the same!" Ruth insisted.

"Not only do they disappear poof into nowhere," Anne mocked the foreman they had left behind days earlier, "they appear that way, too. And they do look alike."

"If Belle could see this, she'd have a fit!" Sarah laughed. "That's probably her jennyass they're tagging along."

The four Chinese, followed by a jennyass with a small load, waved and smiled as the three women passed them, and one of them bowed deeply.

"That one must be ours," Ruth decided.

Day after day, week after week, they moved toward the blue that gradually revealed itself as mountains. The ground became rougher; there was more bush, more water, more trees. Soon they were riding up increasingly steep hills, and old Bess complained more and more often and had to stop and rest repeatedly.

"Come on, you fat old fool," Anne urged sharply. "You're just lazy."

"She's not lazy, you know," Sarah said gently.

"I know," Anne stared steadily ahead, blinking rapidly. "But if you don't say it, maybe you won't think about it. And if you don't think about it, maybe it won't bother you." Anne looked at Ruth, who was riding beside trying not to show her own tears. "She's awful old," Anne added softly.

"Yeah," Ruthie replied, "I know she is."

The deeper they got into the mountains, the harder it got for old Bess. Sides heaving, the mare plodded upward, following Anne with unflagging loyalty. None of the other horses was having any problem and the drays seemed to enjoy having nothing more to do than carry one small woman-child instead of pulling a wagon full of gear.

They had been picking their way carefully for hours, making their way along a rock-strewn trail that wound high above a valley. To their left the mountain sloped steeply upward, to their right it dropped off dangerously, but the path was wide and they were in no hurry. They had been finding increasing signs of other travelers for days, now. A wagon with a broken axle, pushed off the trail and left to the weather. The contents had undoubtedly been divided among the other wagons, the horses taken as relief teams. The previous day they had passed a cairn of rocks and a roughly fashioned cross and had wondered aloud who it was had traveled so far to end up in a grave like that.

The path curved sharply around a huge outcropping of granite, and Dan had to pick his way carefully among an increasing number of large rocks. Anne looked to the right, down the slope, and grimaced. There was no danger, but a careless move could send rocks and bodies tumbling fatally down the drop.

"What's that?" Sarah demanded behind her.

"What?" Anne looked up.

Ahead of her the path was almost blocked by a fresh rockslide, the face of the slope to the left scarred and torn. Roots and dirt, boulders and bushes had rolled down across the path and over the drop.

"Wait here," she dismounted and started to walk forward.

"Something is moving," Sarah called. Anne nodded, moved quickly to where a forlorn, confused and frantic mule was tugging at a rope that disappeared into the messy pile of boulder and earth. Anne walked up to the bruised and scratched animal, and, when she could neither untie nor untangle the rope, she used Andrew's big knife to slash through the frayed lead and set the trembling animal free.

"Come on." She patted the animal and it followed her eagerly, limping slightly and making soft confused sounds. "There's other mules under those rocks," she told Sarah and Ruth soberly.

They inched their way past the tumble of rocks, averting their eyes, ignoring the blood smears on the boulders, trying not to think about who or what lay crushed and buried forever. The mountains looming ahead of them seemed suddenly less beautiful, and they all knew the path they had chosen to take was a long and dangerous one.

The wagon master had explained to them that there were only two or three places where a train had any chance at all of making it through the mountains. The half-obscured trails they had been following merged with other faint trails and became a very definite trail that, after a while, became a wide path over which countless feet and hooves, wagon wheels and sledge runners had passed in the westward trek. The first signs they had seen of others, the abandoned wagon and fatal rockslide, were followed by increasing signs of passage: bits of discarded harness, a coffee pot with a hole in the bottom, a hat blown off someone's head, a child's wooden toy fallen from a wagon. Game became increasingly scarce as they moved higher and the cooled ash of campfires was a common daily sight.

"Look at that," Anne pointed at a jumble of belongings.

"Why would anybody leave all that?" Sarah asked. Anne looked up at the steep slope ahead, eyed the obvious signs of difficult ascent, the tumbled rocks, the scars of metal-shod hooves.

"I guess it was a case of leave the surplus here or never make the grade."

"It seems a shame," Sarah sighed, "to come this far and have to leave it. Look . . ."

"Who'd take a carved wood dresser across the country?"

"Who'd want to leave it behind?" Sarah stroked the carved wood regretfully, tracing the intricate designs with her finger. "Another rain and it'll be ruined," she mourned.

"Want a washtub?" Anne grinned. "There must be something we can use it for." And then she stopped laughing and looked at the sparsely loaded pack horses. "They can carry that easy," she decided, and began rearranging the load, strapping the washtub in place.

"By the time," she announced sarcastically, "that raggedyass pack makes it this far, they'll have plenty of room in their wagon. They'll be able to find almost everything they need right here. But I doubt if their boneracks will be able to haul it far."

It was a temptation, but they restrained themselves, leaving behind household furnishings that had been loved enough to have been carted across terrible distances. A handmade baby cradle, a crate of fine china packed in straw, a spinning wheel they knew someone had wept to leave behind.

"If you see any tools of any kind," Anne insisted, "we'll take them with us. We might need them."

"I wish I could take the spinning wheel," Sarah insisted and finally Anne relented.

"Oh, all right," she snapped, turning Dan around and heading back, "but if the damned thing gets in the way I'm using it for firewood."

"It won't get in the way."

"You don't even know how to use it!" she accused.

"Well, I can *look* at it," Sarah retorted stubbornly.

They moved upward, day after day, the air growing thinner and colder, and at night they were glad of their small fire. The limping mule healed rapidly, and Lucky happily followed BelleTwo and Ruth, sometimes teasing the pack horses, sometimes prancing alongside Dan as if trying to imitate the huge stud.

At night they cuddled together under their blankets, close to the warmth of the fire, their body heat helping keep them warm. In the morning they would hurry on their way, knowing they would warm up quicker moving than sitting. Ruth became almost as adept at catching fish in the bitter cold creeks as Anne. Sarah had learned well from the silent Chinaman, and could spot edible weeds and roots quicker than either of the other women. One afternoon they had to pick their way around the edges of a permanent ice field and Ruth exclaimed in wonder at the sight of small flowers growing right through the ice. She knelt on the dirty glacier, looking up at Sarah and Anne, her tanned face no longer thin, her strange eyes glowing, smiling openly. Anne felt a rush of affection for the girl, reached out and rumpled her short hair, and grinned at her.

They pushed past the ice field and stopped at a small clearing where a dark green pool of water invited them to try for the large, hungry fish hiding in its depths. Anne piled their gear as a windbreak, and turned the animals loose to roll and feed. When she had finished her chores, Sarah had water boiling for hot tea, and Ruth already had four good-sized trout.

"I guess a person could live this way for a long time," Anne sighed.

"Not too long," Sarah contradicted, "unless they had a supply of heavy clothes. It's getting damn cold!"

They sat around the small fire talking and joking, watching the fish cooking in the black cast-iron frying pan, and after they had eaten more than they could comfortably hold, Anne scrubbed the dishes while Ruth played with the small mule and BelleTwo. They didn't go to bed until well after dark, and then fell almost immediately into a deep and dreamless sleep.

"Anne! Quick!" Ruth screamed, panic honing a sharp edge to her voice.

Anne jumped from her blankets, reaching for the rifle, looking wildly for the threat that had the usually calm Ruth terrified. All she could see was Sarah, coming to her feet after a defensive roll from her blankets, and the horses grazing peacefully. Except Bess who lay on her side, her head on Ruth's lap.

"There's something wrong!" Ruth wailed, tears pouring from her eyes. Anne ran quickly, knowing inside herself she had been waiting for something like this, waiting and almost expecting.

Bess lay on her side, panting shallowly, a thin trickle of blood coming from her mouth. Her eyes had rolled half back and she was already almost unaware of anything around her. Anne tried everything she knew to get the fat old mare up on her feet, but no arrangement of ropes, no amount of urging or tugging helped.

"Might as well leave her," Anne said flatly. "We're just making it harder for her by trying to get her on her feet. She's too old, that's all, she's just too old."

"What's the matter with her?" Ruth sobbed.

"I don't know." Anne sighed. "Maybe the air's too thin for her. Maybe she's just . . . old," she finished simply. "But when she doesn't even try to lift her head when BelleTwo nickers, you know she's too far gone for anything we know how to do." And she turned away, sobbing thickly.

"Where are you going?" Sarah asked, taking Anne's arm.

"I'm gonna rig up the gear, and you and Ruth are gonna ride off with them. Tie BelleTwo and take her with you if you have to drag her. Dan and me'll stay behind for a while."

"Oh, Anne, honey." Sarah held Anne close, stroking her back, smoothing her hair, talking softly to her while Anne sobbed roughly, eyes swelling, nose congesting. Finally she wiped her eyes on her jacket, blew her nose, and kissed Sarah softly.

"She *knows*, Sarah," she hiccuped. "Look at her eyes. She knows. And she isn't afraid. She wants to go. And I can't let it drag on any longer, not when she wants to go."

Sarah and Ruth tied BelleTwo to the pommel of Sarah's saddle, and coaxed her with bits of dried apple and soft words, and the young filly allowed herself to be led away, but kept turning back, whickering and demanding her mother get up and accompany them. Ruth, eyes red, face set, sat on Babe's broad back and stared ahead. Sarah knew that behind them a young girl was sobbing and saying good-bye to a friend who hadn't been young when Anne was born. They were well into the tree line when the sound of the rifle came to them faint and sharp, and Sarah got off her mare and pressed her face against the increasingly frantic BelleTwo, and sobbed.

"Don't cry, Sarah," Ruth put her deeply tanned small hand on Sarah's arm.

"It's not *fair!*" Sarah protested. Ruth nodded, and cuddled Sarah comfortingly, and they waited until Anne rode up on Dan, her eyes still streaming, her body still wracked with sobs.

The young filly protested and fought the tether for days, struggling to get back to her mother, but they all closed their ears to the plaintive noises and pushed on grimly. There was a haste to their travel now that hadn't been there before. Every day they covered more distance, every morning they set off earlier, every night they stopped later. There was no Bess to slow them down now, and they all wanted to get as far away as possible from the place where she lay.

They were riding down steep slopes now, having just as much trouble going down as they'd had coming up, the horses' hooves sliding in the shale and rock. Often they had to get off and walk. There were still uphill treks, but the inclines were never as steep as the declines, and the air was beginning to have some substance again. There was more game than there had been higher up, and Anne practiced with the six-gun she'd salvaged from the body of an unknown rider. Sarah could never look at it without being reminded of the young cowboy and the mad marshal, but she could handle the spare rifle easily and well, and Ruth loved to strap the big six-gun to her hip and practice her fast draw.

"One of these days," she promised, "I'm gonna put bullets in it, and draw, and shoot something. A tree maybe."

They knew they were following a pack train. The trail was wide and liberally splattered with mule and horse shit, and the campfire ash was fresher every day.

"We're makin' better time than they are," Anne guessed. "I think we cover in two days what it takes them three to do."

"Should we try to . . . avoid them?"

"Doesn't seem to be much need." She grinned hopefully. "Maybe they'll have some coffee."

It was pouring rain when they caught up with the pack train. The brawny bearded men stared at them for a moment or two, then nodded as if it was an everyday sight, two women and a girl with pack horses, saddle horses, a young filly, a half-grown mule, two powerful drays, a washtub and a spinning wheel.

"You got any tobacco?" one man asked hopefully.

"No, but we've got salt and tea," Anne answered.

"Salt!"

"You got any coffee?" she asked hopefully.

"Yeah. You got potatoes?"

"No," Sarah replied glumly.

"Us, neither. Just that damn rice and beans."

"We've got fresh meat," Ruth said quickly. "We got a small deer yesterday."

"Well, we've got flour for gravy," the leader grinned.

They rode together until it was time to stop for the night. The men watched carefully while the women expertly unsaddled and removed the packs from their animals, and when Anne began to rub them down, the leader nodded and grinned.

"I've seen some people leave the packs on them all night and all day," he growled, "but to me that's worse than never takin' off your boots."

The men, satisfied the women knew what they were doing, set up camp and began to prepare supper. Anne handed over the small buck she had caught drinking at a stream and the pack train cook began to slice thick steaks from the carcass. He nodded when Sarah brought over enough rice for her, Ruth and Anne. "Just toss 'er in with the rest," he suggested, "and if you've got any salt, I'll put your name in my will."

"We've got salt," Sarah smiled. "I brought some and she

brought some. We spent about three months once without any and neither of us wanted to do that again."

"Been about two weeks for us," the cook said, sadly, "and I'm about ready to shoot someone. Even the coffee don't taste right, and, by damn, I like my coffee!"

"I do, too," Sarah said, yearningly, eyeing the big coffee pot the cook was putting over the fire, "but the post was sold out."

"I bought ever' last bean he had," the cook crowed triumphantly, "but some goddamn fool hadda go and fall in the crik with the salt bag . . ."

The coffee was blistering hot and tasted like a mother's kiss. Their appetites were improved by the company and they all ate until they could barely move. One of the men had what he called a juice harp and he twanged tunes for them while they all clapped rhythm and had an extra cup of coffee to celebrate. One of the men offered Sarah and Anne his "rollings," and Anne shook her head no, but Sarah accepted with thanks and rolled and lit a cigarette, smiling happily. The men were mildly surprised when Anne didn't tether her animals but left them free to graze and roam. Then she, Sarah and Ruth rolled up in their bedrolls and fell fast asleep, and only Anne knew she had the big skinning knife in her roll with her.

In the morning there was fried meat, bannock and coffee and an invitation to travel with the pack train.

"It'll be a bit slower," Tom, the leader, invited, "but it's a lot safer, and it's a relief to know if something goes wrong, there's people can lend a hand." They accepted gratefully and took their place at the end of the string of animals.

# Chapter 10

They established a pattern and found their place in the co-operative work load of the train. They would ride ahead of the train, sometimes as much as half a day ahead, and would string a net across a stream or pond, then ride on looking for meat. "If it moves and can be chewed," Sarah joked, "we'll get it. Hide, fur, scales or feathers, it isn't safe with us on the prowl," and the men, after a few sideways looks at some of the land fish and unidentified small animals, just sprinkled some salt on the meat and ate it without asking questions.

The first time Sarah placed the washtub close to the fire and helped Anne and Ruth fill it with water, the men watched slit-eyed, not knowing what to expect, not wanting to ask questions in a country where questions could get you a black eye or worse. When the chill was off the water, Anne and Sarah carried the tub behind a screen of bushes, and Ruth was the first one in, lathering happily with the strong yellow soap, enjoying Sarah's fingers in the thick suds on her head. Anne hunkered casually between the campfire and the men, her rifle resting easily on her knees, waiting her turn. When Ruth and Sarah had finished bathing, Sarah took Anne's place with the rifle, and Anne climbed into the cool water, her skin goose-pimpling, and bathed quickly and efficiently.

"The first bastard who tries to get smart," the leader warned softly, "might never see the Cariboo."

"Why?" a surly man asked. "You figure it's up to you to do something?"

"I wouldn't have to." Tom grinned. "Every one of them is a crack shot with a rifle, and the blonde has got a knife as would lay open a moose."

"I bet she knows how to use it, too," the cook cackled.

"Aw, she's just a kid," someone scoffed.

"Old enough to bleed," the surly man grinned, "old enough to butcher."

"That's right," Tom agreed, "and you make a wrong move and she'll butcher you the way she butchers that meat she brings in." He stood up, stretched, scratched, then sniffed and called out to Sarah: "Could I borrow your washtub when you're finished?"

When Tom had finished his washing, the cook was waiting with his, and that night the bushes were decorated with freshly rinsed shirts and one-piecers. They were still damp in the morning, so Anne bundled them up with her, rode ahead quickly on Dan, and spread them on rocks and bushes to dry in the sun. Then she and Ruth went off hunting and Sarah enjoyed a half-day of rest guarding the wash, turning it to allow the breeze to touch every part, and folding it neatly when it was dry.

That night several of the other men borrowed the washtub and threw their shirts in to soak. Ruth jumped up suddenly, rolled up her pantlegs, and stepped into the tub, splashing happily, stamping on the shirts and grinning.

"That kid can find fun anywhere," Sarah remarked fondly.

"Yeah," Anne agreed, "but we got to find her a pair of shoes somewhere."

Tom came over, sat down beside them, watching Ruth and smiling.

"I got a girl just about the same age as her," he confided. "Sure be glad to get back home again."

"Where's home?" Sarah asked.

"Place called Fort Langley. But before I get there, I got to deliver this stuff to the gold fields."

"Gold?" Anne laughed. "The whole crazy world is chasing after gold!"

"Not me," Tom corrected. "I'm not standin' in cold water up to my ass swishin' gravel around in a pie plate! I've got things on these animals those miners are going to need." He looked around carefully, "Don't tell the cook, but I've even got salt."

"But he said . . ."

"Gotta do it," Tom said sternly. "If people think there's a lot of something, they'll use it so careless that soon you've got nothing. So I told 'em the packs was sealed. They think that all there is in there is mining gear."

"Crafty," Sarah grinned.

"Gotta be," Tom laughed, and rose, still grinning, to walk to the fire.

"He's got a good head on him," Anne said admiringly.

"The rest of him's not bad, either," Sarah answered, and left Anne sitting shaking her head, watching her friend walk after Tom, calling to him.

"Oh, hell," Anne sighed. "Dan ain't the only one!"

Every day brought something different, every day was the same: routine chores and hard work, and a landscape that changed so gradually they were seldom aware of it. Blistering sun and chilling rains, and always the search for food. Ruth was now as adept as Sarah, and both of them almost as skilled as Anne, at the setting of snares, the spotting and capture of game, and she took deep pride in the knowledge she contributed more than her share to the needs of the pack train.

Perched bareback on the placid Babe, inevitably followed by BelleTwo and the calvicating Lucky, Ruth rode off every morning looking for edible roots, streams to fish, rabbit runs to set with traps and snares. Her body filled out and grew firm, her skin tanned and she learned to laugh easily from a place deep in her belly. The tightness around her mouth vanished and the guarded look appeared less often in her eyes. The stiffness in her back and shoulders relaxed and she moved easily and gracefully. She no longer sat apart from the others, compulsively stuffing herself with food until her belly ached with discomfort, and at night she slept easily, unbothered by nightmares born of fear.

All the love and loyalty that for nine and a half years had been locked inside her clamored for release and chipped at the walls of reserve, weakening them. At first it was Belle Two who was the recipient of so much desperate love, and Ruthie openly showered on the long-legged filly all the tenderness and love she hadn't been able to show to anyone in her life. Her mother, worn out by child-bearing and made bitter by disappointment, had never seemed to have time or inclination to cuddle. Ruth couldn't remember the first years of her life, before panic had begun to hone the edge to her mother's voice and bitterness sharpened the gaunt planes of her face. Ruth could not remember being rocked to sleep, cuddled or stroked, but she could clearly remember her mother, her pregnancy pushing at the faded skirt of her worn dress, looking down, dry-eyed, at the still form of the brother who hadn't lived to see his second birthday, staring with dry hard eyes, staring and saying, "Well, that's one less to have to worry myself sick about, one less to have to find a way to feed." And she could remember her mother, months later, handing the newborn to her, not roughly nor angrily, but with quiet, resigned determination. Handing over the newborn, then looking one last time at the unpainted rough-hewn boards on the bare bedroom walls, looking at the grinning face of her husband, smelling the sharp bite of his celebratory liquor, the dark tang of his cigar smoke. Then saying, "I'm tired. I'm just so tired." She rolled on her side, back to the world, and let the breath escape from her body, let her heart stop beating.

"You're the woman of the family now," her father had told her, and she had tried to do what her mother had done, but it wasn't enough to try, and she knew she had never managed, had been a failure from the start. It never occurred to her that nobody could have done what was expected of her. She only knew she had failed.

Sarah had, from the start, treated her as one of the children, one of the pitiable, one of the helpless. If Ruth had never done another thing in her life but be who she was, Sarah would have been kind to her. At first it was a welcome relief to sink into the protected cocoon, to let Sarah cook the meals and worry over the raspy breathing, the deep chesty coughs, the urine-blistered backside of the baby. But Ruth didn't want to live her life as a pitiable child, a perpetual victim. She wanted to be like Anne: able to come and go as she pleased, able to think her own thoughts, catch her own food, skin her own game and depend on herself for everything. Anne's hard-won, slow and grudging acceptance meant more to Ruth than all the easy smiles and protective hugs. Once Ruth knew that not everybody in the world itched, had lice and smelled sour, she did what had to be done to change herself. She bathed with soap as often as she could, often standing goose-pimpled in a mountain stream, scouring herself and her clothes. She asked only that she be given a chance to learn, her bright eyes missed little, and she tried to improve her growing skills.

One of the drovers, a grinning young man with shaggy hair and the sparse beginning of a beard, carried a juice harp in one pocket, a harmonica in another and had a four-stringed banjo carefully wrapped in a blanket and tied to the pack of a sturdy mule. After supper, the young man would take his banjo from its blanket, carefully tune it, and sit by the fire playing and blowing into his mouth organ. When he realized Ruth was watching him with starving eyes, he grinned, his hand left the strings and he reached up and removed the harmonica from his mouth. "Like music?" he asked, his voice bubbling like water coming from a crack in the rocks. She nodded, feeling her face flaming. His tanned and work-calloused hand reached into his pocket. He brought out his juice harp and handed it to her. "Just bite on it, real easy, let your breath slide over it, and twang 'er with your hand," he instructed casually, turning back to his banjo. She tried, and thought her teeth were broken, but he didn't laugh at her; he just moved to sit beside her, demonstrated patiently, and grinned widely when she finally started to make music with it. "Keep it," he said. "I've got another." She slept that night with the harp held in her hand, rode off in the morning twanging happily, inventing her own music, learning for herself the beats and rhythms the young man could coax out of the banjo.

She no longer felt hate for her father. She no longer even thought of him. The nights were for sleeping now, not for lying awake, eyes staring bitterly at the inadequate canvas on the rickety wagon, dreaming new and different ways to kill him and not get caught. It was very important not to get caught. Everyone knew what they did to you when you got caught. Chains around your ankles, and whips, and hard work for the rest of your life. But there were ways to arrange accidents, and she had planned several of them, knowing, even as she was making her elaborate schemes, that she wouldn't carry them out. One little mistake and you'd get caught. As her memory of him faded and her hatred of his weakness turned from a crippling festering sore to a determination never to be that way herself, Ruth found, without even thinking about it, the perfect way to murder her father. He simply no longer mattered. She neither loved him nor hated him. She erased him from her world, as if he had never been in it.

Sarah rode easily, watching the broad back of the pack train leader in front of her. His blue cotton shirt was faded almost white, his skin tanned the color of well-cared-for leather, and his hair grew shaggy on his neck. She knew he was whistling softly to himself, his bright eyes searching the trail ahead for loose stones, sudden turns, places where the ground might slide out from under the careful hooves of the mules. Tom spoke seldom, but when he did the words tumbled from him, laughter bubbled and he made small jokes about unimportant things. She knew it would be easy to start to feel too much, it would be easy to pretend there could be something more for the future, to pretend, just for a little while, but she knew she wasn't going to allow herself to do that. Not only because he had a wife and children at Fort Langley, not just because she didn't want to become anyone's kept woman, but because she could no longer see herself in the dream she had once imagined. She could no longer see herself cooking, cleaning, sewing and caring for children, having another baby every year or two, working to build up a place without ever really feeling it was hers. She could no longer see herself as the passive partner in someone else's dream. She had dreams of her own. A place, certainly; everybody needed a place, but not someone else's place. A child, maybe, but not a lifetime of pregnancy and nursing. Still, it was nice, more than nice, to roll out of her blankets, pad quietly past the embers of the fire, to the prearranged place in the shadows where Tom would be waiting, his blankets already spread, his grin splitting his face. Nice to cling to him for a few hours, to enjoy his body and hers before leaving and returning to her blankets, knowing Anne and Ruth were sound asleep and if any of the men were awake, they would mind their own business. She wasn't sure what Ruth would think if she knew. Probably nothing, and whatever Ruth thought, Ruth would keep her thoughts to herself. It was Anne who might raise hell about Tom if she knew. Or she might not. She might just shrug and turn away, more concerned with the condition of the horses' hooves. Sarah wasn't ever really sure what Anne's reaction to anything would be.

Anne enjoyed the daily solitude as much as the warm fire and grinning company at night. She knew Sarah met Tom almost every night, and it didn't seem to have anything to do with anything. She hoped Sarah had sense enough to realize Tom wasn't a man to walk out on his wife and kids: No man worth his salt would do that, no woman worth hers would expect it. Part of her felt that somehow a wrong was being done to a woman she hadn't even met, but another part of her said Tom's wife wasn't here anyway, would never know, so what difference did it make. Except it made a difference. She tried to convince herself that it was Tom's responsibility to stay loyal to his wife, not Sarah's, but she couldn't fully believe that. And so, confused and without any clear idea of what she thought, or even wanted to think, Anne conveniently pushed it aside, put it in the same locked box as she put the worries about whether or not Uncle Andrew was riding after her, riding to claim Dan from her. Somehow the two problems were linked, and she didn't know how. So she saddled Dan every morning and rode off with her rifle, covering miles daily in search of deer or elk, rabbits or squirrels, anything that could be part of their supper.

---

She was riding back with the body of a half-grown deer lashed behind her. Sarah was riding next to Tom and they were talking and joking. When they saw her, both of them waved. She lifted her arm, grinned and nudged Dan gently. The musical young man Ruth had taken to calling "Twanger" half turned in his saddle to check the mules coming behind him. His horse slipped, a rock rolled, the horse lurched desperately, and then slipped and fell screaming and sliding down the slope. Twanger tumbled awkwardly to the ground, his leg bent unnaturally under him.

"Stay clear of the ledge!" Tom shouted, leaping from his horse. He ran to the side of the path and stared down the wicked rock-strewn slope at the unconscious rider and the screaming, flailing brown gelding trying pathetically and hopelessly to rise on shattered forelegs. Anne leaped from Dan's back and raced to join Tom at the lip of the drop. Less than eight feet from where Twanger lay, the ledge dropped abruptly to rocks a hundred or more feet below.

"Get me a rope," Tom yelled.

"You can't go down there," Anne said softly. "You're too big. You're gonna start all those rocks rolling . . ."

"Can't leave him there!" Tom protested.

"You weigh too much, too," she said carefully. "Someone small has to go down." She started to remove her jacket.

"You sure?" Tom put his hand on her shoulder and squeezed softly.

"Can't leave him down there." She tried to smile and knew her lips quivered.

"Okay." He nodded, took the rope the men brought and began to expertly fashion and knot a chest harness. "You know what you've got to do?"

"Yeah." She nodded, her face white, "I got to use my knife on that horse's throat and get Twanger back up here."

"We can try to get a rifle to you," he offered.

"Only got two hands, Tom." She gulped, and she knew he knew she didn't want to have to do what had to be done. But she knew, and he did, too, that she would do it.

"Okay, Twink. Careful, now."

Twanger was lying unconscious, his leg smashed, a stream of blood coming from a cut on his head. Anne checked him over and turned his face to one side so he could breathe properly. Then she made her way carefully to where the dying horse was threshing in agony. "Easy, big fellow," she soothed, kneeling by his back, patting his head, keeping clear of the thrashing legs. "Just take it easy, it won't hurt much longer." She found the big artery in the side of his neck and slashed deeply. The horse jerked with the first bite of the cut, then lay there, increasingly quiet as life drained from his body. Anne tried to avoid looking at the stream of blood that pulsed from the horse's neck, blood that ran across the slope, heading for the lip where the cliff dropped to the rocks below. She patted his head and talked softly, feeling sick, and not caring that she was crying. "Poor old boy," she soothed, and when it was all over, and the horse was dead, she went back to where Twanger was stirring, moaning.

"Don't you fight me now," she warned.

"Hey, little lady," he tried to smile, but his eyes, soft gray and large beneath his thick black brows, were filled with tears and she realized less than half a dozen years separated them in age.

"I'm gonna tie your hands behind your back, fella," she said calmly, "because if I don't, you're gonna knock my head right offa my shoulders when I move you."

"How bad is it?" he asked, putting his hands behind his back for her to tie them.

"Your leg," she said cheerfully, "is smashed to shit, and you better start getting used to the idea you might not have it much longer."

"Shoot me," he said calmly.

"Got no gun." She smiled at him and started trying to make up a joke about how just because you didn't have your leg much longer didn't mean your life had to be shorter, and when she knew he was concentrating, trying to make sense out of the nonsense she was saying, she put her hands on his shoulders and rolled him suddenly. He screamed like the horse had done and tears flowed from his eyes, curses from his mouth. She wiped his eyes with the tail of her shirt, then tied the mangled leg to the other one, trying not to listen to the screams and curses that poured from Twanger's throat.

"I'm sorry," he gasped, "but dammit, it hurts."

"Be thankful you're not having a baby," she comforted, and even in his pain he managed to grin.

"Now what I figure on doing," she explained carefully, "is sitting sorta under you with my arms around your chest and my legs around your waist, and a rope around us both. And when they start hauling us up, I'm gonna tighten my legs and hang on like hell. What you gotta do is try not to wiggle, because, even with your arms tied, you're a hell of a lot stronger than I'm ever gonna be."

"I'll try," he promised, sniffing, and she loosened his shirt and wiped his nose with the tail of it. "Goddammit," he muttered, face flaming, "I feel so stupid."

"Well, y'are," she snapped, "if a tiny thing like gettin' your nose wiped bothers you!" Then she hollered for Tom to pull them up again.

She was dragged across the slope and then her back was bumped against the rock face. As they started to move upward, she locked her legs around Twanger and scissored tightly. He was pouring sweat, tears streaming from his eyes, mucous coming from his nose and mouth, and though she tried to protect him as much as possible by keeping her own body between him and the rocks there were times when he roared in agony and she had to hang on desperately while he thrashed against her. It seemed to take forever before they were grabbed by strong hands and pulled to safety.

"I can't hold him any more," she sobbed. "I'm just not strong enough."

"It's okay, Twink," Tom said, reassuringly. "I've got him. You can let go now. You did good, you did real good," and then the ropes were being unknotted and she was lying on the ground, weeping, while Sarah pulled the shredded shirt from her back and exclaimed over the cuts and scratches.

"I'm okay," Anne insisted, trying to rise and finding herself unable to stand on shaking legs.

"Sure you are," the cook agreed, handing her a cup of lukewarm coffee, "and you'll be a lot better in half an hour or so."

They made camp early and Sarah gave Anne a fresh shirt. Tom and the cook both said her back would heal quicker without any bandages. "But if the shirt sticks to anything, don't pull on it," the cook warned. "You come to me and I'll soak it off with strong tea."

They stripped Twanger's clothes off, cutting away his pants and one-piece, and when he tried to cover himself with his hands, Sarah shook her head impatiently and covered him with a clean cloth. "I've seen worse," she snapped, and his face flamed bright red. "But I've never seen anything like that leg."

"Jesus, Tom," Twanger begged, "don't cut it off."

"Try not to," Tom promised.

They tied Twanger's arms to two small trees and lashed his body so he couldn't thrash around too much. The cook pulled a bag of some kind of herb from his possibles, and made a tea they forced down Twanger's throat.

"Indian tea," he explained briefly. "Inside 'a five minutes he won't know his ass from his elbow." When Twanger's eyes dulled and his face sagged, Tom and Sarah scrubbed the blood from the ruined leg and started trying to set the smashed bones. Even with the Indian tea, Twanger fought the ropes and screamed until Anne wanted to bend over and just let everything pour up out of her stomach.

"His heart's gonna give out soon," Sarah warned.

"Be finished soon," Tom promised.

When the leg was as well set as it would ever be, they splinted it with pieces of wood flattened and smoothed by the other men, and then they wrapped strips of cloth around the leg to hold the splints in place. A big bull of a man gave them the last shot of

183

whiskey he'd saved "in case of a rainy day," and Sarah, white-faced and shaking now that the emergency was nearly over, smiled her thanks and swallowed hers neat.

"I couldn't have done that," Anne gulped. "I can shoot 'em or cut 'em, but I can't hurt them like that."

"Twink," Tom assured her, "if you'd had to do it, you'd have done it."

For three days they kept Twanger so doped up on Indian tea he didn't feel anything. Every time he opened his eyes or groaned, Ruth held his nose and the cook pried open his mouth and poured more of the strange yellowish fluid down his throat. They rigged an Indian travois behind Babe and moved on steadily, Ruth watching Twanger and fussing over him with touching dedication.

Anne felt stiff and sore, her chest hurt where she'd banged against the rocks on the way down and her head seemed heavy, almost, but not quite aching. She spent more time than usual by herself. She had rope burns on her sides and arms, bruises on her backside, and a new patch on the seat of her pants. At night she tossed restlessly, hearing again the screams of Twanger, screams that in her nightmares blended with the screams of Twanger's horse, the screams of OtherOne, and she woke up covered with sweat and shaking.

"Honey, take it easy," Sarah soothed.

"I don't feel well," Anne confessed. "I feel like all I want to do is just sit down and cry for a whole bunch of stuff that isn't my fault but makes me feel guilty." She climbed out of her blankets and headed for the bushes.

She returned a few moments later, pale and wide-eyed. "Sarah, there's something wrong," she confessed, whispering with a shaking voice.

"What's wrong?" Sarah was wide awake now.

"I must 'a banged myself worse than I thought," Anne admitted. "I went behind the bushes for a pee and . . . I'm bleeding. Something must be . . . broke . . . inside."

"Oh, God!" Sarah sagged with relief. "Is that all?" And she gathered Anne in her arms, stroking her hair, soothing, reassuring and explaining.

---

184

"What's the moon got to do with it?" Anne asked, disbelievingly.

"I don't know," Sarah admitted, "but it does."

"Well," Anne remarked, staring down at the soft strips of cloth padded with moss, "I personally think it's a goddamn inconvenience!" When Sarah howled with laughter, Anne gave her an insulted look and walked back into the bushes, muttering to herself.

The following day Anne kept to herself, obsessed with the worry that the cloth and moss would prove inadequate and she would stain through her clothes, betraying herself to the men. By suppertime she was too tired to eat, and Sarah put some meat aside for her and tucked her into bed early.

"Kid's got a lot of guts," Tom remarked, and Sarah whirled, startled.

"Didn't hear you coming," she confessed.

"Didn't mean to scare you." He looked down at the sleeping girl, her face pale in the gathering dusk. "Is she okay?"

"Just tired," Sarah reassured him, "and her back is sore."

"Soon as we get to a bit of flat land," he promised, "we're going to take us a holiday. Just lie around in the sun and swat flies."

"If you see Saint Peter before I do," Sarah grinned, "tell him thank you for letting us into heaven."

They walked away from the campfire, away from the animals and the drowsy men. "My mother told me," Tom said quietly, "that a full moon was special. Said if you wished on it, you had a good chance of getting your wish."

"Want to try it?" Sarah asked softly, and he nodded, closed his eyes, crossed his fingers like a little kid and scrunched up his face.

The fire was burned down to embers and the camp asleep when Sarah crawled into her bedroll beside Anne. The girl opened her eyes sleepily, raised herself on one elbow and looked around.

"There's food beside you," Sarah said softly, then rolled on her belly, face turned toward Anne, and went to sleep immediately. Anne ate the food hungrily, went to the creek for a drink of water, and went back to her bedroll.

In the darkness she saw the flare of a match as Tom lit a cigarette, but they didn't say anything to each other. She just crawled back into the warm nest and went back to sleep.

They followed the creek for several days, the animals having an easy time of it on the well-beaten path. On the fifth day the creek was swallowed by an intercutting river that defied them sullenly, the thick yellow water effectively blocking their progress.

"There's supposed to be a fording," Tom shouted angrily.

"Well, there isn't," Martin, Tom's foreman, answered sourly.

"Who in hell would lay a path right down to the banks of that bastard anyway?"

"Fools like us, I suppose," Martin sympathized.

"Well, nothing for it but to make a bridge," Tom decided.

"You're out of your head, you know that, huh?"

"You got a better idea?"

"Me? No, I'm outta my head, too."

They made camp in the thick rich grass along the river bank, and tethered the horses where they could eat their fill. Dan rolled happily, then shook himself, his neck swelling and arching, his ears standing upright. The little mare with the spotted rump nickered teasingly, pretended to kick at him, and when he moved closer she bit his neck sharply. He pranced happily, shaking his head and rearing, his hooves striking sparks from the rocks.

"Guess that'll keep him busy for two or three days," Anne remarked. Sarah laughed and reached for the washtub. The little mare with the spotted rump spread her hind legs, half-squatted awkwardly, and spilled a stream of urine to the ground. Dan sniffed and trumpeted a challenge to the world, then chased after her along the riverbank. Sarah filled the washtub and placed it in the middle of the small fire.

"Ask cook if we can use some of his rope for clothes lines," she suggested.

"You know," Anne mused, stringing the rope between two small trees, "when we get where we're going those guys are going to be so busy standing in water getting rich, they won't have time to dry their clothes..."

"The thought had occurred to me, too."

"Well, I think I know how to make soap with ashes and fat..."

"Who does their cooking?" Sarah wondered.

"Can I talk you into doing my washing, too?" cook asked timidly. "I can see to it you get a coupla extra cups of coffee..."

"Sure." Sarah laughed easily.

For days they cut down trees and split them into sections with wedges and heavy mallets. Anne's hands blistered and her shoulders ached; Sarah's hands bled and she cursed angrily. "If I only weighed about sixty pounds more this bastard would split," she raged.

"If you weighed sixty pounds more," Tom teased, "your pants would split." But he didn't insult her by splitting the log for her, he just inserted another wedge and went back to work himself.

The clothes line had to come down; every scrap of rope was used making the bridge. When the day came for them to start putting the bridge across, everyone was very very quiet. Anne looked at the ropes coiled carefully on the bank, then at the massive bear of a man who had given Sarah his whiskey.

"You got the address of my family?" he asked quietly, eyeing the ugly yellow river.

"Yeah," Tom answered. "Listen... I can do it..."

"No," the man shook his head. "You'd never make it, boy. You're too skinny and you don't swim well enough. Me," he swelled his chest, and tried to grin, "my daddy was a shark and my momma was a devil fish. I was born with water in my lungs and a caul on my head. I could swim before I could walk and dive before I could talk and I might die hangin' off a tree by a length of rope, but being wet has never been a problem. I'm the biggest furriest whale you ever saw and this river's just a bit of spit." Then he walked into the hungry water, the ropes fastened securely around his waist, and he headed for the far bank, his arms stroking powerfully.

Nobody cheered, nobody shouted encouragement. They all stood in thick silence watching the man's shaggy head moving with painful slowness toward the far bank. Anne turned away, her throat closing painfully. "I'm not gonna watch," she promised herself, but how could she not watch, and she turned back again, her eyes searching the water until she found the small dot that was the burly man, now more than halfway across the river. Long agonizing minutes later a figure staggered ashore and fell to the ground, then rose to its feet, waved, and sat down suddenly. A ragged cheer rose from the anxious crowd.

"Soon as he's rested," Tom promised, "he'll climb a tree and tie that rope. That's when I start over. It'll be easier for me than it was for him. Then him and me'll set up a pulley over there and the real job'll start."

On the far shore, the burly man was waving his arms above his head. Tom waved back, started into the river, grabbing the rope. They could see the ant-like figure of the burly man, see Tom crossing the river much more quickly, but Sarah turned away, refusing to watch. When Tom was safe on the other side, he and the burly man attached the pulley and Martin pulled, then grinned, and the next volunteer headed into the river, stopping long enough to make the sign of the cross before grabbing the rope and starting across, half swimming, half dragged by Tom and the burly man.

"Okay, line up that bridge," Martin ordered, and they began to lay the rope and cross-bar rig on the bank. Martin and two men waded into the river, quickly tying the bridge, section by section, to the pulley rope. But the hungry water grabbed at the poles and planks, trying to take the first section before it was properly attached, and Martin was having trouble keeping his feet under him. Anne grabbed the rope snaking across the ground, raced once around a tree and braced herself, belly pressing the trunk of the tree. "I can't hold it," she screamed, feeling the rope burning into the palms of her hands, the river dragging it, only the tree keeping Anne from being pulled into the hungry water. A strong pair of arms reached around her, huge brown hands grabbed the rope, and the strain was gone from her shoulders.

"Good girl," a drover said, his teeth flashing white in his dark beard. She looked down at her hands, feeling the pain flaring.

"Guess I'm not much good at some things," she muttered.

"Oh, you'll do," the man grunted, hauling on the rope. Several others grabbed hold and pulled the bridge end back out of the water.

"Didn't even see it," one of them admitted.

"Old Eagle Eye was on the job," the man laughed.

"What's your name?" Anne asked suddenly.

"Dan. What's yours?"

"Dan?" She laughed. "That's my horse's name."

"What's yours?" he repeated.

"Anne."

"That's not *my* horse's name," he teased. "My horse is Clyde." Then he was gone, busy with the preparations for the dispatching of the bridge.

"Here," cook offered, "put some lard on them hands and next time, wear gloves!"

"Yes, Belle," Anne muttered, rubbing the lard on her bleeding palms.

By midafternoon they had the bridge suspended in place. The men on the far shore had heaved on the pulley rope until their backs had strained, and the wood and rope lattice had snaked across the river, the water tearing hungrily at it, pulling some of the crosspieces loose, but in the end the bridge had held together and now it hung over the river, barely clearing the yellow water.

"Goddamn this country," muscular Dan growled. "There's nothin' comes easy!"

The burly bearded man was the first one to use the bridge. He walked back from the other side on the swaying contraption, and when he stepped off the bridge, everyone clapped and cheered. He nodded calmly, then walked over to start preparing his animals for the crossing.

"I couldn't have done that," Anne admitted.

"That's two of us," Sarah agreed.

"I'm not even sure I can lead the horses across," she confessed.

"That's two of us!" Sarah nodded.

"That's three of us," Ruth corrected, face pale. Sarah put her arm around the little girl, hugging her reassuringly.

When it was their turn to cross they hugged each other, and started across the bridge. Anne led Dan with BelleTwo following her father trustingly. Sarah waited with her spotted-rump mare and the pack animals, watching Anne treading her way across the bridge warily. Halfway across she met Tom coming back and he winked at her. "Bet you wish you only had one horse," he teased.

"Don't remind me," she gritted grimly. "I've gotta go back!"

She had to tether Dan to a tree when he saw she was going back over the bridge. He fought the rope angrily, snorting as he watched his Anne step out on the swaying bridge again. Halfway back she met Sarah with the spotted-rump mare and the little mule. They smiled weakly at each other.

"Want me to take them the rest of the way?" Anne offered.

"I'll go back and start with the packers," Sarah agreed.

Dan calmed down when Anne returned and tied the mare next to him, but he still didn't like the idea of Anne starting back across the bridge again. She met Sarah less than halfway over, struggling with the packers who were beginning to panic.

"Whoa, there," she soothed. "Easy." She ripped strips from the tail of her shirt, blindfolded the pack animals so they couldn't see the danger below them, and watched Sarah heading across gingerly. Babe and Sunny were uneasy, unwilling to go near the bridge.

"I'll take them one at a time," she decided.

"I can bring Babe," Ruth said, firmly. "She trusts me."

"Wait until I'm nearly across," Anne suggested. "Then if you have any trouble I can give Sunny to Sarah and come back to help."

But Babe and Sunny gave no problem at all, and once all the animals were safely across, they continued on their way, leaving the swaying bridge in place for the next people.

---

# Chapter 11

$\text{T}$hree weeks later, tired and bruised, they looked down on the mess that was the gold panners' camp. Inadequate, hastily built shacks dotted the hillsides. The creek was fouled with dirt, silt and sand, and jerry-built wooden frames of miraculous invention sprawled everywhere, diverting water and running it over sluice frames, spilling earth and gravel back into the creek. They looked at the half-naked fanatic-eyed men standing in water panning gold or shoveling the gravel banks into the sluice boxes, and they knew that any one of them would kill his best friend for what he thought he had in his poke.

"I don't like this place," Anne decided.

"Can't say I'm too fond of it, either," Sarah agreed.

"Why'n't we just leave?" Ruth asked, reasonably.

"I'll be here two weeks," Tom said quietly. "By then I'll have sold all the supplies and we can head out. But we aren't going back the way we came. I'll never come that way again. From now on it's the Trail up from New Westminster."

"Is it easier?" Anne asked innocently.

"Oh, hell, yes." Tom grinned. "The Cariboo Trail is just a Sunday Stroll."

Within a half day, the teamsters had joined the mad mob in the creeks, fanatically searching for gold.

"Look at them damn fools," cook grumbled. "They don't even realize they drug all that stuff in themselves and then paid like hell to buy it so they could stay here and freeze off their feet this winter."

"I'll be warm," Twanger laughed, slapping the washtub with the flat of his hand.

"You sure you can handle it?" Anne worried.

"I'll make out just fine," Twanger promised. "I won't be able to hunt for meat, but Tom made me a deal on salt pork and dried beef and I can cook as good as Cookie can."

"Like hell you can," cook growled, insulted. "All you know is stew and bannock, beans and bannock and bannock and bannock."

"Yeah," Sarah teased. "You taught him everything you know and he still isn't very smart."

"God," Anne sighed. "I'll be glad to see the end of this place."

Twanger took over the laundry business. He could scour the dirtiest clothes clean in half the time Anne or Sarah could, simply because his hands were bigger and his arms stronger. He had problems hanging them up to dry until he fashioned a crutch for himself and then he became skilled at hopping to the lines with a bundle of wet clothes and draping them, one-handed, balancing on his crutch.

Anne hunted, Sarah and cook made mountains of bannock, Tom provided the flour and coffee, and they divided the profits equally. Anne left at first light and came back with her catch in time for cook to prepare it for supper. After a quick meal, she would join Twanger at the tubs or, if the clothes on the line were dry, she would take them down and fold them. There was no system at all for keeping track of who owned what. It was up to the men to settle those arguments themselves and many a fistfight broke out over the ownership of a pair of socks with fewer holes than usual.

"We could make a fortune here," Sarah mused.

"That's right," Anne agreed.

"But you don't want to stay."

"I hate this goddamn place," Anne flared. "I keep feelin' *eyes* eatin' holes into me. These guys got nothing else to do but act like idiots over some gold and stare at us."

---

"They won't bother you."

"They don't have to touch me to bother me. Just the look on their faces makes me feel dirty." She shook her head, upset. "I don't understand it. Nobody acted like that when we were with the pack train."

"We were all working together," Sarah explained. "Here, they don't trust themselves, let alone each other."

Tom's stock evaporated like liquor at a wake, and when most of his teamsters decided to stay and try to become millionaires over the winter, he offered Sarah and Anne jobs helping herd the pack animals back over the trail.

"I'll work your asses to nubs," he warned.

"Not mine you won't," Anne challenged. "I can out-ride, out-herd, out-talk and out-shoot you any day." Sarah laughed happily and began to pack for the trip back.

The trip out was no easier than the trip in had been, but it was faster. The animals weren't as heavily laden, and if there weren't as many hands to do the work, they were skilled hands, and the work was less. The trail out was almost choked with people determined to get to the gold fields before winter set in, and Tom muttered that if he could just find some way of getting back quicker, he could make a fortune packing in supplies.

"Greedy," Sarah teased. "If it was easy to get in, you wouldn't get the prices."

"I feel like a fish goin' against the current," Anne muttered.

"Now you know why I took the hard way in," Tom grinned. "You get stuck behind some of these fools and you'd never make it in. Bad enough tryin' to get out, unloaded."

"I'd sure hate to be tryin' to bring these animals in with a full load," Anne agreed. "This has got to be the worst place in the world."

Desperate men yelled and shouted, fought and went insane trying to get to the gold fields. They killed each other over real and imagined insults, over food and gold they hadn't even found yet. Roughly hacked out of the sheer cliff, the trail hung over the river below, and the over-burdened mules shied away from the lip of the trail, their eyes wide with fear, their drovers yelling constantly.

The slopes leading from the path to the river far below were littered with scattered supplies and the bones of fallen mules and drovers. In some places they had to put bandannas over their noses to try to screen the stench and the clouds of flies. Ruth refused to go anywhere near the edge, and Babe seemed more than happy to press close to the safe side of the path.

They had little trouble with the in-swarming horde. The bearded and desperate men took one look at the huge stud and his set-faced rider, the rifle in easy reach, the revolver riding comfortably on her hip, and they stopped their shouting, pushing and shoving and stood quietly for a moment while the outward train inched past carefully. Sarah and Ruth rode in the middle of the string of single-file mules. Tom brought up the rear, and both he and burly Dan, with the deep voice, kept their rifles in open sight.

Luck was riding somewhere in the file with them, too. They had just arrived at an unnaturally wide section of the trail and pulled out of the stream of traffic, when Dan started to snort and prance uneasily. Within seconds the other horses and mules were trembling and stamping, and only quick action kept them from stampeding. Anne grabbed Dan, and held his head against her body, talking soothingly, looking over her shoulder, trying to see what it was had the big stud so upset. He had ridden past the smell of blood and death, through swarms of biting flies, past men crazed with greed, rolling in the dirt, fighting and shouting, and never turned a hair. Now he was trembling with terror.

Only the trust their animals had for them saved them all from being dragged over the lip of the canyon.

"Where'd all the push go?" Ruth asked, her face white. "Everybody was pushin' and shovin' like normal just a couple of minutes ago, and now there's nobody." It was true. The trail toward them was empty, the last berserk gold seekers were almost out of sight down the path they had themselves just covered.

"What in Christ is that?" Tom breathed, staring past Anne.

"So help me, God," bearded Dan promised, "if we live through this, I'll never drink myself silly again."

They padded down the cruel trail, two at a time, moving with an ungainly rolling gait, their huge padded feet split like a cow's, their bizarre heads towering above the men who walked alongside, looking embarrassed to be seen in such strange company. The terror of their animals was pathetic, and Lucky spilled his bowels uncontrollably.

"Camels!" Sarah breathed disbelievingly. "I saw them in a circus once."

"Camels, my ass," Anne said inelegantly. "Camels belong on the desert."

"I'm telling you, those are camels," Sarah insisted.

"I heard," Tom said hesitantly, "that they were going to try using them."

"Why?" Anne shook her head. "They scare the very shit out of mules."

"Don't need much water," Tom explained, "and they carry a bigger load. They aren't bothered by flies, ticks or skeeters. They can eat stuff a billygoat'd puke on, and they're as surefooted as a deer."

"They just," Sarah said sarcastically, "stink like hell, and cause good horses and mules to fling themselves over the edge of the ravine!"

By the time the camels passed in front of them they had their hands full of hysterical mules and no breath or time to talk. For five minutes, they had all they could do to control their creatures, and when the unbelievable file had passed them, and the stench from the camels had begun to decrease, they began to feel they had some chance of keeping their pack train intact.

"Whoever had that bright idea," Anne raged, "is probably the son of the man who invented corsets and high heels!"

Dan wanted away from the place, and so did all the other animals, so they mounted and moved away quickly, leaving the scene of panic and terror. Each time they passed a pile of camel shit their animals snorted and jumped, and it wasn't until they heard the sound of a pack train coming toward them that their own animals began to calm down again.

"That's why there was nobody on the trail," Ruth said. "Nobody'll travel with those funny smellin' things."

Even at night the press into the gold fields continued. Men who hoped to make better time on a less-crowded trail pushed each other, shouted and argued and continued the confusion of the day, pushing past small fires where bone-tired men slept in numb exhaustion.

They were a week and a half away from the camel train, working their way downhill toward a valley in which nestled the beginning of what one day would be a small town.

"I'm goin' swimmin," Ruth promised aloud. "I'll be clean from top to bottom and I won't smell like a mule any more."

"Well," Sarah teased, "you'll be clean from top to bottom, anyway."

"How in hell," Anne blurted, "did they make it this far this fast!"

The foreman was cracking his whip, the dust rose like smoke, the small wiry men with the pigtails toiled, the picture was almost the same, but instead of flat prairie, they were toiling to build a roadbed along the very side of the trail the gold-crazed travelers had clawed out of the mountain.

"They couldn't, I suppose," Tom said sarcastically, "just follow the flatland along the river."

"Oh, hell," Ruthie sulked, "look, they caught him!" She pointed at one of the toiling workers.

"That's not him," Sarah decided. "It's another one."

"They all look alike anyway," Anne insisted stubbornly.

The Chinese barely glanced up as the mules and horses picked their way past them. They hammered at chisels, splitting the rock, loading it into baskets slung from long poles across the shoulders of other workers. The baskets of rock were laboriously trudged to where the flat roadbed was being built, dumped to fill holes and hollows and the barefoot, tired men returned for more loads. Behind them, as much a miracle as the mountain from which it was carved, the level grade angled down to the valley and the small town below.

"Gonna be a railroad!" bearded Dan crowed.

"Didn't need a railroad," Tom growled. "Those damn camels did a good enough job of ruinin' the countryside."

Mile after mile they rode past the toiling workers. Anne realized quickly enough they did not all look alike, but there was a similarity that went beyond the shape of their eyes, the color of their hair. They were all rake-thin, they were all exhausted, they were all thirsty and they all hated their foremen with a passion easily understood by one look at the scars on their backs and shoulders.

They made their way down the slope to the lush valley below, and camped alongside the river.

"I," Sarah announced flatly, "am not moving from here for a week."

"Dicker?" Tom grinned.

"What you got in mind?"

"Two days."

"Boy," Anne grumbled, "some people are always in a rush." But she felt a growing pressure within herself to get out of the hills and find a place to settle before the first frosts.

They were finishing their evening meal when the line of Chinese trooped back down the slope toward a cluster of shacks near their camp. Lying on the river bank, letting the evening breeze dry her long yellow hair, Anne watched openly as the workers were fed a meager ration of rice and a few overcooked vegetables, given a cup of tea and then left to their own devices. They pushed the starvation diet into themselves with little sticks, and then with organized precision, split into groups and began to save their own lives in the few hours remaining before dark. A number of them went to the river to check the nets and the wiers they had made in the rapids; others spread out looking for wild vegetables; and a few prowled knee-deep in water peering anxiously at the stones beneath their feet.

"Jade," Sarah explained. "They're looking for jade. It's worth more where they come from than gold is."

---

197

When the women rolled themselves in their blankets, the Chinese were still busy, washing their clothes, cooking the fish they'd caught, sharing the flesh equally and talking nonstop in their sharp, high-pitched voices. They were wakened in the morning by the yelling of the foremen as they herded the Chinese back up the hill to a full day of back-breaking labor on the railbed. Already the nets and wiers were reset, the clothes from the night before airing on lines between the inadequate shanties.

For the first time in days, Anne had a chance to go off by herself for a while, and she quickly took advantage of it. Digging her heels into Dan's glistening flanks she took off along the river bank to spend the day as far as she could from the sight of the cruel rocky trail. Her nostrils welcomed the cool scent of grass and trees. Twice she stopped to strip to her skin and swim in the deep pools where the water ran quietly, contrasting totally with the fierce rapids in the middle of the river. She ate cold food and napped in the sun, and, picking her leisurely way back, she came upon a large buck with an amazing rack of antlers. One shot through his left eye sent him crashing to the thick grass, fresh meat for hungry bellies. She looped her rope around his antlers and dragged him home over the thick green grass, Dan prancing easily, nostrils flared, head high, mane and tail blowing in the breeze.

The buck was hanging from a tree branch, head down, his entrails buried, when the Chinese returned that evening from their day of toil in the dust and heat. They stared, and one of them broke ranks to run to the dead animal, touch the antlers and jabber excitedly.

"What does he want?" Anne asked.

"I think he's just complimenting you on the rack," Tom offered. But when the Chinese returned later with several pieces of green-streaked rock and began to stroke the antlers and jabber again, they knew it was more than that. Finally, a second Chinese came over to translate.

"He wants to buy the antlers," the second man said in good, if accented, English.

"What does he want with them?" Anne wondered.

"At home they are medicine," the dusty man explained. "He wishes to buy them from you and send them home to his family."

"Well, he doesn't have to buy them," Anne said. "He can have them. They're no use to me." She reached for her knife and cut off the entire head of the animal and handed it over, with some difficulty, to the astonished worker.

"Are you sure," asked his companion, "that he cannot pay you for it?"

"Wouldn't be right," Anne said, "taking money for something that's really worth nothing." And she watched the two men walking back to their camp, waddling awkwardly with the antlers and head between them. Shrugging to herself at the strange ways of foreigners, she went back to oiling Dan's gear, and was almost lost in her work when a disgusted exclamation from shaggy Dan jerked her back to reality.

"Them slant-eyed little buggers is cookin' that deer head." He spat in the fire. "I never saw anything so dirty!"

"Try livin' on dust and hope," Sarah said shortly, "and you'll find that even rattlesnake and deer head taste good." She turned away, staring at the carcass of the deer.

"All right, all right," Anne said wearily, rising immediately. "I'll take the damn thing over to them. We can always get another one, I guess."

They took the venison, minus one haunch the cook refused to let leave camp, and went to the Chinese shacks with it. Wordlessly, Anne dropped the stiffened body from the back of a pack horse, letting it slip to the ground, while the Chinese stared at her suspiciously. She looked for the one she knew spoke English, but couldn't see him, so she just bowed, and hoped they would understand. Immediately they all bowed to her, and she and Sarah walked away leading the pack horse, feeling more than a bit foolish.

The one that spoke English was down by the river, lashing logs securely into a raft, and he jumped guiltily when Anne surprised him.

"I didn't hear you coming," he admitted.

"That's because I'm not wearing my boots," she answered.

---

199

"I always hear the foremen before they get here."

"They probably sleep in their boots." She eyed the raft, looked out at the river and then at the raft again. "You'll never make it," she offered.

"I'll make it," he insisted, grimly. "Either I will get to New Westminster, or I will die. Either is better than living like this."

"Why don't you just take off overland?"

"The first person who saw me would know I am supposed to be working on that railbed. They'd bring me back for the reward. Then the foreman would whip me until he was too tired to whip me any more," he explained. "Six men have died that way already. I do not want to be the seventh."

"You'd rather be the first to drown in the river, huh?"

"Nobody has tried the river. Six men tried the other way."

She looked at the raft and shook her head in disbelief. "You built this yourself?"

"A bit every night for the past month. I steal some rope here, I steal some spikes there. Tonight," he smiled openly, "I steal the stove from the cook shack."

"Sure you do," she agreed, laughing with him, knowing he was teasing her.

"Sure I do," he repeated, waving at her as she turned away.

It was still dark when the shouts and gunshots wakened her. She didn't even pull on her boots. She just grabbed her rifle, whistled for Dan, jumped on his back and headed in the direction of the river bank, already sure the English-speaking Chinese had been spotted with his raft.

Two of the foremen were trying to hold the desperately struggling man, while a third yelled conflicting orders at them. As Anne charged up on Dan one of the two glanced up, surprised by the hoofbeats. In that second the Chinese was loose, and a flurry of kicks and blows sent both men to the grass and allowed the wiry little foreigner to shove his raft from the bank into the water, where it began to drift away at increasing speed.

"Stop that Chink!" the third foreman yelled. "He'll drown for sure!"

The Chinese jumped into the water, swam furiously, caught

up with his raft and scrambled aboard. In the thin moonlight Anne could see the potbellied stove in the middle of the raft, spiked to the logs with huge railroad spikes stolen from the supply shed. She wondered what would happen if the spikes the little man had stolen were needed. What if they got the railroad almost built and then ran out of spikes. Would they think to take some of the gold in the river, gold washed from the creeks to the north, and fashion a golden spike to finish their job?

One of the men threw a rope and snagged a log, pulling the raft sideways. The Chinese scrambled to a box near the cast-iron stove, brought out a stolen hatchet, and slashed at the rope. A shot dug into the log near the pigtailed head. Hatchet still in hand the little man ran for the potbellied stove, jumped in and closed the door behind him, bullets zinging from the metal.

"Haul that celestial son of a bitch back in here," the head foreman yelled. "I'll teach the whole pack of them a lesson they'll never forget."

Automatically, the rifle swung to her shoulder, she sighted quickly, fired two shots, and the already frayed rope snapped. The raft swung out into the white water and the railway men cursed viciously. "Sorry," she smiled, "only tryin' to help." And she nudged Dan, swayed her body slightly, and the big stud pranced back toward the campsite. Anne was climbing back into her bedroll when she heard the sound of horses' hooves charging through the night.

"Cut him off at the shallows," a voice ordered. "The river curves, but we don't have to."

"Goddamn fools," she raged, struggling out of her blankets, reaching for her rifle, ready to do whatever needed to be done to slow them down, to give the desperate little man some chance at freedom. In the moonlight, she saw Ruth leap up, ripping open a sealed package she pulled from under her shirt. The girl reached inside the package, pulled something out, molded it with her two small hands, then threw, her wiry arm whipping through the air, a grin already cutting her face. As Ruth wiped her hands on her pantlegs the posse horses went insane. Riders flew through the air, horses squealed and kicked. Dan whickered uneasily and the mules all went berserk, breaking their tether ropes and charging through the night braying and bucking. One by one the members of the posse hit the dirt, one by one their horses ran off into the night, and, one by one, Ruth, Anne, Sarah and eventually even the enraged teamsters, stopped laughing and began the nightlong job of rounding up the terrified mules.

"I know camel shit when I smell it," Anne accused, and Tom stared mournfully at Ruth, his eyes red-rimmed from lack of sleep, his clothes stained and torn.

"Why'd you do it?" he asked.

"So's they wouldn't catch him," she said openly.

"Oh, I can understand that part of it," Tom said carefully. "What I'm askin' is how come you been walking around for a week or more with a package of camel shit stuffed under your shirt?"

"Because," Ruth said reasonably, "I'm ten years old and I never saw camel shit before in my life. None of us ever saw it before. So I figured there couldn't be much of it, and what there isn't much of is usually worth a lot of money."

"You thought," Tom said carefully, "that camel shit might be worth something?"

"Why not?" Ruth asked, puzzled. "If people will fight for some gold dust . . . and there's more of that than there is camel shit . . ." She stared with insulted dignity as Anne rolled on the ground, laughing hysterically.

In the morning, they packed their things, and rode from the valley, moving back up to the trail, watched by the Chinese workers. Nobody waved, nobody smiled, nobody spoke, but Anne knew she felt a kinship with each and every one of them, and she realized she was seeing them all as individuals: They didn't look at all alike after all.

It seemed to rain a lot on this side of the mountains. Sometimes it drizzled, sometimes it spit, sometimes the water poured from the sky in a mind-numbing stream.

"Goddamn," Sarah cursed bitterly, "the rain gets you wet on

the way down and then it hits the ground, splashes back up and gets you wet again. The trees are so big you have to take a four-day detour around them, and the fog is so thick you can catch bronchitis just breathin' it in."

"Pickypicky," Anne teased. "You thought it was real pretty when the sun was shining."

"That whole five minutes the sun shone?" Sarah frowned. "I can hardly remember what it looked like."

But when the rain stopped, the scenery was worth every drop that had fallen. The trees aimed themselves at the heart of the sky, the rocks and cliffs sent minor waterfalls splashing to the creeks, and Anne could not believe the amount of wild game in the woods.

"We could live out here forever and not miss a meal!" she gloried.

"Yeah," Sarah groused, "if we didn't drown in the rain."

Just knowing they were within days of the end of the grinding toil of the mountain trail spurred them all. They barely took time for meals, now, pressing on eagerly from dawn until just before it got dark. Even the animals seemed to know the worst was behind them and trotted quickly down the increasingly gradual, grassy slopes.

Below them, the wide muddy river stretched lazily, the haste and fury of its higher reaches lost in the placid brown. Along the banks, left to bleach dry on the mud, branches, stumps and tree trunks lay under the sun, tangled crazily with bits and pieces of gear that had tumbled from the treacherous trail and been swept away by the churning white froth they had followed for so long. A wagon wheel, spokes missing, tangled in the leafless top of what had once been a tree. Some bones, never identified, lay exposed on a sandbar.

Four days later they sat on their horses staring at the bustle and activity of Fort Langley, unable to believe their eyes.

"Where did they all come from?" Anne marveled.

"Back East, I guess," Ruth answered.

"Well," Anne grinned, "if they did they must have left the jamtarts on the other side of the mountains!"

---

"They say," Sarah teased, "that out here the men are real men and so are half the women."

"That doesn't make any sense," Ruth decided, nudging Babe and riding toward the town.

At the hotel they soaked in hot soapy water until all traces of the vicious trek were scrubbed from their skins, then dressed in new clothes from the skin out. Ruth pranced happily in her lace-front boots, and preened in front of the cracked mirror. They ate mediocre food at the hotel dining room, but it was served on real plates. Their table had a white cloth only slightly stained, and there were flowers in a vase and real glasses for their wine.

"I could get used to this," Ruth confided.

"Really?" Sarah teased.

"Really," the child said firmly.

They slept that night in real beds, with real sheets and blankets. Ruth was in a small bed near the window; Anne and Sarah curled up together in a double bed across the room. In the morning they met Tom and the cook in the hotel dining room for a last breakfast together.

"You're sure?" Tom insisted. "It's just another day or so."

"No," Sarah smiled faintly. "It's easier from here."

"Okay." He nodded, looking away, and signaled the waiter for more coffee.

"You still willing to trade the pack horses and big mule for two riding mares?" Anne asked.

"Sure." He grinned. "But I warn you, I'm getting the better of the deal."

They stood on the dusty street watching the string of mules moving away from them, moving south, to where Tom had his own place. Cook turned and waved repeatedly, but Tom didn't look back once.

"Well," Sarah said suddenly, "that's that. Let's go spend our wages on supplies."

They headed West, with Dan proudly leading the caravan, BelleTwo and Lucky following happily, Sunny and Babe walking stolidly together, the spotty-rump mare and the two new sorrels bunching together companionably.

They rode past homesteads and farms, past incipient towns and bustling villages, and camped just outside the pushing madness of New Westminster. Ships from all over the world were tied up at the rough wharf. Half-naked, sweating men unloaded crates of every possible description and reloaded cargoes of logs cut from the towering green forest surrounding the raw and ugly town. Every language known to woman fought for supremacy in the teeming streets, and Anne complained several times of headache and fatigue.

"I can't stay here, Sarah," she blurted. "I can't stand the goddamn push and shove."

"Just a few days more," Sarah urged. "Maybe we'll get used to it."

"Hey!" Ruthie exclaimed, pointing excitedly. "Lookit that!"

Anne turned, her eyes sweeping the dock, searching for something to look at, discounting the crates and boxes, the net slings and bustling crowd.

"He damn-well made it!" Anne capered, ignoring the muttered curses of the sweating dockworkers. She dodged through the crowd and stood staring down at the battered raft tied to the dock, the bullet-scarred potbellied stove still securely fastened to the rough decking.

"No sign of his box," Ruth remarked.

"He's taken it with him." Anne laughed. "He's taken his damn box of jade and got on a ship and he's on his way home this very minute!"

"How'd you know that?" Ruth demanded.

"I know," Anne assured her. "I just know."

"It's the only thing that makes sense," Sarah agreed.

Anne turned, looked at the sprawling city stretching from the bustling docks, the miles of rich flat land waiting to be tilled and harvested.

"If you want," she said slowly, "we could file a claim on some land and start farming."

"What do you want to do?" Sarah asked carefully.

"We could run a bakery," Anne continued, "or we could open a store, or we could start a laundry, or we could hire out as muleskinners, or we could . . . we could do," she said slowly, "any goddamn thing we wanted to do."

"What do *you* want to do?" Sarah repeated.

"I'm stayin' with you guys," Ruth said flatly, and turned away, her mind made up, her future decided.

"I want to see the ocean," Anne said slowly, "and I want to swim in the salt sea. I want to find exactly the right place to build exactly the house we want, and I want to grow my own crops and catch my own fish and shingle my own roof and never ask anybody for anything. I want," she added firmly, "to get away from this festerin' mess and live my own goddamn life."

"So why stand here?" Sarah grinned. "We can do that. Easy."

Early afternoon sunlight slanted through the trees. Behind them, the frenzy and furor of the growing town receded. Dan lifted his hooves high, neck arched, dancing on the thick under-layer of pine needle and moss. The other horses followed him willingly. Anne looked over at her two friends and grinned, and then they were all three of them laughing together, riding west toward the sea, toward the path the sun leaves when it dips beneath the trackless water, riding toward a tomorrow they would carve for themselves, their laughter spilling like pure water over stones, like golden light or warm love.

"We can do 'er!" Anne promised. "My momma spent all her life scratching rock and dust, and she probably never saw anything like this the whole time."

"You said you didn't give a damn if you never went farming again," Sarah teased.

"Sarah!" Anne was serious. "This wouldn't be farming! This would be the closest thing to fun you could have without a fiddle!"

# Chapter 12

The trees thrust themselves at the blue sky and the horses' hooves sank softly into the thick underlay of mulch and composting leaves. The sun slanted through the half-dark green-tinged air in bright shafts, and the air was rich with the sound of birdsong. Suddenly they were out of the forest and their eyes could see what their noses had been aware of for hours. Rolling and tossing as far as the mind could imagine, a vast sheet of gray, green and blue, bigger than any lake, bigger than anything they'd dreamed, and they just sat on their horses and stared. Then they rode slowly toward the water, not speaking, and dismounted slowly. Anne walked forward, dipped her hand in the white froth at the water's edge and put her fingers in her mouth.

"It's salty!" she shouted happily. "The sea is salty!" And then she was pulling off her boots and socks, rolling up her pants and walking knee-deep into the water.

"You'll get wet!" Sarah warned.

"I don't care."

"It's cold!"

"I don't care!"

"Look out!" Ruthie yelled as she charged past Anne, her bare skin gleaming in the sunlight, the water splashing brightly.

"Come on," Anne invited, diving into the water with her clothes on, reaching for Ruthie and ducking her head under the waves, "come on, Sarah."

"Not me," Sarah said firmly, but after a few minutes of watching safely from the shore she stripped off her clothes and joined the two younger women, splashing and swimming, laughing and teasing.

"There's entire days and weeks of my life where it's as if nothing at all happened," Anne panted. "I know I must have eaten and slept and worked and lived, but I don't remember a single thing. This is something I am never going to forget as long as I live."

"It'll sure be something to tell our grandchildren," Sarah agreed, picking a white shell up and turning it over in her hand. "What kind of thing do you suppose lived in this?"

"I don't know." Anne laughed. "I never saw one before."

The wind grew cold and the waves splashed against the rocks with increasing force. They hurried into dry clothes and walked the curve of the beach, their eyes drinking in every new sight. Ruth's collection of strange shells grew and the horses licked curiously at the wet rocks but wouldn't drink the salty water. They found a freshwater stream running into the sea and caught half a dozen yellow-bellied fish that seemed equally at home in salt or fresh water.

They camped near the stream, the canvas stretched between two strange trees with peeling red bark and leaves that seemed unaffected by the rain. The ground was thick in the unusual leaves, and Sarah kicked at them casually.

"You'd think they'd rot when they fell," she remarked. "Most leaves do."

"Maybe everything's different here," Anne suggested.

They cooked the fish and tried some of the things in shells like the first one Sarah had found. They had no way of opening the oysters but Anne guessed, rightly, that they would probably open in the heat from the fire, and she set them on the rocks.

"I don't know what it is," Sarah decided, "but it's not half bad."

"Sure beats salt pork." Anne reached for another oyster eagerly.

The sound of the waves lulled them to sleep and in the morning they woke to the cry of gulls and breakfasted on more oysters and some oddly shaped blue things Anne tugged off a rock exposed by low tide.

"Don't know what these are either," she admitted, "but they eat good."

They found, to their surprise, that you can't lather soap in salt water and if you wash your hair in it, you have an awful time rinsing the salt from your hair with fresh water from the stream. Anne tried drinking some seawater and was promptly sick. "Won't try that again," she decided. "I feel betrayed."

"You might feel betrayed, but you look green," Sarah teased.

The horses knew they were on holiday. The mare with the spotted rump was getting a bit round in the belly and when Anne said she supposed they'd get an awfully pretty foal in the late spring, Sarah looked surprised.

"Why do you think Dan's a stud?" Anne teased.

"Is it safe to ride her?"

"Why, you afraid she'll go wild and throw you? Of course it's safe to ride her. She's not sick!"

They had seen so little sign of people that when they spied the large log cabin and the stock shed nearby, they weren't sure whether to ride up yelling a greeting or ride by quietly before they got shot.

"No smoke," Sarah observed.

"No sign of much of anything," Anne added. "Don't even see a bloody chicken! What kind of a farm's got no chickens?"

They rode up slowly, keeping to the open ground so that nobody would think they were sneaking up stealthily.

"Haloo," Anne called, but nobody answered.

They dismounted and walked into the cabin. It was empty. No fire in the hearth, no warmth in the small metal stove.

"Hasn't been a fire here for weeks," Anne decided, testing the ashes with her fingers.

"Dishes on the shelves . . . pots . . . table and chairs," Sarah itemized. She walked to a side door and opened it. "Beds . . . with blankets on and everything . . ."

"Here, too," Ruth said, opening the other door. "Looks like kids' beds."

"Anne, I'm scared!"

"Why? There's nobody here!"

"That's why I'm scared!"

There were signs of a garden, started, but destroyed by animals and weeds, and just beyond the garden, side by side, two graves and a single shared wooden cross.

"Who buried them?" Ruth whispered.

"I don't know," Anne tried to keep her voice from shaking, "but it sure explains why everything here is so well started and then suddenly unfinished."

"Maybe we ought to leave," Sarah said.

"The dead won't hurt you," Anne insisted. "It's the living you have to watch out for!"

They pulled the weeds from the graves and placed the shells Ruth had collected and saved on the now tidy mounds of grassed-over earth.

They were subdued the rest of the afternoon and evening. After they had fed, watered and bedded the horses and unpacked their personal gear, they had supper and cleaned up, and then walked on the beach, each one thinking about the quiet graves. Sarah found some more particularly pretty shells and took them back to place with the others.

"I wish we had some flowers," she said softly, then turned and went into the cabin.

Anne spent her days bringing driftwood from the beach and stacking it in the woodshed to dry for winter fuel. She collected and experimented with shellfish and sea life, and found a place where they could string a length of netting between some large rocks and a tree on the shore. At low tide they could go out to bring in the net and remove the trapped fish. Her attempts at making fish hooks had little success, but she did find a way to fashion a crude spear that, once in a while at least, would pierce into a sleek fish.

"I don't know if it's made wrong or if I'm just a poor shot," she complained after a fruitless afternoon. The wind was howling down the inlet, blowing the waves to a froth, and the driftwood crackling in the open hearth seemed more cheerful and welcoming than usual.

"Well," Sarah said resignedly, "you've got the whole winter to practice."

They chinked some cracks in the walls of the cabin, using mud and smoothing it in with their fingers.

"Probably didn't even happen until the place was empty," Anne remarked. "They kept things up real good for as long as they could."

The tools in the shed were in good repair, and Sarah was sure that if the two people sleeping under the grass by the garden had been able, the garden itself would have thrived. Only after they were gone had the deer savaged the crop.

After the first few weeks cursing the eternal rain, Sarah resigned herself to the fact she couldn't turn it off and she put on a slicker and went walking with Anne and Ruth. When the rain finally turned to snow, she cheered with delight and bombarded them with snowballs.

The fogs that rolled in frightened her at first. She insisted she could hear people moving in the fog, insisted there were eyes staring out of it at them.

"Don't be silly," Anne soothed. "They wouldn't see us any better than we can see them."

"What's the matter with me," Sarah sobbed. "I never used to be like this! Nervous and bitchy, crying and sulky."

"Well," Anne said, trying not to sound as if she agreed with her too much, "it's kind of boring here in the winter."

She began coaxing Sarah to join her in the daily walks on the beach. At first Sarah complained that the damp salt air penetrated even the warmest jacket and chilled her to the bone, but she began to look forward to the ever-changing beach. Anne would gather the seaweed that washed up on the tide and take it home to spread on the garden. She didn't know why she was doing it, exactly, "but it smells like something you'd find out behind a barn." She grinned, and Sarah agreed readily. They found rounded worn black rocks on the beach and one day, with nothing better to do with her time, Sarah idly tapped two of them together. Sitting on a damp log, staring out over the slate-gray expanse of water, humming a nameless tune, she rapped the stones to keep time to her own music. The stones cracked and sifted apart in her hands.

"It's coal!" Anne exclaimed happily.

"You're kidding."

"I tell you it's coal! Now nobody has to get up in the middle of the night to stoke the fireplace!"

They began taking a basket from the shed with them when they went to the beach, bringing home coal, clams, oysters, mussels, and the fish they caught in their net.

They hauled water from the well in buckets and carried it into the cabin to heat on the small stove in a big pot and a small boiler, and then struggled to bathe in the washtub that was really just half a barrel.

"Sure do miss the big washtub," Anne grumbled, kneeling in front of the hearth and washing her long blonde hair.

"If your beloved ocean wasn't so salty," Sarah teased, "you could bathe out there and not have to wash crystals out of your hair."

"If it wasn't salty," Anne corrected, "it wouldn't be the sea."

"You sit under this low roof much longer," Sarah warned, "with rain banging almost on your head and fog making everything look different, and you're going to wind up so philosophical nobody is going to be able to live with you."

"Except you," Anne contradicted, "and you only live with me because nobody else'll live with you." Sarah laughed happily and crossed over to help.

"Maybe I should cut it," Anne muttered. "It's down to my backside."

"Yeah, but it's up to your head."

"Oh, wow, listen to who's philosophising now!"

She emptied the soapy water and refilled the half-barrel tub for Sarah's bath. Sarah stripped and began to wash, shivering slightly in the draft that crept under the front door when the wind blew a certain way.

"This sitting around doing nothing but eat and bitch must agree with you," Anne mused, brushing her hair in the heat from the hearth. "You're getting tubby."

"It's not the food," Sarah replied, hiding her face behind the washcloth and hoping she sounded as casual as she meant to sound. She rubbed her face briskly.

"What is it then, the salt air?" Anne asked idly, and then Anne froze and stared at Sarah openly. The silence stretched. Sarah lowered the face cloth, rinsed it, wiped soap from her face, scrubbed her ears, then finally caught and returned Anne's gaze.

"Do I have to guess?" Anne's voice was guarded.

"You might have to guess now," Sarah said quietly, "but in a few months it'd be plain for anybody to see."

The silence stretched uncomfortably. Sarah washed her hair, now down past her shoulders, rinsed it, wrapped a towel around her head and stepped from the tub. She dried herself, and was putting on clean clothes before Anne finally spoke.

"Tom?"

"Yes."

"What about his wife?"

"She'll never know. Neither will he." Sarah began to drag the awkward tub to the door, and in the small bedroom Ruth rolled over, disturbed by the scraping. Anne rose, helped Sarah in silence, and they poured the soapy water outside, left the half barrel on the top step, went back into the warm cabin, and tried to ignore the silence.

"Christmas next week," Anne said suddenly, her voice determinedly unconcerned. "I think Ruth would really enjoy a tree. I would, too," she admitted.

---

"Christmas?" Sarah echoed, puzzled. "A tree?"

"Sure." Anne shrugged. "Why not? We could make decorations with shells and things."

"If you'd like." Sarah stared at Anne, hurt in her eyes, but Anne turned away, twisting her hair into a long braid, ignoring all the questions she refused to ask, all the answers she refused to hear.

Late that night she was wakened by the sound of Sarah weeping. She rolled over in bed, patting Sarah's shoulder gently, and Sarah rolled toward her, cuddling close and crying.

"What's wrong?" Anne asked softly.

"You're disgusted."

"No, I'm not," she soothed, stroking Sarah's shoulders. "Now wipe your eyes and go to sleep. You'll wake Ruth with your crying."

"I don't care." Sarah hiccuped. "You hate me."

"No, I don't."

"Yes, you do. You're disgusted and you hate me. You think I'm a tramp, and . . . and you're mad."

"I am not."

"Yes, you are."

"*Sarah*," Anne snapped, "will you stop telling me I'm mad when I'm not mad? It makes me mad!"

"I knew it." Sarah sat up, accusingly. "I knew you were mad."

"I wasn't mad until you started telling me how I feel. You're always telling me how I feel. Before *I* know how I feel, you're telling me how I feel. And I don't!"

"Well, then, what do you feel?"

"I don't know," Anne said angrily, "but I'm not mad!"

"You are so. You just said you were mad."

"I'm mad at you telling me how I feel all the time, but I'm not mad about you being pregnant. So now will you roll over and go to sleep?"

"Well, if you weren't mad, why didn't you talk?"

"I talked."

"About Christmas trees. Not about what we'd been talking about!"

"I didn't know what to say," Anne admitted. "So I said nothing."

"You always do that," Sarah accused. "Something happens and you don't say anything about it until later."

"Well, what's to say? I didn't know what to say."

"You could have told me how you were feeling about it."

"What difference does it make how I feel about it? Nothing's going to change the way it is. Go to sleep."

"See, you're doing it again! You won't talk."

"What do you want me to say, for chrisssakes!"

"Don't shout."

"Okay. I won't shout. Tell me what you want me to say."

"I want you to tell me how you feel about my having a baby."

"I don't know. I haven't thought about it much."

"I don't want to know what you *think*, I want to know how you *feel*."

"I feel," Anne said angrily, "tired. I feel like if you don't lie down and go to sleep, I'm going to go sleep on the floor in the kitchen. Or in the extra bed in Ruth's room."

"I knew it," Sarah said with grim satisfaction. "You're so disgusted you don't even want to sleep in the same room as me."

"That's just it," Anne shouted. "I *do* want to sleep. Only you won't let me!"

"What are you guys yellin' about?" Ruth demanded from the doorway, glaring at them. "I can't sleep with your noise."

"It's her!" Sarah snapped. "She's the one shouting."

"You were the one crying," Ruth corrected. "That's what woke me up first."

"She was crying because she's going to have a baby," Anne explained.

"I was not crying because of that!" Sarah denied.

"You really going to have a baby?" Ruth's grin spread.

"Yes, I am!" Sarah said defiantly.

"So why were you crying?"

"She thinks I'm mad at her," Anne growled.

"Are you?"

"No, I'm not!"

"Then tell her that." Ruth turned back to her room, yawning. "And let's get back to sleep."

They sat up in bed watching the smaller figure go into her room and close the door.

"I'm not mad," Anne said quietly, "and I am not disgusted. I'm afraid."

"Afraid of what?"

"Sometimes," Anne confessed, "I'm a very jealous person."

# Chapter 13

They cut down a small evergreen and stood it on the table, holding it upright in a lardpail full of stones and wet sand. They decorated it with sea shells, bits of sand-and-sea-carved driftwood, ribbons and bright red berries from some of the bushes in the forest behind the barn. The berries were bitter and they never ate them, but even in winter there were birds in the bushes.

There were trees, too, the names of which they didn't know; trees that had clusters of orange berries that, like the red ones, weren't fit to eat, but made Christmas decorations. Each had hidden in their packs, hidden since they stocked up at Fort Langley, presents for the other. New hairbrushes, bars of mildly scented soap, skin cream and perfume.

"And potatoes!" Anne marveled. "How did you manage to hide them?"

"It wasn't easy," Sarah admitted, laughing.

"Let's eat one each today and keep the others for seed to plant in the garden," Anne suggested.

"They're your potatoes."

Anne cooked the potatoes carefully, baking them in the ashes in the hearth. They had shellfish and sea-run trout caught in the net across the nearby stream, rice and dried beans cooked together, dried-apple sauce and a pot of tea.

"What was it you said your mother said whenever she felt lucky?" Sarah asked, stretching and yawning.

"Wouldn't let the king say he was kin," Anne repeated.

"Well, that's how I feel. I wouldn't let the king say he was kin."


Christmas was followed by several weeks of violent storms. Sometimes the rain washed all the snow from the ground and the horses filled themselves on winter grass; other times the snow fell in thick white soggy flakes and covered everything with slush.

"One thing about the weather around here," Anne tried to cheer Sarah, "if you don't like it, wait half a day and it's sure to change."


By the end of what they figured was February, the snow was as good as gone for the year. It rained day and night, a slow drizzle or a torrential downpour. The wind blew, gentle or strong, and the fog sometimes lasted for days. Sarah threatened to pack and leave but was laughing when she said it.

They woke one morning as the sun was just beginning to brighten the room. Anne stirred slowly, wondering what it was she had heard, or thought she had heard. Whatever it was, she didn't hear it again, and she and Sarah dressed sleepily, then went to the adjoining kitchen. Sitting on the floor, all around the room, with the fire in the hearth newly fueled and beginning to burn happily, sitting almost naked and staring at the two women, were ten brown-skinned slant-eyed black-haired Indian men.

"Oh, sweet Jesus," Sarah gasped.

"Now I lay me down to sleep, I pray the Lord my soul to keep. If I should die before I wake, I pray the Lord my soul to take," Anne said softly, then added, "I'm sorry, Lord, it's the only prayer I can think of right now."

The Indians just sat and waited, eyeing the women with expressionless faces, looking around them as if they had been here before and noticed the changes but didn't find them remarkable at all.

"Do you think they killed those people?" Sarah asked in a whisper.

---

218

"If they did, they buried them, too," Anne replied. "Well, if they aren't going to do anything...I am!" She began to make breakfast. The Indians watched. She mixed enough bannock to feed twice the number of people in the cabin, then sliced and began to fry steaks from the deer she had shot when it came down to see if there was anything left to eat in the garden.

"Make a gallon of tea," she suggested and Sarah nodded, and walked outside to get water from the well. One of the men turned slowly, keeping an eye on her through the open door and when he saw her hauling the bucket from the well he walked out of the house, went over, and took the bucket from her. He spoke rapidly in a language that seemed to be mostly bird calls, clicks and hisses. When she just stared at him he reached out, patted her belly, and scolded gently, shaking his head as if she was the dumbest thing he had ever seen. Then he carried the water into the kitchen and told the others what had happened. They all frowned disapprovingly, shook their heads and seemed to wonder how anybody could expect to get a healthy baby by abusing themselves so.

"I wish I knew what they were saying," she whispered to Anne.

"Well, someone has to be in charge," Anne decided, "and he's got the bear claws."

She handed the young man with the bear-claw necklace the first mug of tea. He took it politely, and stared at her. "Show him what to do," Ruth suggested from the doorway to her room. Anne nodded, took a sip of tea and smiled. The Indian smiled but made no move to imitate her. "Here," she handed the cup to Sarah, "you show him." Sarah sipped tea, smiled, and the young Indian man smiled, raised his mug and sipped tentatively. Then passed his mug to the young man on his right. Who sipped tea, smiled, and passed the cup to the next young man.

"Bannock," Anne said, breaking off a piece and chewing. She was so scared her mouth was dry and the bannock stuck to the roof of it. She was sure she would never be able to swallow. Sarah offered bannock to the men, each one took a piece, smiled and chewed obediently. Anne turned quickly and began to take meat from the frying pan. "Venison," she said with a smile.

"Mowitch," the young man corrected, smiling and reaching for a piece.

"It's hot," Ruth warned, coming from her doorway and sitting near the young man. He smiled, took the meat in his fingers and began to eat it, using a piece of bannock to catch the juice. And suddenly they were all eating, talking, sipping tea and giving every indication of enjoying themselves. They noticed the supply of food was dwindling, and the same man who had taken the water from Sarah put some dried fish on the table and gestured to the women to eat.

"Better eat," Anne suggested. "He might slit your throat if you don't."

"Hey, it's good!" Ruth blurted, and the men all chuckled softly. More tea and more smiles, and then the young man with the bear-claw necklace stood up, spoke to them and gestured them to follow him. He led them to the two graves and began to speak to them, eyeing the sea shells and pointing questioningly.

"He wants to know who put the shells there," Ruth decided.

"We did," Anne pointed at herself, then at Sarah, then knelt and tidied the graves, removing some blown leaves and twigs, setting the shells in place properly and straightening the single shared cross that somehow always tilted in a stiff wind. The young man nodded, spoke to the others who nodded, as if satisfied, then they all moved back to the cabin. When the Indians saw Anne and Sarah automatically wipe their feet on the piece of sacking by the door, they copied the gesture, wiping their bare feet almost ceremoniously. They had two more cups of tea and then rose, obviously ready to leave. Impulsively, Anne cut a haunch of venison and handed it to the man who had helped Sarah.

"Meat," she nodded.

"Mowitch," he agreed.

"He said that before," Sarah remembered. "You said venison, he said 'mowitch.' Now you say meat, and he says 'mowitch.'"

"Deer?" Anne suggested.

"Mowitch," he said firmly, and Ruth laughed suddenly and put her hands at her head like antlers.

"Mowitch?" she asked, and the men nodded. Then as quietly as they had arrived, they were gone, heading down to the beach where long wooden dugouts were waiting on the sand.

"Guess we should go down and see them off," Sarah suggested. "We don't want to insult anybody."

They stood on the beach and waved good-bye. The Indians raised their paddles and whooped in unison, and then they dug the paddles into the sea and the dugouts skimmed across the water, the Indians chanting in rhythm, the paddles digging and lifting as if controlled by one man. The young man with the bear-claw necklace stood in the prow of the lead dugout, lifted his arm in farewell, and smiled.

"They're like no Indians I ever heard about," Anne said, sitting down suddenly. "No horses, no feathers, no guns, and no blankets."

"This place!" Sarah sighed. "Really!"

They tidied up the cabin, washing mugs and plates and trying to explain to each other what the unexpected visit meant.

"What if they come back?" Sarah worried.

"Well, if they don't do anything other than what they did today, all we have to worry about is running out of food."

"Did you notice most of them had earrings?"

"And knives," Ruth reminded.

"Metal knives," Sarah elaborated.

"Wonder if they stole anything?" Anne worried. "Uncle Andrew always said you couldn't trust Indians. They'd steal everything that wasn't nailed down." But though they checked the cabin, the sheds and the barn, they could find nothing missing.

The days were either soft and sunny or overcast and wet. When it wasn't raining and blowing a cold wind, it was warm enough to sit on the beach and plan their garden.

"We have to ride in for seed and shells and stuff," Anne insisted, and Ruth whooped with joy.

"Can't it wait?" Sarah asked.

"No." Anne bit her lip. "And I don't like the idea of leaving you here."

"I'll stay with her," Ruth offered, but her eyes were sad.

"No," Sarah decided, "pot belly or not, I'll go with you."

They tidied the cabin, closed the door, leaving it unlocked. "If anyone comes, which I doubt, they'd only bust down the door anyway," Anne remarked. Then they rode off, easily retracing the route that had brought them here from the ugly little town. They stopped often, and Anne worried privately that all the riding might not be good for Sarah's baby, but Sarah laughed and sang, so relieved to be out of the cabin that Anne believed her when she said if necessary she would have walked the entire way. The sparkle came back to her eyes, the color back to her cheeks, and her laughter bubbled freely again.

Two weeks later they returned with a small mountain of seeds and supplies, and a crate of indignant chickens lashed to one of the patient pack mares.

"You get into the house and get into bed," Anne ordered. "Ruth and I can unpack and do what needs to be done."

"Yes, momma," Sarah mocked, but moved gratefully toward the cabin, holding her back with both hands. "Oh, God, never again. I promise."

"Don't promise," Anne laughed, "restrain!"

"Shut up," Sarah laughed weakly, going into the house.

Anne took the saddlebags into the house and made sure Sarah was comfortable in bed. She started a fire and put water on to boil for coffee, filled the big pot and the small boiler and put them on the little stove to heat, then brought in the saddlebags and the packs that contained personal and household goods. The packs with seeds and supplies she and Ruth moved into the shed. Then they fed and watered the animals, and moved the chickens, still in their lathe cage, into the hen house and fed them. Closing the door to the hen house they walked back into the cabin.

"I'm going to keep all those chickens locked up for about a week," Ruth decided. "Just feed and water them and keep them in that hen house until they think of it as home."

"You sound like you know chickens." Anne grinned.

"I know lots," Ruth agreed seriously.

Supper was bannock and strips cut from the slab of bacon

and fried, with cups of coffee and bannock spread with molasses for dessert. Then Ruth scrubbed herself clean and went to bed, while Anne and Sarah tidied up the kitchen. Then they had a fast bath in the half-barrel tub and fell into their bed eagerly. Sarah cuddled close, moving uncomfortably throughout the night, and the sun was long up before they woke and had breakfast. Anne sent Sarah back to bed while she and Ruth finished unpacking the supplies.

The trip had taken all of Sarah's energy and she sat often in the sun, resting. She ate well and slept well, although she complained she couldn't sleep in any one position for very long. She helped with the cooking and the dishes, but was willing to leave the heavy work to the other two.

And there was a lot of work. They dug grass clumps and established weeds out of the garden plot and spaded it over and over again, turning under the seaweed and kelp, the horse droppings and leaf mulch, enlarging the size of the garden and working the soil until Sarah teased them that all they wanted to do was dig a garden, not plant it, water it or weed it.

"Listen," Anne laughed happily, "if you'd spent as many weeks scratching gravel and dust as I have, you'd know what a treat it is to dig real soil."

Ruth's bedroom with the children's-sized beds became a plant nursery. They made boxes from pieces of wood fashioned into planks with wedges and a mallet, the dry cedar splitting easily, if irregularly. They filled the boxes with soil from the garden. "They don't look like much," Anne admitted, "but they'll do." She planted her seeds carefully, fussing over each baby plant until Sarah asked if she intended to teach them to talk. When the plants were thriving and all danger of frost was past, she transferred half of them to the unheated shed. A few days later she moved them to the garden and placed them lovingly in the soil. "If these take," she promised, "I'll plant the others, too."

"And if they don't take?" Sarah queried.

"I'll put the rest out anyway," Anne shrugged. "My mother did it that way."

She tried to make a cradle and wound up pulling the nails out

---

223

of the cockeyed thing, straightening them, and admitting defeat. "I don't know anything about making a cradle," she admitted. "It didn't rock, it wobbled." She studied the handmade table and chairs in the cabin, looked at how the beds were put together, and drove Sarah half mad fussing over the hand-split planks.

"It can sleep in a bed," Sarah insisted.

"It could sleep on the floor if it had to," Anne agreed easily, "but it doesn't have to." She found the secret she needed in examining the nesting boxes. "It's so simple when you know how!" she roared, and Sarah laughed at the insulted look on Anne's face.

"A cradle that hangs from the ceiling by ropes?" Ruth asked doubtfully.

"I can't get the runners even," Anne said. "And this way we can hang it from a tree and swing her outside."

"Him," Sarah corrected.

Placid Babe delivered herself of a young colt who showed every sign of being even bigger than his father. She had entered the barn early one evening and had seemed to show no sign of distress at all. In the morning when Ruth went to let the horses out of the barn the big mare was standing over a dark-brown colt with a white blaze on his face. Ruth shrieked with excitement and raced for the house cheering.

"Oh, you clever old thing," Anne fussed over the mare, stroking her nose. "Aren't you the good old girl. Hey, BigBoy." She reached down and patted the white nose. "How's the BigBoy?"

They were clearing up after supper, getting ready to have a bath, when the front door opened and the Indians came back, each one carefully wiping his bare feet on the sacking.

"Oh, I'm glad you came now," Anne said with a smile. "Another half hour and we'd have been starkers in the tub, scrambling, screaming and splashing."

"Kla howja." The young man with the bear-claw necklace smiled.

"Put the coffee pot on," Anne said. "I'll go cut up some bacon."

They fried bacon and sliced pieces of bread and the Indians sat on the floor and waited politely. They grinned at the taste of molasses, grimaced over the coffee so Anne made a pot of tea, as well, and they crunched the bacon and nodded approval.

The bread and molasses disappeared rapidly, and when Anne reached for the last loaf the young man spoke sharply, shaking his head no and pointing at Sarah.

"Oh, it's okay," Anne reassured him. "We can make more tomorrow." But he repeated what he had already said and so she put the loaf back and offered them some raisins. They stared at the raisins, suspiciously, and she smiled again, shrugged, took some raisins, put them in her mouth and chewed. The man who had helped Sarah with the water bucket took a few raisins, tried them, nodded approval and they all ate raisins and grinned.

"You do a lot of smiling when that fellow with the bear-claw necklace is around," Sarah teased.

"Don't be silly." Anne's face flamed. "It's just to reassure him."

"Yeah? Well reassure him too much and you'll look just like me." Sarah rose from her chair and moved clumsily to pour more tea. The men looked at the young man questioningly and Anne remembered they had done that when Sarah had offered them coffee and food. Again, as he had done before, the young man shrugged.

"I don't think pregnant women prepare the food," Ruth guessed.

"Too bad what their pregnant women don't do," Sarah snapped.

"She's feeling kind of owly these days," Anne explained, and though she was sure the men didn't understand a word she said, they all laughed softly and nodded.

They showed no sign of leaving and Anne began to think they were going to have to sit up all night and visit with smiles and hand gestures. Then Sarah yawned. The young man stood up, spoke firmly to the others, and smiled at the women.

"Kla howja," he repeated. "Kla howja tillicum."

And they were gone as quickly as they had arrived. Sarah had a quick wash and went right to bed. Anne and Ruth cleaned up the cabin, washed their hands and faces, and got into bed quickly.

In the morning they awakened to sounds from the kitchen.

"Someone's here," Ruth called.

"Jesus, they're back," Anne gasped, reaching for her jeans and shirt. "Here," she tossed Sarah her loose smock and hurried to the kitchen.

"Kla howja," Anne stammered, staring at the table. There was dried fish, smoked fish and raw fish, oysters and clams, things she didn't dare guess at, all neatly piled on the tabletop. The Indian men sat on the floor, waiting politely, while two Indian women fussed at the hearth, obviously preparing a meal.

"They just walked in," Ruth said sleepily, "and started makin' breakfast."

"Kla howja tillicum," the young man repeated. He smiled and opened the front door, waved, and began a long speech in his own language. He spoke with many smiles and nods of approval, and then he stood aside and Anne stared at two very small, very black children.

"Where did they come from?" Sarah asked from the bedroom door.

"I think they come from Africa," Anne blurted stupidly.

"These ones didn't," Sarah corrected. She stared at the children for a long moment then realized they were both very frightened. She moved forward as quickly as her bulk would allow, knelt and held out her arms. "Don't be frightened," she soothed. "We're your friends." The little boy tried to nod, but the little girl smiled and stepped into Sarah's arms confidently. "She's used to cuddles, aren't you, sweetheart," Sarah crooned. "Everybody cuddles you, don't they. Because you've got nice eyes and nice teeth, and because you cuddle back so well. Don't you cuddle?" she invited, pulling the boy to her. He stood stiffly a moment, then relaxed in her arms and the Indians all smiled and nodded and seemed quite pleased with themselves.

"Have you had breakfast?" Anne asked the children, not expecting them to understand any more than the Indians.

"No," the boy said slowly. "We came from bed."

"My God," Sarah gasped, "they're English!"

The little boy's name was James and from him they got enough of a story to be able to piece together and understand some of what had gone on and was still going on. His father and mother were the people sleeping in the grave beside the garden.

"We come in a wagon," he said slowly, searching for words he had nearly forgotten. "And poppa and momma built the house and barn, and started the shed. And then it rained and snowed a lot and momma coughed all the time. Then she got her," he nodded at his little sister, who was happily eating a piece of what looked like raw fish, "and poppa started a garden and built the shed. And then he got hurt."

"What happened?" Anne asked gently.

"I don't know." The boy tried to remember. "We had to lift a tree off him. It fell. He was choppin' and it fell. And momma cried and then she had to dig. And she was coughin' and then she went to bed and cried. Then they came," he added, his frown clearing, "and some of them stayed here and he," he nodded at the young man with the necklace, "he got the women but momma was gone when the women came and I showed them where poppa was and they put momma there too and we went to live with them."

"Why didn't they take any of the things?" Anne probed carefully. "You could have used the blankets and knives. Axes and . . ."

"Only fam'ly can touch what belongs to the . . . gone." He tried to explain and couldn't. "If you aren't fam'ly you get . . ." He talked rapidly in Indian, then shook his head. "We don't know the word. They come at night. And you get scared."

"Ghosts." Sarah cuddled him suddenly. "But there are no ghosts here, son."

He spoke again in Indian and the young man nodded, accepted the cup of tea Anne offered him, and suddenly everyone was smiling and eating enormous amounts of food.

"What's your little sister's name?" Sarah asked.

"Ey-lin-i-kulla," he said easily.

"Eylinik'la?" Ruth tried.

"That's close." He laughed. "Momma called her something else but I forget what it was."

The girl wandered around the kitchen examining everybody's breakfast and choosing for herself the pieces she wanted. A piece of smoked fish from one man, a piece of raw fish from another, a sip of everyone's tea and a corner of Sarah's bread dipped in molasses. Nobody seemed to scold or correct the children, at times it seemed as if they were ignored totally, but when Eylinikulla went too close to the hearth one of the men reached out casually and lifted her away, shaking his head and warning her, obviously, that fire is pretty, but it burns.

Anne showed them some of the fish hooks she had got in town and they watched with interest as she put some bacon rind on a hook, lay on her belly on the rocks and lowered the hook into a dark, shadowed crack between two rocks in the water below. She jiggled the line a few times and then jerked hard and a few moments later brought a large ugly rock cod up, rapped it on the head and laid it on the rock beside her.

"Wanna try?" She offered the line to one of the men. He examined it carefully, then shook his head, cut the line, cleaned the eye of the hook and carefully showed her how to tie the knot properly. Then he lowered the hook in a different place and almost immediately brought up another fish. He examined the hook and when he found it neither bent nor broken, he nodded approval. Anne gave half a dozen hooks of assorted sizes to the young man with the necklace. He took them, stared at her for a few minutes, then nodded and smiled.

"I've got a net, too." She showed them the net and they examined it but were not as impressed as they had been with the hooks. She showed them where she strung the net, and they seemed to understand perfectly what she was telling them, and the young man tried to explain something to her but gave up, laughing, when it was obvious she had no idea at all what he was talking about.

She showed them her garden and they nodded politely but she could tell by the way they talked to each other and looked at the plants they knew little or nothing about gardening and weren't interested in learning. Ruth and the two younger children ran shrieking and laughing, playing games of their own invention, James translating with increasing ease.

The Indians stayed three days, providing most of the food, watching, fascinated, as she and Sarah mixed and baked a big batch of bread. Some of the loaves were odd shapes because they didn't have enough pans to make bread for the entire group, but nobody seemed to notice. The women tried to talk to Sarah and when the language barrier blocked them, they called James. He sat on the floor at Sarah's feet and tried his best.

"She asks when your baby comes," he managed.

"Next month." Sarah smiled.

"How many days?" He struggled to interpret a month.

"About thirty. Maybe more. Maybe less."

"Like a moon turn?"

"I guess."

"She asks where is your man?"

"Gone," Sarah said firmly, and the women nodded, sad-eyed, thinking he had died.

"She asks who helps you?"

"Helps me what?"

"When the baby comes."

"She will," Sarah said with more confidence than Anne felt.

"Who is her man?"

"She doesn't have one," Sarah said, and this caused much talk among the women.

"Does she want one?" James asked, yawning.

"No," Anne said quietly. The women nodded, seeming to understand this very well.

"Not even sometimes?" he asked.

"Not even sometimes," she said, and laughed easily. The women didn't seem to believe this entirely, and chattered between themselves speculatively.

"She says you will," James said flatly, and Anne laughed again.

One of the women reached out and touched the long blonde braid. "She wants to know how you got sun in your hair."

"My mother had the same color hair," Anne explained, "and so did my father."

This amazed them and they looked at her with a different expression on their faces. They commented to each other for a long time, then spoke softly to young James and he ran off, relieved.

Anne went out hunting that night and wasn't the least surprised to have several of the men accompany her. "Mowitch," she said, patting her gun, and they nodded calmly and moved through the forest with her. When the gun fired they jumped, but weren't at all frightened. They examined the large buck, pointed to the hole in the head, nodded approval, and then cut the animal's throat, gutted it and took the heart and liver back with them. They refused to let her carry the deer, and the young man with the necklace smiled at her often, nodding approval. On the way back they spotted a doe. She pointed at the doe, then made a gesture with her hand, as if outlining a bulge of pregnancy, and shook her head. The young man nodded, seemed very pleased, and said something to the other men. They chattered easily in their own language and moved ahead with the dead buck.

Anne and the young man with the necklace walked back slowly. He stopped once to show her a grouse nest under a low-hanging bush. She knelt and looked at the eggs, knowing the mother was crouched nearby, waiting for them to leave.

When they got back to the cabin, the deer was hanging in the shed, the lights were out and only a small fire burned in the hearth. Anne and the young man had a cup of tea, then he left to sleep with the others in the clean loft of the barn.

"Took your sweet time about coming home," Sarah teased when Anne climbed into bed.

"Oh, shut up," Anne growled, and fell asleep knowing Sarah was grinning at her.

The morning they were leaving, the Indians all gathered in the cabin, and James was again called on to interpret. They sat on the floor, the men in kilts, the women in one-piece shapeless dresses of some kind of rough woven fabric, the children nearly naked. Sarah sat on a chair and Anne sat cross-legged on the floor with the Indians, sipping tea, and trying to understand James' faulty and halting translation.

"He says only family can live in the house of dead people and not be afraid."

"But we aren't your family, James," Anne said softly. "You know that."

"I know."

"Then tell him."

"If you aren't family . . ."

"Tell him," Sarah said softly, "we lived in a place with no fish." The Indians were amazed when James managed to translate. "Tell him the dirt was bad, and people were . . . hungry. And we came here and found an empty house and no people. It was cold," she added simply. James tried his best, and the Indians all stared and nodded.

"He says . . . children . . . get things . . . from their mother . . ."

"Oh, God," Anne breathed. "They're scared we're going to steal something that belongs to the kids!" And she thought suddenly of Uncle Andrew and of the raggedyass man who had moved in and taken over.

"James," she felt her eyes brimming with tears, "tell them we are not thieves. If they want, we'll leave and the farm will belong to you and Eylinikulla."

"He says houses . . ." The boy struggled. ". . . like when fish lie on the beach too long or . . ."

"Rot," Sarah supplied.

"He says you work hard."

"But we won't take anything that belongs to someone else," Anne insisted fiercely. "If this is yours . . ."

This touched off a long talk among the Indians, the women having as much to say as the men. James stared at the floor, waiting.

"You mustn't worry," Anne assured him. "Everything will be fine. No matter how it turns out, it will be fine."

"I wanted to live here with you," he admitted sadly. "I wanted to sleep in my room. You've got a horse."

"Anne," Ruth blurted, "I think what they've been tryin' to say is, if only family can live in a place like this . . . and kids belong with their family . . . then the kids go with the place and . . ."

"Oh, God," Anne blurted. "They think we don't want the kids, we just want the buildings and garden."

"Well," Sarah said flatly, "do we want the kids?"

Anne rose from the floor and walked nervously around the kitchen, aware every eye in the room was fixed on her.

"They're a big burden," she said slowly, "and we'll never be able to just pack up and go again. In some ways I feel like I did when that raggedyass bum expected me and you to look after his pack . . . but . . . this is a lot different, isn't it? Well, isn't it?"

"One hell of a lot," Sarah agreed. "Starting with the color of their skin."

"I didn't mean that, I meant . . . nobody gets something for nothing . . . or shouldn't . . . and I didn't like it when Andrew just walked in and took over without ever . . . sharing, I guess. I mean he just *took over!*"

"Well, we've sort of taken over, too."

"Not the same," Anne insisted.

The young man with the necklace rose suddenly and began a long speech, obviously more for the benefit of his own family than for Anne and Sarah. One of the women stood up and answered him. Everybody nodded and then they all rose and moved toward the door, smiling and nodding, chattering among themselves.

"Kla howja," the young man smiled, showing Anne the fish hooks.

"Kla howja," she echoed, wondering just what exactly was going on. She and Sarah walked with them to the beach where the dugouts were packed and waiting.

"They'll be back," James promised, and he waved and shouted happily.

"Don't let Eylinikulla get wet," Anne said absently, watching the dugouts speed across the water.

"Does this mean the kids stay here for good, or does it mean they'll be back to get them in a day or two?"

"I don't know." Anne sighed. "I don't have any idea at all

---

what's going on around here." She scooped Eylinikulla up and carried her back to the cabin under one arm, James and Ruth running excitedly to the door and opening it for her.

"You want to feed the horses tonight?" she asked James, idly.

"Yes!" His eyes shone.

"Okay. You and 'Linc'la play near the cabin with Ruth. And don't let 'Linc'la go too far into the water, you hear?"

"You sound like a grandmother," Sarah teased.

"I feel like a grandmother." Anne shook her head. "Except I think grandmothers are less confused than I am."

Bit by bit, day by day, the baby's name got shortened until everyone, including James, was calling her Lin. She chased the chickens until the rooster turned on her and scared her into tears with his exhibition of ruffled feathers and widespread wings. She ate a bit of whatever they were having at mealtimes and napped whenever she felt sleepy. There was no problem about toilet training, she never once wet or messed on the floor of the cabin, but might make it no further than the side of the house before squatting and relieving herself. "Well, she might as well do that," Anne sighed. "She'd probably just fall through the hole in the privy, anyway."

"And who'd want to wash her off, eh?" Sarah teased.

James spent his days with Ruth catching fish, pretending the logs on the beach were dugout canoes, gathering shellfish, helping Anne with chores, and diving off the rocks into the sea.

"What if he gets hurt?" Anne fussed.

"What if he doesn't?" Sarah mocked.

"How come you're always sort of laughing at me lately?"

"You're the one didn't want to be bothered with raggedyass hangers-on and now you're the one fussing over a boy who's doing quite well without any fussing."

"That's about the dumbest thing you've said all day."

"Just think on it," Sarah said placidly, moving her chair into the sun and settling herself, hands folded across her swollen belly. Anne sighed and walked off, mumbling to herself. She found James leaning on the fence, talking to BigBoy, the colt.

"Come on," she invited. "I'll teach you how to ride a horse properly. I know you're trying to climb on them out there, and you'll only get hurt if you don't know what you're doing."

"What if he gets hurt?" Ruth fussed.

"He'll get some bruises and scrapes and maybe even break his arm," Anne suggested. "On the other hand, he might not fall off at all. You didn't fall off. . . ."

She lifted him up onto the back of Mabel, one of the riding mares. He sat stiffly, trying hard not to be afraid.

"Awful high up, isn't it?" Anne grinned, and he nodded gravely, looking down at her and swallowing quickly. "Well, don't sit stiff. Pretend she's a chair. Put your hands here, like that, and hold the reins like that . . . now touch her real lightly with your heels, just a tiny bit, that's the way . . . now move this rein a bit . . . see, she turns the way you want her to turn. You don't have to yank hard, you don't have to *make* her turn, just let her know what you want her to do and she'll try her best to do it."

"She won't run, will she?" he quavered.

"Not until you tell her to," she assured him. "You just ride around the corral for a while and then I'll take you for a ride with me. On Dan." James' smile flashed, the prospect of a ride on Dan stronger than his uneasiness.

When he was seated in front of her, safe in the circle of her arms, he began to laugh happily.

"Faster," he urged.

"How fast?"

"Real fast!" and Dan charged down the beach, James' laughter dying in his throat, his body stiffening, pressing fearfully against Anne. She slowed the big horse to a gentle lope.

"How'd you like that?"

"Okay." He was trying to grin.

"Still a bit too fast, huh?"

"Everything was . . . like a big blur," he confessed.

"You watch, by this time next year you'll be riding all over the place. A real cowboy. Now let's go back and give Ruth a ride on Dan, shall we?"

"Can I ride Mabel again?" he asked eagerly.

"Sure. Or, if you'd rather, you can ride Sunny when Ruth rides Babe."

The quick grin flashed, and she knew she had touched on one of the corners of James' dream. She gave him a quick hug, nudged Dan, and turned him back toward the small cabin. Later, looking up from the garden, holding her hoe handle loosely, she watched James and Ruth trotting the two gentle drays along the beach where the first waves of the incoming high tide were slapping against the sand. Suddenly James stopped his horse, slid off recklessly, knelt, dug his fingers into the sand, then whirled, screeching happily, racing back on bare feet, forgetting his horse, forgetting Ruth and Babe, forgetting almost everything in his excitement.

"Dzadza'wanx!" he shrilled, "Dzadza'wanx!"

"What?" Anne raced toward him, almost stepping on the sturdy little plants. What could have happened? Had something bitten him?

"It's the oolichan," he panted, "they're back. It's Dzadza'wanx time!"

"I don't know what you mean," she said helplessly.

"Dzadza'wanx," he explained carefully, as if to a simpleton, "is when the oolichan come back. Not just one oolichan, or a hunnerd oolichan, but . . ." He turned and waved his arm at the sea, "all the oolichan. A sea full of oolichan."

"But what," she tried to be patient, "in hell are oolichan?"

"Fish," he snapped, "little fish!" And he was gone, heading for the barn, disappearing inside and coming out seconds later with the feed buckets and an empty sack, hurrying for the beach, almost shaking with excitement. "Well, come *on*," he demanded.

The oolichan were silvery fish, four to six inches long, riding in on the big waves, flopping on the sand, burrowing into the soft wet grains, slithering frantically as James reached for them, picking them from the sand like so many silver berries, plopping them in the buckets, dancing happily among the writhing small forms.

"Count the waves," he panted, laughing. "Watch them. See,

some of them come further up the beach. Those are the big ones. The next seven won't come as far up; watch. Then there'll be a big one again and the oolichan on the sand will ride back out with the big one, other oolichan will ride in on it. They're laying eggs," he added, as if that explained everything.

"There are hundreds of them," Ruth marveled.

"When it's night," James promised, "we'll have lots. Lots and lots and lots and lots."

"What are you going to do with them?" Ruth asked.

"Eat 'em," he promised. "We've got to catch as many as we can."

"Got to?" Anne urged.

"Got to," he repeated. "Old Woman sends 'em. Now, and again before the leaves fall from the trees. And you've got to catch as many as you can, to tell her thank you. She sends 'em," he explained, "so's we won't get hungry, and so's we won't have to take all the salmon and because soon the berries will start and when the berries start you aren't allowed to eat clams or oysters or mussels or anything that lives on the rocks in the water."

"Why not?" Ruth asked.

"Because," James said, patiently, "if you do, you might die." He started scooping up oolichan by the handful.

Sarah brought Lin down to the beach, and the baby squealed happily, chasing oolichan, sometimes even catching one and putting it carefully in the buckets with the others. When the sun had gone down and the first cool dark of evening was rising from the water and staining the evening sky, the oolichan came in such masses that Anne couldn't believe her eyes. She stood in water to her knees, swishing her bucket through the sea, lifting it, full of fish and water, pouring it into the sack James and Ruth held open, a sack full of wiggling silver oolichan. When the sack was full, they dragged it to the barn and dumped the fish out onto the big tarpaulin stretched on the floor. Then they headed back to the beach, to again stand in water and scoop oolichan by the bucketful, pouring them into the sack, the water draining out quickly through the rough weave. Lin fell asleep on the grass and Sarah took her back to the cabin and tucked her into her small cot. Then, leaving the door open in case the baby should wake and call out, Sarah went back to the beach and started a small fire. James took time from the oolichan gathering to explain and demonstrate to Sarah how to cook the small silver fish, then he went back to his job of holding the mouth of the sack open. When Anne's arms were tired, James scooped with the bucket and when his arms were tired, Ruth took her turn.

"Supper's ready," Sarah called, and, arms heavy, they dragged the last sack of oolichan out of the water, then slumped around the fire, grinning at each other.

"I did what you said," Sarah hesitated, "but are you *sure* you don't clean these fish first?"

"You eat 'em like this." James demonstrated, reaching for a fish, holding the head between the thumb and forefinger of one hand, the tail between the thumb and forefinger of his other hand. The body of the fish disappeared into his mouth, he tossed the head and tail into the fire and chewed happily.

"Guts and all?" Ruth grimaced.

"That's how you do it," he insisted. Sarah reached out, took a fish, copied James, chewed and then smiled. "Guts and all," she agreed, reaching for another.

"You can use 'em for candles, too," he confided, sticking an uncooked fish in the sand, head first, and lighting the tail with a burning branch from the fire.

"Well, I'll be damned," Anne breathed, watching the flame flicker from the stiffened body of the dead fish.

"Sometimes," James mumbled around a mouthful of oolichan, "you can put 'em in a big wooden box-thing, and let'em sit until they turn into oil. But you gotta take the other stuff out every day. They kind of fall apart."

"Oh, wonderful." Anne shuddered, imagining a wooden box full of rotting fish. "Then what do you do?"

"They go to oil," James repeated, "and you can eat it, or make lamps with it, or rub it on your skin if you get too dry in the sun, or . . . whatever you want," he finished, reaching for yet another oolichan.

They ate until there wasn't room for another small fish inside them, then waded back into the water and scooped for another couple of hours. When they were chilled and tired, and the barn doors were safely closed, they washed the fish scales from their bodies, left their soggy, fishy clothes on the front porch, and crawled into bed gratefully. Anne fell asleep thinking of the wave after wave of living silver crashing on their beach, spawning, returning to the sea, leaving a wealth of fertile eggs to incubate in the sand. When the moon was right again, the highest tides of the cycle would take the newly hatched oolichan back to the sea, to feed and grow and return the following year.

"If it wasn't for James," she mumbled, "we'd never have known." And her breathing deepened, her lips parted and she never knew she had spoken, never knew Sarah had already been asleep and hadn't answered her.

The next day they strung oolichan by the thousands on cords through their gills and hung them over the smoldering fire in the smokehouse, hung them to dry out in the sun, packed them in layers of salt, and ate them for breakfast, lunch and supper.

"They come again tonight?" Anne asked.

"Yes," James grinned.

"We've got more already than we can smoke."

"Yes." He grinned again. "Tonight we can watch them, and sing to them, and tell them thank you."

"Next time they come we'll be ready," Anne promised. "I'm going to build another smokehouse."

"Yes," James nodded. "Maybe two. Then we can do some salmon, too."

The oolichan run lasted a week, and not all of the spawners made it back to the sea. Between tides the beach was littered with dead bodies, the gulls swooped frantically, trying to get to the fish before the children did. Sack after sack of dead fish, some of them mangled by birds, was carried behind the barn and dumped into the compost pile, then covered with seaweed, and left to decompose.

There was no time for working in the garden. Anne was kept busy drying, salting and smoking fish, and by the time the oolichan run was finished, the weeds were demanding attention. Before the weeds were finally pulled, James was glowering and casting longing glances back at the water.

"You're not much of a gardener," Anne teased.

"I'd rather," he grumbled, "pull fish from the water than weeds from the dirt."

"You wait," she promised. "When the corn is ready, you'll be glad you did this." But she knew James would have to be convinced by the corn; he didn't believe her. She relented in the afternoon and he and Ruth raced to the beach, already stripping off their clothes, heading for the water that was still too cold for Anne and Sarah.

James and Lin were in the tub, Ruth and Anne bathing them, Sarah resting with her hands contentedly clasped across her swollen belly, when the door opened and the young man with the bear-claw necklace entered with two older women. "NaiNai," James shrieked, rising from the water, clambering over the side of the tub, running, dripping on the floor, to throw himself at his friends. Lin was slower getting out of the tub, but her shrieks of welcoming joy were louder, and she hugged the old women happily. "Nan," she blurted, "Nan." James chattered in Indian, telling all about his horseback riding, and Lin sat on the women's laps, alternating from one to the other happily, patting their lined faces, kissing them wetly, smiling until her eyelids fluttered and she popped her thumb in her mouth and fell asleep, her naked legs sprawled, her head resting on the ample bosom of one of the old women. Anne made tea and Ruth sliced bread and spread it with molasses. Sarah sat, smiling and nodding. The young man looked at her and smiled, pleased, certain she had finally learned that a woman has enough to do just carrying happiness, and ought not to work at anything else, but allow others to share her joy by doing for her the chores that need to be done.

They drank tea and ate bread and molasses, then the women took sleeping mats into the children's room, spread them out on the floor, and lay down calmly.

"He says," James interpreted sleepily, "that if you want to sleep with him you can."

"Tell him I'll be sleeping with Sarah," Anne said carefully, her face flaming, "but he can sleep in the kitchen, or in the loft, or in your room, or anywhere else he likes. Except with Sarah and me," she added firmly, eyes averted.

James translated and the young man laughed softly. He said something and James stumbled off to bed leaving the young man alone in the kitchen with Anne. He rose and moved to stand beside her, reaching out to touch her hair, speaking softly, teasingly. She shook her head, her face still brick red, and he shrugged regretfully, stroked her face and walked out the door. Without even washing her hands and face she hurried to the bedroom, undressed and crawled into bed beside Sarah.

"What was that all about," Sarah asked, laughing.

"You were awake and listening!"

"So . . . you can sleep with him if you want," Sarah said gently, "but you didn't want . . ." Then her voice changed and she propped herself up on her elbow. "What's wrong? Anne?"

"I don't know," Anne confessed finally, finding shelter in Sarah's cuddling arms, "I was . . . not scared, really, but . . ."

"Oh, baby," Sarah crooned. "You're such a damn fool at times! The poor man likes you!"

"Well, I like him, too," she admitted, "but . . ."

"Don't be silly about it," Sarah soothed sleepily. "You can do the most dangerous things without worrying and a thing as natural as this has you in a dither. Go to sleep and try to wake up smarter in the morning."

But she wasn't any smarter in the morning. She made breakfast and took some in to Sarah but Sarah didn't want to eat anything. The Indian women walked into the bedroom uninvited and looked at Sarah's pale face, then called James.

"Are you bleeding?" he asked, and Sarah blushed.

"No," she answered.

The next question took a lot of questioning and explaining from the women before James could ask, "Has any water come?"

"No."

---

240

"They ask if you have pain . . ."

"My back," Sarah admitted. "It feels like it's broken." And when James translated, the women nodded, then sent him from the room and very casually lifted Sarah's nightgown and began to feel her swollen abdomen.

"Do you think I should feel shocked?" she asked Anne with a faint smile.

"I don't know about you," Anne said fervently, "but I'm damn glad they know what they're doing! You aren't a horse."

"I'm as big as one, though."

The women talked seriously with the young man who nodded gravely, smiled reassuringly at Anne, and had James translate for him that they were going to stay until the baby was born.

"The women say tomorrow," James added casually.

Anne worked in her garden, looked after the stock, gathered eggs and tried to settle to the task of ringing the bark off some of the trees she wanted to clear for next year's garden. The young man sat in the sun watching her, shaking his head at the amount of work she was doing.

"He says you will hurt yourself," James teased.

"Tell him I won't either."

"He says you must be angry with him."

"No, I'm not." Anne was surprised. "Why does he think that?" But the young man only laughed and walked away toward the beach. She put down her axe and followed him, unaware that James had gone into the house.

"Tell him I'm not angry," she said, then turned around and realized James wasn't there. "I thought . . ." She fumbled. The young man nodded, and sat down on a log, staring out at the sea. He began to speak to her in Indian, and they laughed together when she obviously did not understand. She shrugged and sat down beside him, and they talked all afternoon in different languages.

Sarah was feeling better at suppertime. She got out of bed and joined them, eating well and smiling often. Lin climbed on Sarah's lap and chattered away happily in her own private baby language, and the women helped Anne and Ruth clean up after

241

the meal. The young man joked and laughed with the women, and one of them spoke sharply to him, then patted Anne on the shoulder approvingly.

"Was he talking about me?" she snapped.

"Yes," James admitted.

"Well, of all the nerve!" And she walked out of the cabin angrily. The young man followed and tried to talk to her but she wasn't going to listen, not even to words she didn't understand, and she went back into the house.

Sarah was back in bed, the women, Ruth and James talking with her, and Anne worried there might be something wrong. Then the women came from the bedroom, smiled calmly and sat down for another cup of tea. They began talking seriously with the young man, who listened carefully, looking often at Anne.

"Were you talking about me?" she asked Sarah.

"Yes."

"What about?"

"Sometimes their men have two and three wives at a time," Sarah said, twisting uncomfortably on the bed, "but he has no wife at all. He wants you for his first wife."

"I hope you told them no!"

"Oh, I told them a lot." Sarah grinned. "I think they understand perfectly. Or as perfectly as you can understand with a five- or six-year-old boy as interpreter." She squirmed again.

"What's wrong?"

"I'm pregnant." Sarah was tired. "That's what's wrong."

She began having pains at midnight, and the women talked reassuringly and prepared to go to bed.

"Not yet," the boy translated, falling asleep in his chair, "not for . . . hours."

"How did they know when to come?" Anne asked.

"The moon." The boy yawned. "It's full. Babies always come when the moon is full. Almost always."

By noon the next day Sarah was sweating and walking stubbornly around the main room of the cabin. She didn't want to talk to anybody, but she didn't want to be alone.

Anne was half frantic with worry. The young man came in

with some straw from the loft and some soft moss he had gathered in the woods. Then he went down to the beach and went out in his dugout, coming back with some fresh seaweed, which he gave to the women. They put it in fresh water and made a tea out of it, talking quietly, nodding often. They spread a sleeping mat over the straw and moss, then waited patiently for Sarah to have enough sense to lie down and relax. At suppertime only the children and the Indians ate anything. Anne was too upset and Sarah didn't feel the least bit hungry.

The women put Lin to bed early, and she lay in her bed singing to herself. Then they took the small boiler down to the sea, filled it with sea water and put it on the small stove to heat. Sarah got out the baby clothes she had sewn herself, and showed them to the women, who nodded, but seemed to feel all these clothes were totally unnecessary for one small baby. The young man tried to talk to Anne, but James' interpretation wasn't as reassuring as the young man's tone of voice tried to be.

"He says not to worry," he piped. "These women are magic women. They know everything."

"I hope so," Anne muttered, fretting.

James fell asleep and Ruth took him to bed, while Anne sat on a chair and tried to reassure Sarah, but had no more success than the young man had with her.

"I think I'd better go to bed," Sarah gasped, but the women wouldn't let her get into her own bed. They made her lie down on the cedarbark mat on the floor of the bedroom, then they sat cross-legged beside her, talking softly and stroking her abdomen. They motioned for Anne to sit by Sarah's head and hold her hand.

"How do you feel?" Anne asked, wiping Sarah's brow.

"Awful," Sarah admitted. "Awful and scared."

"Nothing to be afraid of," Anne soothed. "We're here."

"Maybe you're not," Sarah rambled. "Maybe I'm all alone. Maybe there's no James and Lin, no Indians and no farm. Maybe I'm out by the tree where they hung Keno. Maybe I'm all covered in tar on that horse."

"What about me?" Anne tried to laugh and couldn't.

"Maybe you got bit by a snake or something. Maybe you're lying on the prairie and maybe we're both dying. Or already dead."

"How did we meet each other?" Anne felt goosebumps on her arms and knew her eyes were wide. The Indian women looked sharply at her and Sarah, spoke quietly to each other and one of them began to hum softly.

"You heard him," Sarah mumbled, straining with pain. "Only family can live with the dead. Maybe we're dead, too. And maybe we died at the same time so we met each other that way . . . Oh, God, Annie, it hurts!"

"Then you're not dead," Anne said firmly wondering why she had been so frightened. "Don't fight like that, Sarah, you'll just make it worse."

"It's tearing me apart, Annie!" Sarah cried. "Oh, God, I'm sorry. I'm so sorry for everything. I can't have a baby!"

"Well, you're having one," Anne said flatly.

"I can't! I can't even look after myself. How can I look after a baby? Oh, God, never again, I promise."

The women spoke sharply, then grabbed Sarah by the shoulders and hips and rolled her on her side with her knees drawn up. They seemed appalled that a woman would not know what to do giving birth. They put her hands on her knees and when the next pain hit she grabbed her own legs and curled almost in a ball, gasping.

"Oh, Jesus," she moaned.

"Hey, lady," Anne soothed. "It's easy, just relax and think of something nice. My mother always told me Think Nice Thoughts. Old Bess did it, and Babe did it, and they weren't any more special than you." Her voice ran up and down like a half-sung song. She stroked Sarah's head and dried her face, and the Indian women nodded and smiled at each other.

"Annie?"

"I'm here, honey, I'm always here."

"What if it's dead."

"Don't be such an asshole," Anne teased. "A minute ago you had us all dead. Just do what you're here to do."

"Oh, you're a fine one to talk," Sarah snapped, then bent double with cramp again.

She didn't scream, but deep-throated sounds grated from her, not a growl, not a moan, but similar to and different from either. The women talked softly and one of them knelt at Sarah's shoulders, reached over and grabbed her knees, pulling them tightly toward her chest, and then Sarah was straining, her face red, sweat pouring from her body.

The lamp was turned low. There was a sudden gasp of relief from Sarah, and then, in a gush of fluid and some blood, the baby emerged. One of the women spoke sharply and Sarah pushed again, tears streaming from her eyes, and then the baby was in the strong hands of the second woman, and the first woman was rolling Sarah onto her back. They lay the baby on Sarah's now flat belly, and smiled at each other.

"I thought you were supposed to hold them by the feet and slap them," Anne whispered in awe.

"Oh," Sarah breathed, "let them do it their way."

The little girl coughed and stirred, tried to raise her still-wet head and wriggled.

"It's alive." Sarah's face was radiant. She lifted her head and looked down at her daughter. The women were whispering to the baby, cleaning Sarah and assuring each other this was undoubtedly the most beautiful baby they had ever helped catch. Sarah touched her child's hand and the small head turned curiously. The little face began to pucker.

"Ah," Anne sighed. "She's scared. She's never done this before." And the baby began to cry, not loudly, irregular little whimpers of protest. The older woman rose and left the room, returning moments later with the small boiler of water. She tested it with her inner elbow, nodded satisfaction, then moved the baby and examined the cord. The big vein had stopped pumping, the cord was collapsed, and the women quickly pinched it shut, wrapped a piece of . . . something . . . around it and tied a knot, then cut the cord. The baby squirmed, not liking the touch of their hands, and she mewed in protest again. And the women lifted her and placed her in the lukewarm sea water.

---

"She likes it," Sarah whispered, resting on her elbow and watching. The little girl moved her arms and legs. The women stroked her rhythmically, talked softly, and with smiles and nods encouraged Sarah and Anne to touch and stroke the child. Instead of howling and protesting, the little girl relaxed and almost went to sleep.

"Oh, she's beautiful." Sarah wept happily. "She's just beautiful."

The women lifted the baby slowly from the water, dried her with a soft cloth and placed her beside her mother.

"Look," Sarah sighed, "she's smiling."

"*She's* smiling? You should see yourself." Anne blinked back tears. "God, you're beautiful," she said to the child and the child's mother.

They cleaned away the afterbirth and blood, changed Sarah's nightgown, bathed her with warm sea water, then padded her with moss and the soft strips of boiled cloth she had prepared. Anne helped Sarah, one of the women held the baby, and they put Sarah to bed in the big soft bed. Then the woman put a piece of cloth under the baby's bare bottom and handed her to her mother.

"Help me off with this damned nightgown," Sarah muttered suddenly. "I want to *feel* her, too." The women nodded approval and helped remove the nightgown. Sarah and her daughter snuggled together in the big bed, skin touching skin, and then the small mouth began searching and Sarah instinctively adjusted her position and the baby found the swollen and darkened nipple and nursed.

"Oh, Annie," Sarah sighed, "I have never . . . I mean *never* . . . felt anything as wonderful as this."

"Just enjoy it," Anne whispered, kissing Sarah's cheek, "and get some sleep."

The sleeping mat and all other evidence of the birth were gone. The women were in the kitchen having tea and talking with the young man. Anne walked over to them and cuddled the women gratefully, not needing words.

"Thank you," she wept, and they patted her hand and said soft things. Then they went to the children's bedroom and left her alone with the young man. They drank their tea and then he patted her shoulder, smiled, and went out to his bed in the loft. She tidied the kitchen, tiptoed past the sleeping Indian women and checked on James and Lin, pulled the covers over their bare shoulders, then went outside, got the half barrel, took it into the kitchen and poured warm water in it. She stripped off her shirt and knelt on the floor, soaping herself and rubbing her hands along her arms.

Her mind was in a turmoil, her head full of images of Sarah and the baby. She heard herself so long ago talking about trash and dirtiness. She shook her head self-mockingly and rinsed the soap from her arms and upper body, stripped off her boots and socks, pulled off her jeans and underclothes, and sat down in the half barrel. She was sitting in the barrel, washing one lifted leg, when the door opened and the young man walked into the cabin. He stared at her.

"Close the door," she snapped, "preferably behind you."

He closed the door, then quickly muttered something in his own language, opened the door and left, carefully closing it again. She finished her bath, dried herself with a towel, picked her clothes up off the floor and took them into the bedroom.

"Awful lot of in-ing and out-ing in that kitchen," Sarah teased.

"You ought to be asleep."

"I can't sleep. I'm too excited."

"Let me look at her . . . Oh, Lord look at those little fingers." She sat on the side of the bed, gently touching the small child. "Her skin is all crinkly. Like a little old woman. And look at the hair! Hey Puddins," she crooned. "Hey, how's the big girl?"

"Want to hold her?"

"I thought you'd never ask!" Anne took the sleeping baby and held it close against her skin, lowering her face and holding her cheek against the baby's head. "Was she worth it?" She grinned.

"Yes," Sarah said flatly. "I'd do it all again tomorrow."

"Bet you sleep all day tomorrow."

Sarah watched Anne crooning to the baby, smiling softly, totally unaware her towel had fallen off and she was naked on the edge of the bed.

"You ever think of having one of your own."

"Never thought of it before," Anne confessed, "but I thought about it tonight when that guy walked in on my bath."

"I told you you smiled a lot when he was around."

"Yeah? Well don't hold your breath."

"You going to sit there getting goosebumps all night?"

"No. I was going to get dressed and empty the washtub." Anne cuddled the baby happily. "But to hell with the washtub, it'll be there in the morning."

Sarah held back the covers invitingly and Anne crawled into bed. She handed the baby back to Sarah and watched as she settled back with a happy sigh.

"You're doing a lot of sighing and smiling," she remarked softly, cuddling close.

"I couldn't begin to tell you how it feels. I thought being with Keno was the nicest feeling in the world, for a while. And then I thought waking up at night and knowing you were here and that we could fight and argue but never be mean was the greatest feeling . . . but this tops them all." Sarah laughed suddenly. "I thought it was the ultimate when I was lying here with the baby, but now that there's the both of you . . ."

"Oh, for God's sake, go to sleep. You're rambling again." Anne nudged Sarah and Sarah turned on her side, the baby sleeping against her breast. Anne curled herself around the curve of Sarah's back and buried her face against her shoulders.

"Don't do it again tomorrow," she mumbled. "I couldn't take it!"

In the morning the children stared at the baby and Lin wanted to hold it so they sat her on the bed and lay the baby on her lap and she giggled and crooned. Then it was James' turn. He held the baby gently, and touched her head softly, then turned to Sarah with sad eyes.

"Are you gonna die, too?" he asked.

"No, my precious, I am not," she promised. "Not for a long time."

"I missed it," Ruth flared. "I went to sleep and missed it!"

Anne took the baby into the kitchen and the Indians fussed over her while Anne emptied the half barrel, then took it and warm water into the bedroom. While Sarah washed, Anne changed the bed linen and tidied the room.

"Now into bed and I'll bring you some breakfast."

"I don't feel sick," Sarah insisted.

"Oh, get into bed and let me fuss!"

"Jennifer," Sarah said, cradling her daughter and smiling down at her. "Jennifer, because I never knew a nasty Jennifer in my life, and Anne because . . . because I never knew a Jennifer at all!" She laughed happily, not the gentle and placid laugh of the last few months, but the full-bodied and self-mocking laugh Anne remembered best.

"You mean to tell me you're calling her Jennifer because you never knew anybody else named Jennifer?"

"That's right."

"That's not right, that's silly!"

Four days after the baby was born the Indians went back to their village. Anne and Sarah walked to the beach with them, hugged the women gratefully, and nodded thanks to the young man.

"He says he will be back," James translated.

"Tell him," Anne said firmly, "that brothers are always welcome."

"He'll be sorry to hear you call him brother," Sarah teased, but the women nodded approvingly and the young man smiled.

"Kla howja," he said, waving.

"Kla howja tillicum," Anne waved.

# Chapter 14

Jennifer had dark hair and eyes, a slow smile and seemed to want nothing but warm milk, cuddles, smiles and the sound of friendly voices. At first she did little but sleep and the children would happily swing her cradle gently for hours at a time. James helped with Jennifer's bath every night. When she was very small he would stand on a chair and talk to her while Sarah bathed her in the same big oval bowl they used to mix their bread. When she got too big for the oval bowl, they bathed her in the half barrel. The little girl took one look at this big strange container, her face crumpled and she got all set to cry bitterly.

"She's scared," James announced calmly. Then he whipped off his short pants, climbed into the half barrel and held Jennifer, her back pressed against his belly, his arms wrapped around her. She looked up, saw the grin she knew so well and began to relax. James had grinned at her over the side of the cradle, from beside the bread bowl, across the room, he had grinned at her from every possible angle and now even if this was a strange place to take a bath, James was grinning and holding her. She moved her hand and the water splashed. She recognized that, too. All thought of tears vanished and before long the cabin floor was damp and the children were splashing and laughing. Lin wanted to get into the bath, too, but there wasn't enough room so after a while James got out of the half barrel and dried himself while Lin climbed in and splashed with Jennifer, and after Lin, it was Ruth's turn.

They hung her rude cradle from the branches of a tree and Sarah and Anne weeded the garden while the baby laughed at the touch of the wind on her skin, laughed at the movement of the leaves and branches, laughed at the sound of the birds and stopped laughing only when she began to feel hungry. Then she called to her mother with the tearless cry that is every baby's first communication and Sarah left the garden and sat under a tree nursing her daughter.

"I don't think there's anything more annoying than a new baby's crying," she confided. "Even if you didn't want to, you'd break down and do whatever you could to stop that noise. That's probably no accident. It's probably nature's way of making sure you don't forget there's a baby to be fed. Or changed. Or rolled over in its bed. Or whatever."

"You figure that out yourself," Anne asked, "or did you read it somewhere?"

"We're lucky she doesn't cry very often. It must be awful for people whose baby howls all the time. I've heard of women going crazy because of a howling baby. And someone always has stories about some baby with colic . . ."

"I bet babies get colic because their mothers aren't happy about something," Anne contributed, pulling the buttercup roots out angrily. "The only baby I ever heard of who cried all the time was Charlie Petersen. They say he howled night and day until even the neighbors were ready to move. But Ina Petersen, Charlie's mother, was the most nervous thing you ever saw. Not the kind of nervous that twitches or has a tic or anything, but the kind of nervous that never knows from one minute to the next what she's doing. If I'd'a been Charlie, I'd'a cried, too. That woman could have taken him in the basement to get cucumber pickles and forgotten him there until the next week when she wanted preserved pears."

"You made that up!" Sarah laughed.

"Me? Would I tell lies about Charlie Petersen? Or his poor mother May?"

"You said her name was Ina."

"Yeah. Ina May. Ina May Henderson."

"Petersen."

"Who?"

"Ina May Petersen."

"Oh, did you know them, too?"

Anne looked up from the unending war with the buttercups and chickweed, her capable hands stained with dirt and weed juice. James and Lin were playing on the swing she and Sarah had made with equal lengths of rope and a plank wedge-split from a cedar log. The horses were grazing along the grassy beach and browsing in the bush. She gazed at Sarah and Jennifer, threw the weeds aside and walked over to stand looking down at them. The baby's head snuggled against Sarah's milk-swollen breast, the small hands pumping rhythmically, stroking and caressing, the small mouth sucking, soft slurping sounds and frantic hasty swallowings. Jennifer gasped for air, then nuzzled close again, greedy and happy. "God," she breathed, "you're beautiful."

"She is," Sarah agreed, smiling down at her daughter.

Anne made a funnel-shaped box, much bigger at the top than at the bottom, then she placed it in a tray on the floor of the hen house. She poured grain in the top and it sifted down to the bottom, a thin layer of it spreading into the tray. As the hens ate the grain from the tray, more sifted down from the top.

"We can leave them for up to three weeks," she announced proudly, "and they won't wander away because there'll be food here."

She built rough bins in the storage shed and hauled sand up from the beach in buckets. Then she set the buckets on the stove until the sand was actually hot to the touch.

"Why you cookin' sand?" James asked, puzzled.

"I'm not cooking sand," she explained, "but there are bugs in it: sand fleas and sand lice and things I don't even know the name of. If we don't kill them they'll eat the vegetables. And even if they don't, would you like to eat buggy beets?"

"What's beets?"

"You know the greens we have at supper? Well that's beet top. Beets are the bottom part. When they're bigger, I'll show you."

When she was satisfied there were no bugs left alive in the sand, she stored the sand in the bins in the storage shed.

"If we had a cow," she said, "we could churn butter from the milk. If we had a churn."

"Put it on the list," Sarah reminded her absently.

"It's going to take *two* wagons to bring all this crap back," Anne complained.

"You're sure you told them to order wool for the spinning wheel?"

"Yes," she muttered, "but damned if I'm having sheep around here! Dirty, smelly things, and we'd never keep them out of the garden!"

"Did I say I wanted sheep? All I asked was did you order wool!"

"I ordered wool! I ordered wool! But I'm not ordering any goddamn sheep!"

Anne flatly refused to let Sarah do any lifting, and for two months Sarah listened to her. Then one day, while Jennifer was sleeping and James and Lin were playing in the shallows, Sarah came from the cabin in pants and a faded shirt and grabbed the other end of the split rail Anne was trying to lift into place.

"You'll hurt yourself," Anne blurted.

"How?"

"Lifting, stupid."

"You're lifting. You aren't hurting."

"I didn't just have a baby!"

"Neither did I. Jennifer is more than two months old."

"Your belly muscles."

"Never you mind my belly muscles. Lift your end, mine is getting heavy!"

"Well, okay, but if your milk dries up, don't blame me."

"I am not," Sarah said gravely, "lifting this fence rail with anything that has anything at all to do with milk." And Anne burst out laughing.

---

"If only we could," she giggled, "it'd be like an extra pair of hands."

Lin learned to swim, after a fashion. She fell off the rocks, where she wasn't supposed to be, into the water. James was torn between the need to get help and the desire to save his sister. He threw her a piece of driftwood and she grabbed it with her hands.

"Kick!" he yelled, so she did. "And hang on!" Then he ran for Anne and Sarah. "I can't get her out. I can't get her out," he screamed. Anne dropped the wedge and hammer and ran for the beach, her heart in her throat. When she saw Lin happily paddling around holding onto a piece of wood, Anne didn't know whether to sit down and cry with relief or drag the girl from the water and warm her backside.

"I told her to go home," James quavered.

"Why didn't you bring her back to the cabin?"

"If I did, I'd never get any fishing done. She'd just come back and I'd take her up and she'd come back and I'd take her up . . ."

Anne and Sarah discussed the choices that night. Did James have to have his life ruled by Lin's babyish lack of what in someone older could be called responsibility, did either Anne or Sarah spend most of the day watching over Lin and keeping her from learning there were dangers in the world, or did they tie Lin to a tree, out of harm's way.

"I guess," Sarah ventured, "we have to sort of do a bit of everything. It's the water I'm afraid of. There isn't much else can happen to her."

"Except the fire in the hearth, or an animal in the bush, or banging her head on a rock, or . . ."

"Don't!" Sarah shuddered. "Next year it might be Jennifer!"

They all tried to keep an eye on Lin but there were times when the little girl eluded them. She ran around naked most of the time, stubbing her toes on rocks, skinning her elbows and knees and trying to catch the small beach crabs that always seemed to scuttle sideways under rocks before she could get them.

\* \* \*

"It's a box made out of sticks," James explained, "and the door only opens in, not out. And you take something good, like a fish head, and put that inside. And a rock to hold it down. And a rope up to . . . a thing . . . it floats."

"What thing?" Anne asked patiently.

"A thing . . . You get it out of a . . . sort of an animal . . . like a dog, but it lives in water . . ." He tried in vain to describe a seal and finally, nearly in tears, he blurted "Cocoa-quitza . . . We call it cocoa-quitza."

"And it floats?"

"You blow it up and tie the end . . ."

"Couldn't we use a sort of a raft . . . or a log?"

"I don't know," he sobbed. "We used cocoa-quitza thing."

And so, one evening, with nothing better to do, Anne took the sticks James had carefully chosen, and with much laughing and redoing, experimenting and arguing, they got a start on the underwater trap. It took two nights just to figure out how to make a door that only opened one way.

"Well," Sarah decided, "if there was a thing here to keep it from swinging back out . . ."

"How stupid can I be!" Anne laughed, and she and James built a stopper to keep the door from swinging outward.

They had no boat or raft and Anne wasn't going to try to make a dugout, not when James insisted it all had to be carved in one piece from a living tree and never touch the ground or it would sink.

"They drag them up on the beach," she protested.

"Only after," he insisted, "only after it's been in water!"

So she rode out on a log with James rolling on the beach with laughter and Sarah pretending to weep and wail a farewell. Then lowered the trap to the floor of the sea, hoping the two fresh cod heads would do what James insisted they would do, and that the two rocks would keep the contraption from floating away immediately. She paddled her log back to shore, and dragged the laughing Sarah into the water.

"I'm not the only one wet now," she laughed. That evening she paddled back out, dragged the trap up onto the log and stared in distrust at the large green-shelled creatures with pinchers on their bigger front legs.

"What are these?" she demanded of James.

"Ah-Sam," he replied.

"Ah-Sam? Is that what the Indians call them?"

"That's what they *are*," he insisted. He told them Ah-Sam had to be boiled alive or the meat would make you go cross-eyed. "You can't kill him any other way." And he stuck by his story. Anne didn't believe that killing the crab first and then cooking it would make her go cross-eyed but she knew of no other way to cook it, so they did what James said. Then, feeling uneasy about it all, she, Ruth and Sarah copied what James did with his Ah-Sam. They cracked open the shells on the legs, picked out the white meat and tried it tentatively.

"I don't care if it did scratch and try to get out," Sarah vowed, "I'd eat it any time, boiled to death or not!"

In the middle of summer the Indians came back for another three-day visit. Ap-jei, whose name, James said, meant happy man, the young man with the necklace, smiled and nodded when he saw the smokehouse, but laughed long and loud when he saw the rough crab trap.

"It works," Anne insisted, laughing with him. When she showed him how her piece of netting was getting frayed and at times ripped, he nodded, then said something in a reassuring tone of voice. The next morning, for the first time, she saw the Indians actually doing what she considered work. They were driving poles the size of a strong man's wrist into the mud beneath the shallow water at low tide. The women were busily cutting lengths of supple tree branches.

"Ask them what I can do," she told James, and he waded out to talk to Ap-jei.

"He says to watch and learn," James reported back to her. She studied everything they did and even before the wier was finished she knew what it would do. "There's a door," she explained to Sarah, who wasn't allowed near the work because she was a nursing mother, "and you can open the door thing by a sort of pulley. And then you can close it again."

"Why?" Sarah asked calmly.

"You open it when the tide is coming in," James explained, "and you leave it open until before the tide is going to go back out. Then you close the door and the fish can't go out with the water. In the time of salmon we put them at the river mouth and catch lots and lots and put them in the smokehouse. This one will catch a few fish each day, enough for us."

They used the last of the flour making sourdough bread and when James inadvertently told Ap-jei it was the last, Ap-jei spoke angrily to Anne.

"He says what you did was foolish," James translated.

"Tell him I can get more when we go to the trading post."

"What's a trading post?" James asked.

"It's where we can go and . . . we can give them smoked fish," she said, knowing neither James nor Ap-jei would understand money, "and they will give us things we need. Like flour."

"Ma-cu-co!" James triumphed, and Ap-jei straightened as if he had been pricked with a pin.

"Ma-cu-co? U-yi?" he asked eagerly.

Poor James had a difficult time trying to explain how far it was to the trading post. The fact it was inland meant he had to try to translate days on horseback into days afoot, and when Ap-jei heard how long it would take him, he slumped unhappily. Sarah and Anne were deep in conversation while James was trying to translate for Ap-jei.

"Tell him," Anne said quietly, "that if he will have someone stay here and keep the deer out of the garden, we will go to the trading post and get some of the things he needs."

Ap-jei wasn't sure he wanted to look after a garden, but he did know he wanted fish hooks like the ones Anne had given him, and a good rifle. And he had seen how much more easily the saw cut through wood than the rough tool his people had. He had a metal knife, most of his people had metal knives they had obtained by one means or another, mostly from Island tribes who had traded with the Spanish, and they all knew of the town growing along the big river far down coast, but the town was in territory belonging to another tribe and neither Ap-jei nor his people had any wish to start another bitter tribal battle, with huge navies of dugout canoes heading out to challenge first the sea, then a rival navy. In the end he agreed to stay with several of the women. But, he wanted a large boiler like the one on the small stove.

"If you will not marry him," James teased, "he will marry someone else."

"Tell him he's my brother," Anne said easily, "and brothers don't marry sisters." Ap-jei shrugged and pretended he didn't really care one way or the other.

"He has to go home first," James translated, "and he will be back in two fours of days."

So when the Indians left, Ap-jei left, too, but he returned eight days later. He, James translated, would keep the deer away from the garden. The women would keep the weeds out and feed the chickens. But he, Ap-jei, would not nursemaid any birds.

Sarah left the spotted-rump mare and her new foal in the corral, ignoring the desperate cries of the mare who wanted to accompany them. She rode one of the now-pregnant saddle mares, with Jennifer strapped to her chest and held in place by a wide band of cotton. James rode the other saddle mare bareback and Lin rode up on Dan with Anne. They had full saddlebags and the rifle that was once Uncle Andrew's. The other rifle and half the remaining shells, they left with Ap-jei for the deer who might threaten the garden.

"He'll kill every deer for six miles," Sarah guessed.

"Probably," Anne agreed, "but I bet they come from ten miles to try for the garden."

It didn't take as long this time as it had last time, when Sarah was pregnant with Jennifer. At first James' backside hurt him, and sometimes he fell asleep on the horse and Sarah had to ride alongside and lift him onto her horse, holding him with her free arm and letting her horse follow Dan, reins wrapped around the pommel of the saddle. Lin complained bitterly at not being able to run around, and she often fell asleep against Anne, and Lucky and BelleTwo pranced happily, keeping up with them but not tethered, both of them reluctantly accepting the pack frames.

The trader took one look at Dan and his eyes lit up, he hesitated only briefly, and then blurted an offer.

"Tell you what," Anne said quietly, "we'll just leave him in the corral for as long as we're here. If you cheat me, I'll know, and you'll never get a chance to put one of your mares with him again. If you treat me fair, I'll bring him down twice a year, and you'll have the best bloodstock for miles." She walked off, certain they wouldn't have to dip into their cash reserve for the supplies they needed.

They stayed a week, the children at first fascinated by the growing pile of things in the wagons Anne had ordered on their last visit, but gradually the fascination faded and they became bored, began to look around for things to do, began to talk about missing the sea, missing the fun of fishing, began to talk about going home. Dan pranced and trumpeted happily in the corral, and Anne and Sarah carefully picked over and chose the things they thought they would need.

Dan didn't want to leave when it was time. He bucked and kicked, bared his teeth and danced away from her.

"What's wrong with him?" Anne asked.

"Honey," Sarah said softly, "he's a stud. A stud with a very small harem of mares, all of them pregnant. Pregnant mares don't come in heat. And he's a stud," she repeated.

"But he never acted like this before!" Anne protested.

"He's been months and months with only pregnant mares around him," Sarah said flatly, "and what you don't know, you don't miss. But there are at least six mares here who are still in heat, and . . . he's a stud."

And so, after going behind the buildings and weeping bitterly, Anne took the saddle off Dan and turned him loose in the corral again.

"Pick any horse you want," the trader offered, and Anne took a long time before finally choosing a large, deep-chested gray mare with a long off-white tail.

"I'll be back," she promised the trader.

"We could make a deal," he said quickly. "I'd keep him without charging for his feed, and I'd split the stud fee with you . . . there's lots of people are going to want to put their mares with him."

"Sure," she said shortly, throwing her saddle on the big gray mare. "I guess I'll just have to trust you. But you be careful with him, and don't let anybody try to ride him." Then she swung up on the mare, dug in her heels, and rode off, not really caring if the wagons followed her or not. Babe and Sunny didn't wait for Ruth and Sarah to urge them forward, they followed Anne immediately.

"Look at it this way," Anne said coldly. "We'll have a good credit here come springtime."

The trip back was quiet. Anne missed Dan so much she couldn't even spoil and pet the other animals. She felt betrayed and lost, and very very angry.

"It's not her fault," Sarah snapped when Anne threw the saddle on the big gray.

"I know."

"You haven't even given her a name."

"Okay, so I'll call her . . . something."

"I hope I never get on the wrong side of you!" Sarah exploded. "Because when you set your mind to it you're a bitch!"

"Sarah!" Anne was shocked.

"Well, you are. You're as sulky as a little kid whose sugar-tit fell in the dirt! For chrissakes, can't you look at it from Dan's point of view! *He's* happy! He's got a good home, an unlimited harem, and you said it yourself, he's a stud. That's what he's supposed to do."

"How am I supposed to feel?"

"Spoiled baby, wants everything her own way. She isn't happy. She wants to be happy even if everyone else is living unnatural lives!"

"Are you talking about Dan or about yourself?" Anne flared.

"I'm talking about *you*, honey!" and Sarah got on her horse and rode off, James following and Lin sitting in the wagon wondering why everybody was mad at everybody else.

261

"Come on, Nelly," Anne muttered, "let's catch up with those bad-tempered people."

"Nelly?" Sarah shrieked. "Nelly?"

"Nelly Gray, you dummy," Anne teased. "She's my Darlin' Nelly Gray. What else?" and though she knew Nell would never be to her what Dan was, it wasn't Nell's fault. Or Dan's. Or anybody's. It was just how it was.

Ap-jei ran out to meet them, a wide smile creasing his face. "Kla howja. Anne grinned.

"Kla howja." He gestured to the garden, then to the smoke-house, and released a flow of happy sounds.

"He says he got many deer," James interpreted.

"Tell him we knew he would." Sarah laughed.

Ap-jei grinned wider when he saw the array of fish hooks. And when Anne handed him the new rifle, he was so pleased he couldn't smile, only nod his head and repeat some words beneath his breath.

"And this," Sarah announced, "is the biggest boiler we could find."

He helped them unload the wagon, grinning when he saw how much flour they had brought back.

"Well, we had to," Anne laughed. "We're making bread for a lot of people."

They started a big batch of bread as soon as the supplies were unloaded, before they were unpacked. Ap-jei was in a hurry to get back to his village and show off his wealth and Sarah wanted the women to take some loaves back with them. She gave each of them the length of bright cloth she had chosen for them, and they ooh'ed and aaah'ed in a language everyone under-stood.

# Chapter 15

Anne complained bitterly that the wool smelled as if the sheep were still wearing it, but Sarah just pursed her lips, pretended not to hear and continued working the spinning wheel, awkwardly at first, then with more and more skill. The wool wasn't soft and fine, there were strange lumps and knots in it, but it was undeniably wool.

"By the time there's enough wool to knit a sweater for Jennifer, there won't be enough wool to knit a sweater for Jennifer. She'll be a grown woman," Ruth teased.

"That sentence makes no sense at all."

"Neither does fussing around like that." Ruth laughed and headed off to help Anne with the chores. The garden thrived, the corn grew tall, and they were kept busy cutting, splitting and stacking wood for the winter stove and for the smokehouses. One section of the barn was cleaned and turned into a storage shed for the smoked and dried meat and fish, and Anne was so tired at night she sometimes wished she hadn't been so ambitious.

The oolichan returned, and even though they still had strings of them from the spring run, they worked until late each night catching the shiny treasure and celebrating.

"Oolichan only come to special beaches," James chanted, his feet dancing, "and we have a special beach. When visitors come they will know ours is a special beach. Mother fish lays her eggs in the sand, father fish gives seed. When the highest of tides comes again, baby fish swim to the sea."

"That sounds like a song." Anne laughed and Ruth ran for her juice harp, while James strutted happily, translating the ancient Indian prayer of thanks, waving a kelp tail and laughing. Soon they were all dancing on the beach, and the juice harp was joined by the sound of Anne's clapping hands, Sarah's two kitchen spoons and the happy shrieks of Lin and Jennifer.

Autumn settled on them grimly, the wind howling and biting, the rain pelting down constantly. The children stayed in the house, complaining there was nothing to do and Anne and Sarah took turns going out to the barn to enjoy the peace and quiet of the animals.

"God, if they don't stop moaning about nothing to do I'm going to stuff something in their mouths." Anne poured herself a cup of tea, then walked to the bedroom door and looked in on the sleeping children. "Except, they're so damn sweet when they're asleep."

"Anne, we've got to find a better way to dry diapers," Sarah insisted. "I'm going berserk with these things flapping in my face all the time. Isn't there room in the barn for some lines?"

"We can try," Anne said, "but they won't dry as fast."

"As long as I'm not walking around with the damn things slapping me in my face. How in God's name do people survive with more than one child in diapers?"

"With difficulty." Anne laughed. "Come on, forget about it. We'll have a hot bath and a cup of tea and go to bed and . . . and in the morning it will still be raining."

"I wish I had a cat," Sarah said, for the umpteenth time. "And a dog," she added firmly.

"Now a dog! First a cat, then a dog!"

Anne lifted water from the boiler to the new big washtub, laughing gently. Then she stripped off her clothes and climbed into the tub, her feet and lower legs hanging over the edge.

"Remember that tub at Belle's place?" she mused, "and how you could get all of you into it at one time?"

"There was a lot less of you to get in then, too," Sarah remembered fondly. "And you were so sure that your belly and breasts were . . . dirty . . . that you washed with your underwear

264

on. Remember how you were going to run away rather than bathe with someone watching?"

"And you just whipped off your . . . Belle's . . . gown and stood between me and the door. The only way past was to touch you and I'd never seen so much skin in my life. I was scared to touch!" She laughed happily.

"Oh, Annie," Sarah sighed, "you were such a . . . strange . . . little girl. Stiff-necked and oh, so moral!"

"What's wrong with being moral?"

"Well, don't take it to extremes."

"I told you, there was no room to take a bath in private and you never knew when Andrew would just saunter in all eyeballs and grin."

"There's no room to take a bath here, either."

"Yeah, but nobody is ogling and grinning, either."

She soaped and rinsed herself, then stepped onto the floor and began to dry herself.

"You want that water, or do you want fresh?"

"That's fine. Any dirt you've got, I've got," Sarah said casually, adding some warm water and then climbing into the tub to sit, feet and forelegs hanging over the edge, soaping herself eagerly.

"What you said . . . when I was mad about Dan pulling the stunt he pulled . . . about living unnatural lives . . . did you mean it?"

"Half of it, I guess. Does it bother you?"

"A bit." Anne poured tea and handed a cup to Sarah. "Do you miss . . . Tom?"

"Tom? No, I don't miss him at all," Sarah said easily.

"Well . . . other men?"

"I don't know. Sometimes I feel as if this is kind of a . . . waste of time, I guess. I mean . . . I don't know."

"It never bothers me," Anne blurted. "I mean, I feel as if I've got everything I ever want. Do you get . . . lonely?"

"No. Not lonely." Sarah stepped from the tub and reached for the dry towel warming on the oven door. Anne pulled on clean underwear and clean clothes, then took the washtub to the front door, opened the door and dumped the water onto the already soggy ground. "A bit more water won't hurt us," she muttered, "and I'm not walking out into that damn rain!"

Lin wakened in the middle of the night and Anne padded to the children's room, lifted Lin from her bed and set her on the chamberpot.

"Okay, baby," she yawned, "let it drip." The floor was cold and there was a draft blowing from somewhere. Her bare skin prickled with cold and she hugged herself, shivering slightly. When Lin smiled, Anne lifted her from the chamberpot and tucked her back into bed, then placed the chamberpot under the edge of the bed. "Remind me to empty that in the morning." She pulled the blankets up over James' shoulders and on her way back to bed dropped several pieces of beach-salvaged coal onto the fire in the hearth. When she got back to bed her feet were cold and she was chilled.

"You're like ice," Sarah mumbled.

"Baby sleeping?"

"Like a log. And not just your feet, your legs, too!"

"It's bitter cold. I put coal on the fire. You feel as warm as toast." She sighed, cuddling close. Sarah wriggled slightly, adjusting herself to Anne's body, and Anne placed her arm across Sarah's waist, hugging her tightly.

"You've changed," she said softly. "You even feel different."

"Because of Jennifer? What do you mean?" Sarah half turned toward Anne. "I might be a bit . . . bustier, but my waist is back where it was and my stomach's as flat as a board again." Then she giggled softly. "Flatter than some of those boards we've been trying to make."

"Not that." Anne shook her head slightly. "But something. I don't know what it is, you just feel . . . different."

"It's not me," Sarah whispered, "it's you."

"Me?"

"Yes, dumb person, you. Stupid person," she teased, turning toward Anne and smiling at her. "Idiotic person," her hand touched Anne's face. "Moron of a person."

"Sarah . . ." Anne tried to speak and couldn't.

"Such a frightened person," Sarah said softly, her hand lost in Anne's hair. Anne's hand on Sarah's back felt burning hot, and trembled. It moved, stroking Sarah's shoulder.

"Are you sure?" Sarah whispered.

"I don't know," Anne admitted, her leg rubbing against Sarah's leg. "I don't think I know very much of anything at all. I don't even think I know what it is I'm feeling or what it is I'm supposed to do about it."

"Just don't start fighting." Sarah smiled down at Anne, her lips moving softly against Anne's skin. "Because I'm damned if I want to leap up and block the door again."

"It wouldn't work this time anyway," Anne said with a new sort of gentle firmness. "This time, I don't think I'm afraid of skin at all."

She had kissed Sarah hello and good-bye, kissed her for luck, kissed her to soothe and comfort, be soothed and comforted, kissed her goodnight and good morning, but never more enjoyably or eagerly.

"I know what I want," she confessed, her hands stroking the soft skin of Sarah's hips, "but I don't know what to do."

"Don't worry," Sarah laughed softly, her breath warm on Anne's breast, her fingers gently stroking the inner thighs of Anne's strong legs. "Belle was the best teacher in the world. All you have to do is be willing to learn from me."

"Well," Anne's voice trembled, and she searched for a joke, however weak, to hide her sudden shyness. "I learned to play the piano. And even if we don't have a piano, yet, if we ever do get one, I'll just need some time to practice and . . ."

"You going to babble all night or are you going to learn how to make love?"

"I'm learnin'," Anne muttered, her shyness evaporating, her lips hungry and searching.

Hours later, cradled happily in each other's arms, they watched the first sun begin to dissolve the mist, heard the birds cheeping, the rooster begin his morning ritual. Then Jennifer began to stir and moments later Ruth padded to the kitchen and started the fire in the cookstove.

"Another day," Sarah smiled, stretching like a cat and sighing contentedly.

"I love you," Anne whispered.

"You sure do," Sarah teased. "You love me very, very well, indeed. You learn fast," she stroked Anne's hair, "and you learn good, and," she continued, kissing gently, "you're wonderfully inventive. I can see where my nights are going to become so damned wonderful I'll get so content and happy I'll stagger out of bed in the morning all smiles and yawns and so pleased with the world everyone will wonder what I'm drinking in my tea."

Jennifer began to mumble and squirm and Lin came into the room rubbing her eyes. Clattering from the kitchen suggested James had decided to help with breakfast. "Up and at it," Sarah laughed, "the day is upon us."

"I love you," Anne repeated, swinging her legs from the bed and reaching for her clothes.

They hung the diaper lines in the barn and then spent an hour or two bridle-training BelleTwo. Anne whistled and Nell trotted over, nuzzling Anne's pockets, searching for grain. Lin was stamping her feet, splashing in the puddles, and down by the rocks James, in his new winter pants, new shirt and warm jacket, was picking coal and putting it in the bucket. Sarah grabbed a shovel and began to heave the richly smelling manure from the floor of the barn to the compost pile.

"That's a far cry," Anne teased, "from the high heeled shoes and tinkling piano."

"Look who's talking," Sarah teased back, lovingly. "Just listen to her. Wasn't what you were saying last night." And when Anne's face burned, Sarah started to laugh. Anne turned away suddenly, and the laughter died.

"You okay?" Sarah asked.

"Yeah, fine," Anne mumbled, and walked away quickly. Sarah finished cleaning the barn, then went into the cabin where

Anne had started making lunch. Jennifer was awake and crawling on the floor, smiling and chattering to herself. Lin came in, complaining that her feet were cold.

"Wash and dry your feet, then put on your socks and shoes," Anne said firmly.

"Don't like."

"Then don't complain to me about cold feet." And everyone, including Lin, knew that very soon she would get over her dislike of shoes. Anne called James in for lunch and they ate quietly, the children talked sporadically, but Anne had very little to say to anyone.

"Okay," Sarah announced, "as soon as Jennifer's had her drink, she and Lin are going to bed for their nap."

Anne washed up the dishes, watching Jennifer nursing lazily. The baby wasn't hungry. She had sampled some of everybody's lunch, and while she couldn't eat anything that required much chewing, she did well with mashed potatoes and carrots or finely chopped beets. She fell asleep, her mouth opening and releasing the dark nipple, and Sarah wiped herself with a clean damp cloth, buttoned the front of her shirt and carried the baby to her bed.

"Lin," she said in a very subdued voice, "bed," and Lin scampered off, protesting that she wasn't tired at all.

"She'll be asleep in five minutes," Sarah said. Anne nodded and threw the dishwater out the door into the yard.

"What's wrong?" Sarah blurted, her eyes brimming with tears.

"Nothing." Anne seemed surprised.

"You've hardly spoken! All I said was . . ."

"I know what you said."

"And you went all red in the face and walked away."

"I thought you were laughing at me."

"At you? *At you.*" Sarah didn't know whether to laugh or cry. "You idiot, I thought I was laughing *with* you."

"And anyway," Anne's face began to burn again, "it made me start thinking . . . remembering . . . and," she stammered a bit, looked down at her hands, then pushed ahead, "and I remembered the night Ap-jei walked in the door . . . the night Jennifer was born . . . and I felt . . . almost . . . the same way then as I did when you said what you said. But not the same."

"You aren't making any sense at all." Sarah laughed.

"I'm not supposed to." Anne looked into Sarah's eyes. "Aren't you the one told me that one of these days, when I was big . . . You said, one of these days, when you're a big girl, you'll make a damn fool of yourself just like everybody else does."

"Oh, baby." Sarah crossed the room and cuddled close to Anne, realizing suddenly that the little girl was taller than she was. "If you're a fool, I'm another."

The ground was white with snow and the moon full and round. Anne walked from the barn to the cabin, opened the door, then closed it quickly and dropped the new bar in place across it. Then she stuffed the crack at the bottom of the door with the sacking, took off her jacket and warmed her hands by the fire. She checked the sleeping children, smiling at Jennifer curled up in bed with James, and she pulled the covers up under their chins. She went into the main room, put coal on the fire, then poured two cups of coffee and took them into the bedroom with her.

"Where have you been?" Sarah asked sleepily.

"Walking," Anne said briefly, stripping off her clothes and climbing into bed. "Thinking."

"You fool, you're frozen."

"I'll be warm in a minute. It's lovely out there. The trees look like something out of a storybook. And it's so quiet!"

Sarah cuddled close, Anne's arms wrapping around her comfortably, their legs entwined, their breath warm against their faces.

"Anne?"

"Huh?"

"Can I ask you something without you getting mad?"

"What?"

"Promise not to get mad?"

"Promise."

---

270

"The night Jennifer was born . . . when Ap-jei walked in . . . Why didn't you . . ."

"Because," Anne said firmly, holding Sarah close. "Because I didn't love him. And you said it, I'm a moralist: If you don't love someone, it's dirty, and if you do, it's not."

"Love you, Anne."

"Love you, Sarah."

# Chapter 16

The cabin was warm, the scents and smells of breakfast still hanging in the air. Sarah was measuring flour for her bread baking and Lin and Jennifer playing on the floor with the chicken-wheat ball, rolling it back and forth to each other, giggling. The door opened, the cold draught blew in, and Anne entered with an armload of wood, followed by Ruth and James, similarly burdened.

"We," she grinned, "are going to get a Christmas tree."

"I," Sarah mocked, "am going to stay here, warm and toasty, and wait for you to do just that." And she tucked Anne's scarf around her throat, hugged her, leaving floury handmarks on her jacket. She waved good-bye to them, mixed her bread and set it to rise, then sat down with the present she was embroidering for Anne. It wasn't easy, in a small cabin, to find the time or space to be alone and work on a surprise, and Sarah wanted Anne's shirt to be ready. Lin and Jennifer threw the ball across the room, Jennifer crawled after it, laughing. Just before she got to it, Lin ran, snapped it up and threw it back across the room, then dropped to all fours and crawled beside the baby, pretending to race, their laughter loud and shrill in the small kitchen. The riders who came from the south, along the beach, arrived at the cabin door unheard. Sarah's first inkling of visitors came when the door swung open and the chill air swept across the floor.

"Back already?" She tried to hide the embroidered shirt, then looked toward the door, her jaw dropping when she saw the two men.

"What . . . do you want?" she asked.

"Oh, a cup of coffee, something to eat!" The first man smiled, coming into the cabin, knocking the snow from his boots and clothes. The second rider stepped in and, closing the door, walked toward the table, trailing snow and mud.

"Had hell's own time finding you," he said pleasantly. "Where's Anne?"

"Oh, she's . . ." Sarah froze.

"She's where?" Uncle Andrew asked, sitting at the table, ignoring the children as if they didn't exist.

"Do you want some eggs?" Sarah stalled for time, rising and moving to the stove, pushing the coffee pot closer to the hot end of the stove, hoping neither man noticed how badly her hands were shaking.

"We thought we'd lost you all together," Andrew continued, "but then I saw my horse at the trading post, and after that it was easy."

"Yeah," the second man said softly, stepping over Jennifer, unconcernedly, and sitting easily at the table.

"Eggs?" Sarah repeated stupidly.

"Sure," they nodded. The second man pulled his tobacco pouch from his pocket and rolled a cigarette.

"Took me a while," Andrew volunteered, watching Sarah nervously cracking eggs and whipping them, "to find out which way you'd gone. Guess I was either drunk or hung over for the better part of a week, and then when I did wake up neither that fat tub'a'guts nor her fancy woman would tell me so much as the time of day. But the whole town was laughin'," he grinned wolfishly, "and that stupid bugger Luke Wilson was playin' songs on the banjo, and I just stayed real quiet until they stopped har-har'in' long enough to brag to each other, and bit by bit, I figured it out."

"Coffee?" She poured two mugs of coffee and knew they saw her hands shaking.

---

274

"I'd'a maybe never found you," Andrew said agreeably, dropping honey into his coffee and sipping noisily, "but I run into this band of frog-croakin' half-breeds, and when I said as how I'd once seen a big black stud that was more horse than I could begin to describe, they all grinned and agreed as how he was one hell of a horse. A jug of whiskey later, I knew which way you'd gone from there. So I just kept goin', and sure enough, run into two very pissed off men with a passel of crabby kids. From there it was easy. Only one way to go from there."

"Your eggs." Sarah put them in front of him, turned and filled a second plate for the silent smoker.

"Ran into Simon, here, and me'n him teamed up. Simon, he used to ride with Luke Wilson, didn't you, Simon?"

"Yep," said Simon, shoveling eggs into his mouth.

"Learned a lot from Simon, I have," Andrew bragged. "Simon was there the night they strung your cardshark boyfriend, wasn't you Simon?"

"Yep," Simon agreed.

"Oh, God," Sarah gasped.

"You should'a let 'em kill you then," Andrew said pleasantly. "You're the child of the devil and he looks after his own, for sure." He ate quietly, his eyes darting to the two frightened children, then to the quiet sandy-haired killer, Simon. "Simon didn't believe you was alive, did you, Simon?"

"Nope," Simon agreed.

"But you are." Andrew giggled suddenly, choking on his half-swallowed coffee.

He hawked and spat on the floor in disgust. "Still alive and spawning more just like yourself," he growled, glaring at Lin and Jennifer. "Who left that black one in you?" he shouted suddenly, frightening the children and making them cry.

Sarah moved to comfort them, hushing them and telling them everything would be all right. She didn't like the way the sandy-haired man with the gentle smile was eyeing them and so she quickly gave each of them a piece of bread and molasses and sent them into the small bedroom.

"What do you want?" she managed.

---

275

"Told you. Coffee, food, and . . . finish what ought to have been finished a long time ago."

"I'm not doing anything wrong!" she protested. "I . . ."

"Shut up," he said quietly, and she did. "You're trash and trash don't talk, it just lies on the ground and smells bad. And makes more trash like itself. A while ago there was only you, wearing short dresses and sinning. Sinning and making others sin. Now there's you and them two in the other room. If I leave you here before long you'll have a swarm of baby whores, training them and making them just as trashy as you."

"No!" Sarah gasped.

"Yes," he said calmly, "because you're all alike. All of you. Born like that. Born to temptation and sin."

"You heard the man," the sandy-haired killer smiled. "He's been looking for you the way a preacher looks for a repentant sinner."

Sarah wished she could get at the spare rifle, but it was in the bedroom, on a shelf high over the bed, kept out of sight and out of reach ever since the day Anne had caught James trying to load it. He had wanted to practice with it so that he, too, could go hunting. The knife in her hands was long and sharp and she was certain she could get at least one of them with it, but what of the other one, and what of the two children.

"Don't try anything foolish," Andrew grinned, enjoying her fear, toying with her, feeling his blood warm at the sight of her pale face and trembling hands. Simon pulled his long skinning knife from his boot and began to pick his teeth, clean his fingernails, his soft eyes belying the madness that flamed in his can-of-worms brain. "Simon," Andrew bragged, "can use that knife so good he can take all the skin off a living woman's tit and leave the nipple in place. Until he cuts that off, too," he added happily.

Sarah looked at the knife in Simon's hands and remembered Andrew's comment about baby whores, and her panic grew, thinking of the soft baby flesh of Jennifer and Lin. Andrew looked at the bedroom door, as if reading her mind. "Don't try it," he warned, "they squeal just like dying rabbits."

"Oh, God!" Sarah bolted for the bedroom door, hoping to

get on the other side, slide the bolt in place and escape through the window with the babies. Andrew stood up quickly, back-handed her, splitting her lip and knocking her to the floor. Lin ran from the bedroom, shouting and trying to defend Sarah. Simon picked her up casually, then threw her across the room.

"Little black bitch," he cursed softly, and Lin's body hit the wall with a crash. She fell to the floor, her neck twisted, her body still.

"Lin!" Sarah screamed, trying to rise, hearing Jennifer screaming with terror.

"Grab her," Andrew shrilled, "and bend her over that chair. I'm gonna show you," he promised, tugging at his belt, "there's more than one place to visit a whore!" The leather swished through the air, bit into the flesh of her back and buttocks. Simon was dragging furiously at her clothes, ripping them off, and then she was slung from the chair to the table, the edge biting into her belly. Simon pushed her face down, her cheek smearing blood onto the plate still greasy with scrambled eggs. The table edge was hurting her, the belt was slashing at her, and Andrew's breathing was sour and hot against her face. And then she could smell the sweat of him, feel his hands digging at her breasts, his fingers pinching, pulling her backward against him, her buttocks trying to escape the prodding thing that was forcing them apart, and then a pain like nothing she could remember stabbed through her, and the sound of their laughter swelled, blending with her scream and her sobs.

The scream froze Anne in her tracks. She dropped the butt end of the Christmas tree in the snow, her hand reaching for the revolver on her hip.

"Stay here," she commanded Ruth and James, and she raced through the trees toward the cabin.

Two horses standing slope-hipped and cold, their reins trailing in the snow, and from the cabin the sound of Jennifer wailing in terror, and other sounds, bumps and moans and deep grunts. Anne moved toward the cabin slowly, remembering the stories she had heard of waiting for the bear to charge before shooting, forcing herself to move slowly, carefully.

From the corner of her eye she saw James and Ruth come from the trees, Ruth's gloved hands firm on the rifle Anne had given her when she had grabbed the butt end of the fir tree. James clutched the double-headed axe, his young face tight with fear, his eyes fixed on the cabin door.

Anne motioned to them to lead the two wet, tired horses away from the front of the cabin. If the men inside came outside, they would be easier to catch if they were on foot. James nodded, said something to Ruth and, while she kept the rifle aimed at the front door, he moved the horses behind the barn. Anne crept to the door and tried to peek inside, but could see nothing. If the new bar was in place she wouldn't be able to open the door anyway, and they would hear her and know someone was outside. She moved to the window and used the edge of the hatchet to pry one of the boards, not enough to remove it, the added light might warn them, just enough so the edge of the sharp knife could dig into the dry cedar and shave a piece away. She peeked inside carefully. Someone had Sarah bent across the table, and what he was doing made Anne feel sick. Sarah was bleeding and gasping for breath, and a man Anne had never seen before was standing by the doorway to the children's bedroom, his knife in his hand, warning Sarah that if she made any more noise he was going into the bedroom to paint the walls with blood. Anne couldn't see Lin where she lay on the floor.

The man by the bedroom door had a knife in his hand and a gun in a well-oiled holster at his hip. The other had his hands under Sarah and his pants down around his ankles. Anne aimed the revolver carefully and fired through the cedar planking, blowing Simon's guts all over the wall behind him.

Before the other man could fumble himself free of Sarah, Anne was in the cabin, her revolver pointed at him.

"Annie?" he gasped, staring at the gun.

"Uncle Andrew?" Anne gaped, staring at the ghost. Wanting to pull the trigger, wanting to blow his sweaty face all over the wall, unable to move, unable to so much as twitch her finger. In the doorway Simon was dying noisily, but Anne couldn't tear her eyes from Uncle Andrew's face, she didn't even notice Andrew had pulled up his pants, fastened his buttons, and was sneaking looks at his gun. She thought she'd killed him once, by burning, and he'd lived. Now he was here again and she wanted to kill him and couldn't, not a second time.

The roar of the rifle filled the room with sound, and jerked Anne out of her paralysis. Andrew was flung across the room, his chest blossoming red, and then Ruthie was walking into the kitchen, the rifle still in her hands, her face white with rage and shock.

"Bastard," Ruth said flatly.

"Linnie!" James shrieked, running past Anne to the crumpled little body.

"Jennifer," Anne said, and Ruth headed for the back bedroom, stepping over the now-silent Simon, and disappearing behind the blood-stained door. Jennifer's screams diminished to sobs, and Anne still stood, staring at James cradling the body of Lin, staring past Sarah who held onto the edge of the table as if it was her only hold on life.

"Come on," Anne said finally, "let me check you."

"I'm all right," Sarah sobbed. "I won't die because of it. But Lin . . ."

Anne carried the small body into the bedroom, and laid her on the bed, straightening the limp little arms and legs, trying not to look at the awkwardly lolling head, the broken neck.

"What's wrong with Lin?" James asked.

"She's dead," Anne said honestly, giving him the full shock at once, giving him the dignity of knowing the worst, like an adult, not trying to lie to him. Whether he learned the truth now or later, the pain would be the same.

James' eyes brimmed and he lay down on the bed next to Lin and cuddled her, trying to pretend she was just asleep. Ruth sat on the bed holding Jennifer, staring white-faced at Anne.

"Why?" she asked, finally.

"Because the world is full of snake-hearted bastards," Anne said, moving to the door.

In the kitchen, she grabbed Simon by the feet, dragged him across the floor to the front door, opened it and took him outside, dumping him in the snow, and leaving him there like garbage. Back in the kitchen she grabbed Andrew by the boots, and dragged him from the kitchen, not caring that his head bumped on the edge of the porch, not caring any more than if he had been a wheel-crushed snake, dumping his body beside that of Simon. When she went back in the house the sound of soft crying from the bedroom told her that Ruth and James were trying to console each other.

"Come on," she said flatly, "give me a hand with this washtub."

"What?" Sarah said dully.

"The washtub," Anne said. "You've got to get cleaned up. You're all over blood and shit and you're cut."

But Sarah just stood with her hands on the tabletop, staring down at the blood-smeared plate, eyes hollow with shock. Anne filled the tub with water, led Sarah to it, stripped off the last of her ruined clothes and pushed her into the water. Gently, soothingly, she washed the belt welts on Sarah's back, bathed the split lip, the cut above her eye, wiped Sarah's back and legs with a warm soapy cloth.

"Don't look at me," Sarah pleaded. "I feel so dirty!"

"That's exactly how he wanted you to feel," Anne said, her voice soft. "Don't give the son of a bitch the satisfaction!"

When Sarah was washed and her cuts cleaned, Anne led her to the bedroom and tucked her into bed, then went to where Ruth and James were still lying cuddling Lin. Jennifer was staring from her cot, her thumb in her mouth.

"Sarah needs you," Anne said quietly. They looked at her, eyes red-rimmed. "Lin doesn't need you," Anne urged. "Sarah does." And they moved from the bed, went to the other room, crawled in beside Sarah and held her, stroking her, talking softly to her, cuddling her until she began to cry.

Anne swilled buckets of water on the floor, sweeping the water, blood and bits of splattered flesh outside. She worked her rage off with the scouring brick, moving all the furniture and dragging the brick across the boards furiously, scraping clean the mud from their boots, their blood and mess, scraping it all off the boards and swilling it outside with more water. She built up the fire in the hearth and in the small metal stove, then sat by the table, waiting for the floor to dry, waiting for the sound of weeping to stop. All this time the two bodies lay stiffening in the snow and mud, ignored totally.

When the floor was dry, Anne scrubbed the dishes and table, then cooked supper and took it in to the three in the bedroom.

"I can't," Sarah said weakly.

"You have to," Anne said sternly, "because Jennifer is going to want to nurse and if you haven't got a grip on yourself . . ."

"I'm not nursing her any more," Sarah insisted. "He made me dirty! I could have a disease! She'd get sick."

"Bullshit," Anne snapped, needing to keep things as much like normal as possible. "I'm not having that kind of shit come into this place and throw everybody for a loop! Okay, they came. And they did their goddamndest. And we're all hurting. But it's not going to mess up our lives. Drink the coffee or wear it!" And then she, too, was crying, holding onto Sarah and apologizing for snapping at her.

"I didn't mean to yell," she sniffed.

"It's okay," Sarah insisted, sipping her coffee.

"Can you look after the kids?" Anne asked quietly, and Sarah nodded, understanding without needing words.

"See if you can get her to eat some of your egg," she whispered to James.

"Where are you going?"

"To get rid of that trash."

"Then I'm going, too," he said firmly.

She got the dugout Ap-jei had given them, and lengths of rope from the barn.

"Empty their pockets," James said suddenly.

"I don't want anything of theirs!" she snapped.

"That's foolish," he replied. "Ap-jei says you don't give an enemy anything to take with him when he goes. You send him out the way he came and that way he can't lie his way into the good place. They just look at him and know what kind of a

---

281

person he was. Everyone else shows up with . . . presents. And you put their best thing in their hands. When they show up, the others know this was someone who was Somebody . . ." And so they stripped the bodies completely and dragged them by ropes to the beach, then placed several large rocks in the dugout, got in and paddled straight out to deep water, dragging the two naked corpses behind the dugout.

"Pull them alongside," Anne grunted, reversing her paddle and reaching for the rope. James pulled the naked body of Andrew beside the dugout, face down in the water, then, with shocking swiftness, rolled the corpse on its back and bent over the side of the dugout, his sharp knife in his hand.

"James!" Anne protested, horrified.

"They don't get sent over with their dings," he said coldly. "If they got their dings, even if they're naked and got no presents or treasures, they might fool some spirits who were never very smart, anyway. They might find some woman who showed up with nothing, just like them, and they might find a way to be not too lonely, maybe even have fun. Without dings, they'll never enjoy anything. Not ever again."

"What about people who lose arms and legs and show up without them?"

"They'll have presents and clothes," James gritted, sawing with his knife. "Others'll know it was an accident. These naked things with no dings . . . everyone'll know they're nothin' but driftwood. Never been nothing but driftwood, never will be nothin' but driftwood. And they won't ever get to come back again!"

He dropped the fleshy bundle to the bottom of the dugout, hauled Simon's body alongside and quickly slashed away the genitals.

"What will you do with . . . that?" she asked, feeling as if she were about to vomit.

"Gonna burn it," James said coldly. "Gonna burn it to ash and let the wind scatter it all over everywhere. They can search 'n' search 'n' search but they'll never be whole again. Never gonna fool anybody else, either."

They tied rocks to the bodies and watched them sink out of

sight in the gray heaving sea, then paddled swiftly back to shore, James grimly carrying his bloody burden.

Sarah, Ruth and James helped Anne bathe Lin and dress her in the bright red dress that was to have been her Christmas present.

"Don't put shoes on her," Sarah sobbed. "She hated shoes." And so they left her feet bare.

"No box," James insisted. "Momma and Poppa don't got no box holding them in."

The four of them dug a small grave beside the other two, and they wrapped Lin in her own quilt from her own bed. Ribbons in her hair and the Christmas locket gift from James around her neck, her hands holding the rag doll they had all worked on, they lowered her into the wet ground.

"It looks so cold."

"It's not," James said surely. "Not for her. Here, we're in one place and where she is is another place and things are different in different places and she's not cold."

"Ap-jei?" Anne asked.

"No, Na-nis," James answered, his sorrow under control. "She isn't hurting and she isn't crying. We can't see her but she can see us. And she can see Momma and Poppa, too." He placed her toys and Christmas gifts in the grave, arranging them carefully. "So she's got her things and they know she was Somebody," he explained. But he could not watch when they began to cover her with dirt. "We don't do that." He shook his head sadly. "We don't put dirt on their faces or mud in their nose. We put them in a tree where they can smell the sea and feel the wind." And he walked into the house sadly.

When Sarah went back out to the grave that evening she found ribbons dangling from the cross and food on the grave.

"James," she said softly, "we don't put food out like that."

"We do," he said quietly, "until we know they made the trip."

That night the driftwood fire on the beach blazed hungrily and James sat beside it, eyes streaming, chanting the prayer for the dead. The cedar driftwood had been slow to ignite, but James had carried coals from the fireplace and dry kindling from the woodshed and when the wet cedar finally began to burn the sparks leaped to the cloudy winter sky and the smoke billowed fiercely, blown on the strong wind.

They watched from the small window in the kitchen, their faces strained and worried.

"It's . . . heathen," Anne whispered.

"Oh, for God's sake," Sarah said wearily. "If it makes him feel better, what difference does it make? The dead are dead and the living console themselves as best they can and try not to wish that they were dead, too."

Ruth turned from the window, walked to the door, and, without putting on her coat or her hat, went out into the wild December night. The mist was damp against her face, the smell of woodsmoke from the cabin mixing with the smell of cedar smoke from the beach. She moved toward James' fire, her skin prickling, but not from the cold.

She sat next to him on the sand, immediately aware that it was not cold and damp, as she'd expected, but warm, still steaming slightly as the heat from the huge blaze evaporated the water, rose and mixed with the smoke. James didn't even look at her. He was staring into the fire, chanting, weeping. There was no sign of the bloody rags or the genitals of the two killers, and Ruth knew he had already burned them. She didn't know the meaning of the words he chanted, but deep inside she recognized the message. She took her juice harp from her pocket, and began to twang softly, keeping the rhythm of the chant. James reached out one small hand, laid it on her leg, and continued singing. The cedar sparks raced to the sky, carrying the prayer upward. We who have loved you, he sang, send prayers and thoughts. We who have loved you and are now alone. Trees and shore, fire and earth sing with us. We who have loved you and are now alone. Seasons will come and seasons will go and we who have loved you will be alone. In our lives and in our deeds, we will remember you. We who have loved you and are now alone. Fire and water, earth and sky carry our love, we who have loved you and are now alone.

---

The next afternoon Ap-jei and eight pullers beached their dugout near the still smouldering logs. They nodded, the spotter had been right, something had happened, but they didn't know what until they got to the cabin.

They sat on the floor holding their untouched cups of tea, listening carefully to James' words. Ap-jei cried openly, but when he tried to comfort Sarah and be comforted by her, she pulled away from him, her eyes burning and inward-turned. Ap-jei sighed, turned away sadly, and went outside to stand by Lin's grave and mourn freely.

The pullers nodded with satisfaction when James told how he had marked the killers, and they told him he had done well and honored his family. They each went to Ruth and held her closely, stroking her shoulders and arms, calling her Little Sister, accepting her freely into their clans and families. Then they, too, went outside and joined Ap-jei by the grave. James sat with them, translating the words they spoke as they gave witness to the spirits that this was a child of the people, a person of worth and value, a person who was loved and would be missed.

Anne expected they would all stay to share a meal, but they left without even saying good-bye, each of them leaving a token or gift on Lin's grave. Some beads, several knives, some fish hooks, a bracelet made of natural copper, the designs etched deep and clear.

"When he gets home," James explained, pointing to a small stick of cedar with freshly cut notches on it, "he will break three kettles so they can never again be used on this earth. The spirits of the kettles will join Lin and all the others in that place will know she was a person of importance. And this," he lifted a shell lovingly, "this is a promise that he will have a fine dugout carved for Lin, and he will fill it with bowls of oil and otter pelts and fine treasures and light it on fire and turn it loose on the sea, and it will change from wood to smoke and float to where she is and will be able to go through the air in it and travel all over the world. She will fly in her spirit dugout and watch us from the stars, and be more free than the birds."

"Does he really believe that?" Anne asked.

"Do you really believe 'I am the Resurrection and the Life and whosoever believeth in Me shall not perish'?" Sarah asked.

"I don't know," Anne admitted.

"I don't know if James believes this or not," Sarah sighed, "but I'd rather think of Lin zipping from star to star and laughing and swimming in the clouds than think of her sitting on some goddamn leaky cloud with white wings coming from her shoulders playing a twice-shat-upon harp and singing Oh Holy Jerusalem."

"Sarah!" Anne protested, shocked.

"Life," Sarah turned away, "is just like a shit sandwich: Every day another bite, and all of them stick in my throat." And she walked away, face set and cold.

Christmas was a sad and quiet day. Jennifer didn't know what it was supposed to be about, and both Ruth and James were too aware of the fresh grave to be able to enjoy anything. Anne and Sarah had considered letting Christmas just pass them all by unnoticed, then had decided the day, and the idea behind it, was too important to be ruined by the kind of people the two men had been. Sarah finished the embroidered shirt she was making for Anne, and Anne brought out the warm wrapper she had bought at the trading post and hidden away for so long. New clothes for Ruth and James, and bright new jacknives for both of them.

"I want you both to stand on the porch with your eyes shut," Anne said, and the two children put on their coats, squeezed their eyes shut, and allowed Sarah to lead them outside. "Hold out your hands," she said, her eyes damp with tears. Anne put the leather reins in their hands, and still they stood, eyes shut.

"Open up," she said, trying to smile.

They stared, not understanding, looking at the new leather.

"Not just the bridles," Anne said. "The horses are yours, too."

"Mine?" Ruth breathed, looking past the new bridle to BelleTwo.

"Yours," Anne said firmly. "BelleTwo is your own horse, to train your own way. And now James has his own horse, too," she smiled. It didn't matter to James that the big brown gelding used to be Simon's horse. He was James' horse now, and that was all that mattered.

"Oh, thank you," Ruth said, holding Anne tightly, wiping the tears from her cheeks. "I promise, I'll be real good to her."

"I know you will," Anne said. "Now why don't you and James go off and have some fun? After all, it's Christmas." And while the two children rode off down the beach, Sarah sat in her rocking chair watching Jennifer play with her toys on the floor, and Anne sat in a kitchen chair by the stove watching Sarah watch Jennifer. The silence in the cabin weighed heavily, while both women tried hard to forget that there were now three graves instead of two.

# Chapter 17

The memory of the two men and what they had done hung over the cabin long after the sea had reduced their bodies to nothing. Jennifer had bad dreams for weeks, and would wake screaming with fear. James sometimes lay on Lin's bed in the evening and stared damp-eyed at the ceiling, missing her terribly. Even after the belt marks and bruises, bites and scratches had healed, Sarah could feel Andrew on her skin, remember him driving dryly into her, and she grew in on herself, scarcely speaking, not wanting to touch or be touched. Every night she would climb into the washtub, but her nightly bath was different now. Where before she had washed in warm water, relaxing and smoothing soap onto her body, now she climbed into a tub of hot water and scoured at her skin. When Anne tried to speak to her about it, Sarah would turn away, her eyes shadowed, her face drawn.

"You can't know," she said bitterly.

Anne tried in every way she could think of to help Sarah, but it seemed as if everything she said or did was the wrong thing.

"Sarah?" she said softly, moving closer in bed and cuddling Sarah's stiff back. "Please don't cry."

"Don't touch me," Sarah said coldly.

"Sarah . . ."

"I'm sorry," Sarah said, getting out of bed and going into the kitchen to sit staring into the embers in the hearth. Much later Anne followed her.

"Isn't there anything I can say?" she begged.

"I just want to be left alone, that's all."

"Sarah, for God's sake, you didn't do anything wrong!"

"Maybe not. But I can still smell that man's sweat, and I can still feel his fingers. I can't get the stink of him off my skin or the thought of him out of my mind, and as long as he's still there, I don't want to be touched or looked at or spoken to!"

Anne busied herself with work, turning the manure pile, cleaning the hen house and clearing all sign of grass and weeds from the garden plot. She enlarged the garden and cut down several of the trees she had ringed previously. She repaired the fish wier and began enlarging the barn, making ready for the cow she intended to bring back from the trading post.

"We've got too many horses," she said one night.

"If you say so," Sarah replied, cuddling Jennifer tenderly.

"I'm going to trade the others. Lucky, too. The last thing we need is a damn mule anyway."

"When do you want to go?"

"When do *I* want to go? Aren't you coming, too?"

"No," Sarah said quietly. "I want you to take James and Ruth with you and just leave me here with Jennifer."

"But, Sarah!"

"Please," Sarah begged, "Anne, please listen. I know it isn't my fault, and I know it isn't your fault and I *know* all that . . . but it happened. And it changed me. And it changed you, too."

"I love you."

"I know you do. I love you, too, but . . . you feel *sorry* for me, Anne! You tell me not to worry, but you fuss over me. You touch me and I think it's because you're trying to convince me of something!"

"Well, I'm not!"

"Maybe not, but . . . we need to take another look at . . . everything."

"Jesus Christ!" Anne raged. "If we hadn't taken so long picking that damn tree! If I'd been able to get here even three stinking minutes sooner!"

"See," Sarah said grimly. "It isn't *your* fault, either, but you still blame yourself."

"Okay," Anne said after a long, hurtful silence. "Okay, we'll go in without you."

"Thank you," Sarah said simply. As they were getting ready for bed she spoke again, very softly, "And anyway, I have to find out if I can look after myself alone or if one of the reasons we're together is that you're always there when I need you and you always seem to be able to figure out a way to do what needs to be done."

"Oh, for God's sake," Anne said wearily.

It was bitter cold but the snow was light and the horses were in excellent shape. Anne and Ruth hitched the big mare to the wagonload of bedding and provisions, then Anne went into the house for one last cup of coffee, one last attempt at conversation with Sarah, while James and Ruth saddled the horses.

"We'll sleep in the wagon," she said into the heavy silence between herself and Sarah. "And I don't know how long we'll be gone. It depends on the weather."

"I'll be okay," Sarah said quietly.

"Well . . ." Anne stood awkwardly at the door, a scarf over her head and covering her ears, thick gloves on her hands and her heavy jacket buttoned tightly. She cuddled Jennifer, wanting to squeeze the warm little body, then handed her back to Sarah. They nodded at each other and Anne hurried to climb on Nell, blinking her eyes rapidly.

"Ready?" she asked, and James and Ruth grinned eagerly, perched high on their horses, their saddles cleaned, gleaming and fine. "Okay, we're off." And she nudged Nell forward, afraid to look back in case Sarah wasn't at the doorway, waving.

It was a hard and bitter trip to the trading post. The last storms of winter blew down on them and their breath froze and hung in the icy air. Frost gathered around the horses' nostrils and mouths, and James, huddled in his clothes, looked like a little ball of wool and flannel, his face protected by a warm woolen scarf, his knitted toque pulled down over his ears. Ruth, similarly dressed, sat on BelleTwo silently, only her eyes visible from behind the woolen scarf wrapped around her face.

"By God," James muttered. "I can think of warmer ways to have fun."

"You sound like an old man of seventy instead of a boy of seven," Anne teased.

"Maybe I'm eight," he insisted, "or even nine."

"And maybe you're only six," Ruth interjected. They bickered briefly over how old he was. He insisted he could remember too much of the wagon trip up to be only six or seven. "My mom made biscuits in the ashes," he recalled, "and my dad shot a . . . a . . . thing . . . It lives in the ground."

"Gopher," Ruth supplied.

"Maybe. And we had to float over some rivers, too."

"Well, maybe if you can remember all that, maybe you are older than six or seven."

"Don't worry about it." Anne tried to smile. "We'll know how old he is when he starts to grow whiskers."

"My poppa had whiskers," James bragged, "black whiskers that curled on his chin, and my momma called him a bear. He was black like me," he added unnecessarily.

"Can you remember his name?" Anne asked gently.

"Poppa. His name was Poppa."

"What did your mother call him?"

"Lover." He grinned. "She always called him Lover. Or Sugar. Or Honey. One time she was mad at him and called him Mister Man. 'You just listen to me, Mister Man,' she said, and Poppa laughed, and then she did, too."

"Too bad you don't know his name," Anne said casually. "Then you could be more than James."

"What name do you have besides Anne?" he asked.

"Gray." She reached out and patted Nell's neck. "Anne Gray and, oh, my Darlin' Nelly Gray."

---

"You made that up," Ruth accused.

"Did not." Anne shook her head. "My father's name was John Gray, my mother was Martha Gray, and I'm Anne Gray. That's why I called my horse Nellie. Didn't you know?"

"Well," Ruth said flatly, "I'm not calling myself Ruth Smithers." Anne remembered John Smithers and his weak-chinned whining, and nodded, understanding.

"What was your mother's name before she got married?" Anne asked.

"I don't know," Ruth shrugged. "But if you're supposed to have two names, I guess I can make up any name I want for the other one."

"Maybe I'll call me James Black," the little boy laughed, nudging Simon's horse and riding on ahead, laughing happily.

"Maybe," Ruth muttered, "maybe I'll call myself Ruth Sunshine. Maybe it'll make me feel warmer. Or Ruth Hotday, or Ruth Summertime."

"That's nice," Anne agreed. "Nelly Gray, could I introduce you to my good friend and sister icicle, Miss Ruth Summer?" And she and Ruth grinned at each other in spite of their shivering, and if the only part of the grin that could be seen was in the crinkling of their eyes, each knew the other was smiling behind the thick woolen scarves.

At night they shivered together in the wagon while the horses pawed at the snow looking for the long yellow winter grass beneath.

"Will it be this cold on the way back?" James asked miserably.

"No," Anne promised, "it won't be."

"It'll prob'ly be pourin' rain," Ruth muttered.

The trader was cheating her, she knew that, but Dan was sleek and happy, and, after a short talk with the trader, she knew he knew she was aware of his borderline dishonesty, and they both knew it would diminish. He would never be totally honest, but Anne no longer expected to find anybody who was.

"Can't get near him to ride him," the trader sighed. "He's kind of wild."

"You were told not to try," Anne said coldly. "He's only got one job in life, and he does it just fine. If you aren't happy with that, I can take him back with me."

"No need," he blurted, "no need for that."

"Fine," she nodded. "You draw up the papers making me one-third partner and I'll leave him here. If ever I decide to take him back, the partnership is dissolved."

"One third!" the trader exclaimed, shocked.

"One third," she said coldly. "I happen to know that there's a trading post at Fort Langley run by a guy name of Tom. And he's getting the trading business." She leaned on the corral watching Dan prancing and tossing his head. "Cariboo gold won't last forever," she pointed out carefully, "and when that craziness has died down, the only real future for you is raising good horseflesh. Which you can't do without that stud."

They argued and dickered about it the full time she was there, and in the end the trader agreed. Anne knew he agreed because he had no real intention of keeping his books honest, but she also knew the agreement would keep him from cheating her too outrageously. And anyway, Nelly Gray was hers now, and had spent enough time in the corral with Dan that Anne knew there would be a foal born, a foal that would combine the best of both parents, a foal that would give her back what she had thought she had lost when Dan had refused to accompany her. When she went to the corral the big stud whistled shrilly and ran up to her, searching her pockets for treats, rubbing his head against her, but she knew, happy as he was to see her, there was no way he was leaving his mares.

"Silly fool," she mumbled, scratching his head. "They'll be the death of you one day. Wear yourself out, and what thanks will you get?" She rode him several times, more to prove a point to the trader than for any other reason, and found herself thinking even while astride Dan that Nelly had a smoother gait, and was more dependable, less apt to be distracted. Still, there was something special about Dan, and the bond between them would always be strong.

Two weeks later the wagon was packed, the two milk cows

were tethered to the rear of the wagon, and a very indignant, very pregnant cat yowled from inside a lathe cage similar to the one in which the chickens had made their trip. Tucked under James' arm was a squirming hound puppy he said was for Sarah, but both Ruth and Anne knew it was really for himself.

The cows slowed them down and the wagon rims bit into the wet spring earth. James fretted that his puppy would be a dog before they got home and Anne expected the increasingly stony-eyed cat to either chew her way out of the cage and rip them all apart in their sleep, or else give birth in the wagon and train her kittens to do it for her.

Sarah did the chores, cared for Jennifer, tended the fires, walked the beach with her basket gathering the coal deposited by each tide, and, once a day, reminded herself to eat. Every morning and evening she would sit by Lin's grave and weep, and each time she bathed her own child, she remembered the laughing little girl who had loved her bath, loved the beach and the water, and who had died so suddenly, so needlessly. Everything in the cabin seemed to remind her of something. As soon as she stepped out of the cabin she was confronted with the evidence of Anne, the children, their lives together, and how terribly everything had changed. She bathed, dressed and brushed her hair out of habit, but the sun only shone thinly outside and not all the coal or wood in the world could make a blaze warm enough to thaw the ice growing in her belly. Even Jennifer's laughter came to her as if from a distance.

By day she moved mechanically through the routine of life on the coast in late winter. The rain washed the snow away and more snow fell, never more than a few inches, an inconvenience and a bother, rather than a hardship. When a fierce gale blew in off the sea and several of the hand-split cedar shakes tore loose, Sarah donned warm clothes, and spent the morning splitting replacements from the dried slabs in the woodshed. Then she got the ladder from the barn, climbed to the roof and repaired the damage.

At night she sat in the quiet cabin and cursed the puddle of light from the oil lamp and wished she could, for just one evening, be in a place where the shadows didn't obscure everything, a place where she could look across the room and actually see the far wall.

She lost weight, the smudges deepened under her eyes and Jennifer's laughter came less frequently with nobody to play with, nobody to tease her, tickle her, or laugh down at her.

The wind was moaning fitfully, the waves slapped viciously at the rocks, the light flickered sickly from the soot-darkened chimney of the lamp. Sarah supposed she ought to clean it, but it would wait until morning. She sat staring at the blue and orange flames licking at the coal in the fireplace, her mind numb, her thoughts scattered.

The door rattled but the bar held. Sarah stared, eyes round, her flesh goose-pimpling. Who now? Who in the middle of the night, unannounced, trying to open the door, trying to get in the boarded-over window, trying to enter the cabin where Jennifer lay asleep? She wanted to run for the rifle, shoot the intruders, shoot herself, shoot the baby so the recurrent terror would stop.

She watched, disbelieving, as her body rose from the chair and moved to the door, lifted the bar and stepped back to allow the door to open, the intruders to enter.

Ap-jei looked at Sarah, shook his head and stepped aside to allow the old women to enter. Then he left the cabin and moved to the barn where his paddle pullers were already bedding down in the warm hay, their bodies chilled and exhausted by hours of fighting the rising storm, the freezing spray.

It didn't matter that James wasn't there to translate. Even if he had been, he would not have known the language the women were using. There was a common language, shared by all, spoken and understood by men, women and children. Then there was a language known only to the men, taught to the young boys by their uncles when the boys had demonstrated their willingness and readiness to leave childish things behind and begin to assume the responsibilities of manhood. The language of the men had a low form known to all men and a high form known to the nobles and royalty, the spiritual and instructed. At the same stage of development the girls began to learn the language of women, a language James had never heard and never would hear, and this women's language, like that of the men, had a low form and a high form. The fourth language was known to the shamans and healers, the spirit-callers and sanctified, possibly one person out of twenty or thirty. The fifth language, the arcane language, whose roots were lost in the mists of time and the confusions of creation itself, was known only to the most holy, and it was this language the disciples of the matrilineal society spoke, to each other, and to Sarah.

Her mind whirled with fear and confusion but her body allowed the women to do what they felt necessary. They heaped wood on the coals in the fireplace and blew out the feeble and ineffectual lamp. Then they stripped her clothes from her and washed her with warm water into which they had dumped a powder made of dried seaweed. She saw one of the women carry a sleepily smiling Jennifer from the cabin, and before she could formulate the question, she knew the answer. The child would sleep with and be cared for by the men who had been chosen to bring the old woman, the priestess, the earthly embodiment of Old Woman herself, and her disciples, through the storm to the soul that had been crying its need.

They rubbed her skin with hemlock branches until the blood rose to the surface and she glowed pink, then they smeared her with oil scented with bracken fern and into her hair they brushed the boiled juice and leaves of a plant so sacred and healing its leaves, stems and roots are protected by a foul-smelling yellow flower, a plant that grows in profusion in the damp and swampy places and is all too often ignored because of the odor that guards it.

One of the women gave her a faintly yellow flavorless tea to drink while another ignited leaves and herbs in a small stone bowl shaped and fashioned to resemble a whale. The acolyte blew this smoke into Sarah's face and for the first time she became aware of the sound from the small drum a disciple was stroking with her fingertips.

She sat naked on the floor facing the old woman, waiting,

trusting, knowing she needed help and it had arrived, knowing
all she had to do was accept the help being offered and everything
would work out as it ought to, perhaps for the first time in her
life.

The old woman sat cross-legged, her hands resting on her
knees, thumbs and forefingers forming circles. Her eyes glittered
like chips of black diamond, and the lines and wrinkles in her
face told more clearly than words how old she was, what all she
had survived.

Sarah began talking, certain, in a place deep inside herself,
that she would be understood in spite of the language barrier.
She told of her childhood, of never feeling she belonged or was
welcome. She told of leaving home, finding, always temporarily,
a place for herself in someone else's bed, under someone else's
straining body, welcome for as long as it took her to satisfy the
need, drain the hunger. She wept for the dead young cowboy,
for Keno, for all the dreams smashed before they could be
realized, for all the chances lost before they were even tried. She
cried for Lin and for the horror Andrew and Simon had brought
into everyone's lives, and then she cried for herself. The old
woman sat, blinking thoughtfully, and then she nodded.

The disciples joined hands, and the old woman pulled Sarah
to her, the gnarled hands gently guiding Sarah to lie down and
place her head on the old woman's lap. Sarah curled on her right
side, still trembling, shaken with sobs. The smoke from the whale
bowl drifted past her face, stung her eyes, and she closed them.

*Ships in the fog and men with fierce eyes, glittering
chestplates and metal helmets. A cross held high. A
sword stained with blood and the people reeling in confusion, their bodies invaded by sickness, so desperate
with raging fever they plunged into the sea to cool their
flesh and their hearts stopped with the shock of the icy
water. Babies dead before they lived and children tor-
tured to convert them to a new religion, their bodies
mangled to save their souls. Entire villages emptied and
the ravens of death fat in the cedars. And as the ghosts*

*swirled in Sarah's mind, the lined face of the old woman*
*dominated her vision, a face that changed but never*
*altered, not one woman's face, nor two, nor three, but*
*twelve thousand years, forty thousand women's faces,*
*students who became acolytes, acolytes who became*
*disciples, disciples who became priestesses and priest-*
*esses who became the old woman who represented on*
*earth the wisdom of Old Woman, and all of them*
*enduring.*

The fog faded, the nightmare dimmed and Sarah thought of
the empty prairie, of herself, more dead than not, and suddenly
the tough little face under the ridiculously huge hat. She told the
women of the rifle and the food it provided, of the long hours
scrubbing clothes because the young blonde woman expected and
demanded what Sarah had wanted to hear and never heard from
Keno, an end to the trading of her flesh and her respect in return
for fleeting comfort and money. And then she saw herself as she
had never seen herself before, giving comfort as often as she
needed it, teaching at least as often as she was taught, sharing
and giving, washing away more than trail dirt in Belle's big tub,
discarding more than outgrown and tattered underwear when she
stripped Anne of the shame and shyness of a blighted childhood.
She saw herself strong and laughing, capable and courageous,
as able to endure and overcome as anyone, a woman to be
respected, a woman to be loved.

The old woman spoke and Sarah heard bird calls and chirps,
whistles and clicks and she felt herself relaxing, welcoming healing
peace. The wrinkled old hands, the knuckles swollen with age
and hard work, stroked the tear-swollen pale face. Sarah smiled
and was already asleep when the strong young acolytes lifted her
from the floor and took her to bed.

In the morning, there was no magic, no wonder, just Ap-jei
and the pullers, and Nai-Nai, his grandmother, and some of
her friends. They breakfasted together, and laughed together.
Ap-jei looked at the newly repaired roof and grinned. He nudged
her, clowning, preening himself comically and held out his hand,

and she knew he was teasing her, inviting her to be one of his wives, knowing before she told him, that she would refuse. Sisters never marry brothers.

"One of these days," she promised, "you'll make that offer once too often and someone will say yes, and you'll be sorry."

Ruth and James rode together, taking turns holding the puppy, chattering to each other, leaving Anne with all the time in the world to examine her own thoughts. She missed Lin, but the change in the relationship with Sarah hurt her even more. She knew, without ever trying to put it into words, that she would be able to survive the end of any friendship, the end of any relationship. She just didn't want to have to. On the other hand, she didn't want to live in silence, or depend on mutual civilized politeness to keep things in the cabin on an even level. Sarah would never be able to run the place on her own, and there were the children to think of, too. Ruth and James loved the place and belonged on it for as long as they wanted to stay. Until they could look after everything, Anne was needed. But if she stayed with Ruth and James, did that mean Sarah would leave with Jennifer? Perhaps another cabin was the answer. Perhaps she could live with Ruth and James in a new one, and Sarah and Jennifer live in their own. What if Ruth or James, or even both of them, wanted to live with Jennifer and Sarah? What if Sarah wanted to move closer to town? What if Sarah wanted another child? Over and over the unresolved questions turned, until Anne was tired of listening to the voice in her head, tired of questions without answers, tired of the knot of anxiety in her stomach.

"What's a nigger?" James asked suddenly.

"A what?" Ruth asked.

"A nigger," he repeated, eyes fixed trustingly on her face.

"Where'd you hear that?" Ruth stalled, thinking furiously.

"That man. That trade man. He asked me what was a nigger doing on a horse instead of walking behind a plow."

"What did you tell him?"

"Told him I was riding it." He shrugged. "What's a nigger?"

"Someone who's black," Ruth said bluntly.

"Then why don't you call me nigger?"

"It's an insult," she replied. "You're supposed to feel bad when someone calls you a nigger."

"Why?"

"I don't know," Ruth admitted. "Ask Anne."

"He's an asshole," Anne explained. "The world is up to its ass in assholes."

One day they began to recognize the outline of the rocks along the shore.

"That's where we saw that thing with all the arms," James exulted. "And that's where we paddled to with the dugout when we set the traps and caught those real big crabs!"

"Smoke!" Ruth shrilled, and then they were urging their horses forward, racing for the place, the puppy chasing after them, tripping over her own feet, trying to catch up, whining eagerly, afraid of being left behind. Anne leaned over, grabbed the pup and desposited her in the wagon where the cat tried to come either out of her skin or out of her cage, spitting and raging while the pup peered innocently through the slats. "Don't get too close," Anne warned the pup. "She'll eat your nose."

James was in the house cuddling Jennifer, and Ruth was impatiently waiting her turn when Anne arrived with the wagon and supplies. Sarah was standing in the front yard, waiting.

"Have a good trip?" she asked calmly.

"Some of it was good," Anne dismounted, rubbing her rump, "but a lot of it was a pain you-know-where. I brought you something," she said quickly, hoping to bring the dancing lights back to Sarah's eyes. "We had to go to five farms before we found one, but here it is," and she swung the lathe cage from the wagon.

"That," Sarah said positively, "is the goddamndest ugliest cat I ever saw in my life."

"I just knew you'd love it," Anne said, disgusted, putting the cage aside. "And we got the worst cows we could find, too." She immediately led the maligned beasts to the barn and turned them loose in their roughly-made stalls where they began to eat hungrily.

She had imagined a much different homecoming. She had imagined Sarah laughing and hugging her happily. She had dreamed of a warm family meal and then a leisurely unpacking of the wagon. Instead, she gritted her teeth and began to haul things from the wagon, moving most of it into the shed, hauling some of it as far as the porch. Sarah watched her speculatively for a few minutes, then wordlessly began to help.

"Aren't you coming inside?" James asked.

"No!" Anne snapped.

"What about supper?"

"I'll make it," Sarah said coolly, walking past Anne and into the house. Anne unpacked and unloaded until it was too dark to do any more work, then she went into the house, still insulted and angry, and ate her supper wordlessly. Jennifer climbed on her knee and babbled lovingly, and Anne's anger dissolved. "Precious wetbum," she crooned. "I missed you so much the birds didn't sing."

James was highly insulted when his puppy had to sleep in the barn.

"I'm sleeping there with her," he warned.

"Well you go right ahead," Sarah said calmly, "but she's not sleeping in here and leaving her calling cards all over the floor."

"She wouldn't do that," James said doubtfully.

"You want to bet everything you own on that?" she dared, but he just reached for his jacket, grabbed his bedroll and headed for the barn. "And take that ugly damned cat out there with you!" Sarah ordered.

She bathed Jennifer and put her to bed with her new doll, then went back into the kitchen to find Anne already stripped and in the tub.

"You look tired," she commented casually.

"I am." Anne's voice was flat. "I'm afraid if I get into bed I might not move for a month. No. I'm not afraid, I'm hoping! Not one muscle. Not a twitch. I might not even bother blinking my eyes."

"That bad, huh?"

"Worse. I'm getting too old for this."

"Old?" Sarah hooted sarcastically. "You must be all of, what, twenty?"

"Well, you know how it is. An hour dancing is like no time at all, an hour sitting on a hot stove is forever." She stepped out of the tub and began toweling herself dry.

"Your hair looks nice that way," Sarah commented.

"Thanks," Anne said absently, pulling her embroidered nightgown over her head and reaching for the coffee pot.

"You want one?" she asked.

"Sounds good." Sarah stripped off her clothes, tossing them in the same heap as Anne's things. "I bet we've got a mountain of washing to do tomorrow."

"You'd win the bet." Anne handed her the cup of coffee, then sat on a chair with her feet up on another, sipping reflectively and staring at her feet.

"Something wrong?" Sarah asked carefully.

"Yes," Anne said frankly, "but I don't know if it would be better or worse to tell you."

"Might as well tell me." Sarah shrugged. "Nothing could be any worse than the way it's been since . . . Christmas. I did a lot of thinking, too, while you were gone," she added quietly.

"And you're leaving. Is that it?" Anne asked, waiting in vain for an answer. The silence lengthened.

"You want me to go?" Sarah asked finally.

"I guess what I want doesn't really matter," Anne mumbled. "It's what you want."

"I don't know what I want until I know what you want," Sarah said stubbornly.

"You didn't even want your goddamn cat!" Anne accused, angrily.

"I never said that!" Sarah raged.

"You did so. You just said it was ugly. Without even looking at her, you said she was ugly. You just froze me out."

"*I* froze *you*? I? . . . You ride up here looking like you just . . . all stiff-backed and hardly speaking, and when I try to make a joke you come down off that damn horse of yours and start throwing boxes and barrels around like a madwoman. I can't even take a look at the cows without . . ."

"The cows!" Anne sat erect. "Jesus, I forgot to milk the cows!"

"Name of god," Sarah muttered, reaching for her clothes, "if it isn't one thing it's another. Can't even have a good family fight around here without someone else's tit needing pulling."

They hurried out to the barn with the lantern, opened the barn door and burst out laughing. James was sound asleep in the hay, the cows were contentedly chewing their cuds, and James' puppy was guiltily withdrawing her muzzle from a pail of milk.

"James did it," Sarah sighed. She grabbed the bucket of milk, looked at Anne and shrugged. "If we don't tell the kids, they'll never know."

"Even if they did know, they wouldn't care," Anne agreed, and they headed back to the cabin with the pail.

"Not much milk from two cows," Sarah muttered.

"Only one is milking," Anne explained. "The other one is pregnant and won't come fresh for months."

"A pregnant cow, a pregnant cat . . . What next?" Sarah grumbled, putting the milk pail on the table and heading for the bedroom, her dark hair falling past her shoulders, her brow furrowed in a frown. Anne followed her, very carefully saying nothing, not sure if Sarah was angry again or not. They got into bed, the lantern burning dimly on the floor, and lay beside each other, stiffly, staring up at the ceiling.

"You look nice in that nightgown," Sarah said quietly, and Anne could think of nothing to say. Sarah waited, then rolled on her elbow, facing Anne accusingly.

"That's once more," she said quietly.

"What's once more?" Anne blurted.

"One more compliment I paid you that you ignored, that's what!"

"I don't know what to say."

"It doesn't matter," Sarah snapped, rolling on her other side, back to Anne. "Just see if I care!"

"Well, what do you want me to say?" Anne stormed. "Jesus, just tell me what you want me to say and I'll say it. Every time I open my mouth you jump down my throat! If I said it was raining, you'd say it wasn't! If I told you I'd chopped my foot off, you'd say No you didn't it was just your toes. Without looking to see!"

"What are you babbling about?" Sarah gritted. "You haven't hurt your toes."

"I said I didn't know what to say," Anne snapped, "and you said it didn't matter what I said, you didn't care anyway, so I'm just saying any old thing at all because it won't matter, no matter *what* I say."

"Don't you shout at me." Sarah sat up in bed and turned her face toward Anne.

"You're crying!" Anne accused, suddenly happy. "You're crying because I'm mad at you!"

"I don't care," Sarah said. "I don't care if it makes you smile because I'm crying."

"I'm smiling because if you're crying it means you still care."

"Well, of course I do! Did I ever say I didn't?"

"You said," Anne said sternly.

"Will you guys shut up?" Ruth called angrily. "You're gonna wake the baby."

"We're having a fight," Anne answered happily. "We're having a family fight. If the baby wakes up, you look after her." And she turned to Sarah, smiling, reaching for the arms that were reaching for her. "I can't stand it when you get all quiet and sulky and won't talk to me," she admitted. "I'd rather yell and shout."

"I hate yelling and shouting," Sarah murmured, snuggling close. "I just needed some time to myself, that's all."

"You should have said so," Anne whispered.

"I still think that cat is as ugly as sin," Sarah teased, reaching to turn out the lantern.

Her shirt was stuck to her skin with sweat, her arms felt heavy, her hands swollen with hard work. Anne heaved, and the last of the cedar split rails fell into place. The fence was finished. She grinned across the fresh-scented yellow cedar rail at Sarah, face flushed, beaded with sweat.

"We've done 'er," Anne panted.

"Well," Sarah pretended to grumble, "if you've got another job in mind for today, you can just forget it. I," she turned away, wiping her brow, "am going to die."

Anne looked at the large garden, the young corn growing tall in the summer sun, the silky tassels blowing softly in the breeze that came from the sea. Rows of beets, turnips, parsnips, carrots, an entire plot of potatoes, rows of lettuce and tomato plants tied to strong sticks. The trader had told her tomatoes were poison, but nobody had even got sick yet, let alone died from eating them. The squash grew thick around the base of the corn, and the patch of greens was going to seed quicker than they could cut it and eat it. The split-rail fence would keep the cows and horses out of the garden, her rifle would take care of the deer and the smokehouses were enlarged and ready. Out in the bay Ruth was sitting in the dugout jigging for cod, and James was playing in the shallows with Jennifer, helping her build a small fish wier that might even trap a few sand crabs. There was flour, coffee, tea and salt enough in the cabin, and lately Anne had begun to listen when Sarah talked of maybe finding a way to grind their corn and be less dependent on the trips to the trading post. Nelly Gray was standing under a tree, swishing flies, and, though there was no external sign of it, Anne knew that the foal who would be the best animal ever seen on the coast was growing inside the powerful gray mare. She sighed contentedly, rubbed the stiff place in the small of her back, and fastened her gaze on the slender figure of Sarah, walking away from her.

"Hey," Anne called, putting her tools aside, "betcha I can get there before you do." And Sarah raced for the water, laughing, already stripping off her shirt. Anne chased after her, pulling off her clothes and throwing them aside, shouting with joy and satisfaction. They hit the water at the same time, diving under the cool green sea, bubbles of air from their laughter rising from their mouths, hands reaching, clasping, fingers intertwined.

Anne's head broke the surface first. She spit sea water and shouted with pleasure. Sarah's head broke water, her smile warm, all pretense of grumbling gone. For a brief moment the two women looked at each other, then, together, they swam lazily toward the shore, toward their home.

*Anne Cameron* was born in 1938 in Nanaimo, B.C., a Leo with Leo rising, five fixed planets, no water signs. She is the mother of two sons and two daughters.

Her previous books include: *Dreamspeaker* (published in Canada by Clark-Irwin and in the U.S. by Avon); *Daughters of Copper Woman* (Press Gang, Vancouver, B.C.); *Earth Witch* (Harbour Publishing, Madiera Park, B.C.); *How Raven Freed the Moon* (Harbour Publishing); and *How the Loon Lost Her Voice* (Harbour Publishing). *Dreamspeaker* won the Gibsons Award for Literature and the screenplay won the Canada Film Award for Screenplay in 1977.

"I live on 7 acres of rain forest with a small clearing in which we have fruit trees, grape vines, turkeys, chickens, one duck, 50+ rabbits, three dogs and three cats. Two toads live under the house, the larger, brown one is called Agnes, the smaller green one doesn't have a name yet. I've been living with my partner for over five years and in my next life I want to be a country and western singer like EmmyLou Harris. My main wish in this life is that women would stop volunteering, stop being Candy Stripers and joining the Ladies Aid, would stop serving coffee and donuts, and, instead, use their energy to just go out in the streets one day a year and YELL. The "ululululululul" was the war cry of the Celtic amazons, the north African amazons, the amazons of the Caucasus and the Cherokee women. The mythology of each says no man could endure the power of that yell for more than a few minutes. Weapons shattered. Men dropped dead. Armies fled. Makes more sense to me than coffee, donuts and peanut butter cookies!!"

*Photo: Eleanor Miller*

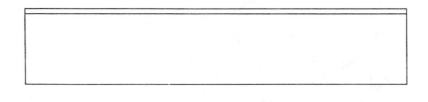

# spinsters | *aunt lute*

Spinsters/Aunt Lute Book Company was founded in 1986 through the merger of two successful feminist publishing businesses. Aunt Lute Book Company moved from Iowa City to San Francisco in 1986 to join with Spinsters Ink. A consolidation in the best sense of the word, our recent merger strengthens our ability to produce vital books for diverse women's communities in the years to come.

Our commitment is to publishing works that are beyond the scope of mainstream commercial publishers: books that don't just name crucial issues in women's lives, but go on to encourage change and growth, to make all of our lives more possible.

We also want to thank you, our readers, for your commitment. Whether you support us by buying our books or choosing one of the many other ways to invest in Spinsters/Aunt Lute, you enable us to bring out new books. Write to us for a free catalog of our 26 titles and our women's art notecards. Or let us know of your interest in an investors' brochure.

Spinsters/Aunt Lute
P.O. Box 410687
San Francisco, CA 94141